Theatre under Louis XIV

THEATRE UNDER LOUIS XIV

CROSS-CASTING AND THE PERFORMANCE OF GENDER IN DRAMA, BALLET, AND OPERA

Julia Prest

palgrave
macmillan

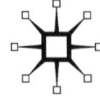
ISBN: 978–1–137–32081–0

The Library of Congress has cataloged the hardcover edition as follows:

Prest, Julia.
    Theatre under Louis XIV : cross-casting and the performance of gender in drama, ballet and opera / Julia Prest.
       p. cm.
    Includes bibliographical references and index.
    ISBN 1–4039–7518–3 (alk. paper)
      1. Performing arts—France—History—17th century. 2. Performing arts— France—History—18th century. 3. Female impersonators—France—History—17th century. 4. Female impersonators—France—History—18th century. 5. Male impersonators—France—History—17th century. 6. Male impersonators—France—History—18th century. 7. French drama—17th century—History and criticism. 8. French drama—18th century—History and criticism. I. Title: Theatre under Louis 14. II. Title: Theatre under Louis the fourteenth. III. Title.

PN2632.P74 2006
791.0944'09032—dc22   2005057634

A catalogue record for this book is available from the British Library.

Design by Newgen Imaging Systems (P) Ltd., Chennai, India.

First PALGRAVE MACMILLAN paperback edition: April 2013

10 9 8 7 6 5 4 3 2 1

To my parents,
John and Susan

CONTENTS

LIST OF ILLUSTRATIONS

ACKNOWLEDGMENTS

I would like to extend my sincere thanks to the Principal and Fellows of Jesus College Oxford, where, as a Junior Research Fellow, I undertook the bulk of my research for this book, and to the Department of French at Yale University, where the book was completed. It is published with the generous assistance of the Frederick W. Hilles Publication Fund of Yale University. I am grateful to Nick Hammond, Joe Harris, and Hannah Thompson who read and commented on an early draft of the manuscript, and to Ned Duval for his meticulous reading of a subsequent draft. Becky Harris-Warrick's comments on my opera chapter improved it beyond measure, while Colin Timms, John Powell, and Ellen Rosand were always quick to respond to my music-related queries. Thank you to Claire McMurray, who drew my attention to Roger Herzel's article on *Les Femmes savantes*, to Christina Elefteriades, who was an excellent checker of references and enthusiast, and to Susannah Carson for her painstaking proof-reading of the final draft. I would like to thank the staff of the Beinecke Library at Yale University who were infinitely patient and helpful during my quest for illustrations, and my helpers in Paris, Brian Reilly and Fabien Cavaillé, without whom the picture of Louis XIV's ballet costume would never have been reproduced in time. Matthew Bailey of the National Portrait Gallery and Libbi Lee of the Globe Theatre dealt with my requests for illustrations with efficiency and good humor while all the time Joe Roach cheered from the sidelines. My thanks to all of you. Finally, I would like to thank Julia Cohen at Palgrave for dealing with my many queries about the technical side of things and especially Farideh Koohi-Kamali, also of Palgrave, for her interest in the project from the outset.

My warm thanks to Desiree Browne (Editorial Assistant at Palgrave) for all her help, and to Robyn Curtis (Associate Editor at Palgrave) for her unwavering support for this project. St Andrews, November 2012.

INTRODUCTION: CROSS-DRESSING AND CROSS-CASTING

The stoning scene (sc 4) in *Monty Python's Life of Brian* (Terry Jones, 1979) is attended by a crowd of female characters (all played by male actors) who have dressed as men in order to be admitted to the ceremony. This combination of cross-casting (male actors playing female roles) and cross-dressing (the female roles disguising themselves as men *within* the fiction of the film) is particularly effective within this chaotic comic context and it operates at a number of levels. The fact that the women wishing to attend the stoning are cross-cast (i.e., played by men) immediately renders them comic, with their wobbly falsetto voices, and ill-concealed masculine features. The fact that they are, moreover, incompetently cross-dressed (disguised) as men in order to participate in a ceremony from which they would ordinarily be excluded renders them doubly comic. Their multilayered performance of gender is as anarchic as the ceremony itself in which the Roman official finds himself unable to control a group of rowdy, violent women. The fact that the official does not recognize them as women (despite their obvious fluctuations between falsetto and ordinary speaking voices, and between masculine and feminine pronouns as they perform their various identities) establishes a special complicity between these characters and the viewer, while simultaneously serving the comic and satirical purposes of the film. Here as elsewhere, the cross-cast actor brings into relief the crucial question of reality and falsehood in performance—and in this way he is a quintessentially theatrical figure.

Writing about cross-casting, Dorothy Keyser makes a useful distinction between a "convention" and a "device" in the theatre: the former she defines as "discrepant elements that the audience is expected to ignore" (such as the fact that in a proscenium theatre, a square room has three walls), and the latter as "discrepant elements introduced deliberately to draw the audience's attention to some aspect of the production."[1] One of the aims of this book is precisely to examine when cross-casting is used simply as a convention and when it is used as a device, and to what effect. Monty Python's use of cross-casting in the stoning scene of their *Life of Brian* is a device used to highlight questions of sex and gender, and also of truth and fiction, as they draw the viewer's attention to the powerful theatricality of their satirical take on this period of Roman history.

A convention and a device are not mutually exclusive. In theatrical traditions involving all-male casts, such as the theatre of Ancient Greece or that of Renaissance England, the convention of cross-casting was sometimes, if not systematically, *additionally* exploited as a device, often generating dramatic irony. Aristophanes, for example, wrote for all-male casts, with every actor wearing a mask. His comedies include a variety of female roles, the most sympathetically portrayed female figure generally being the reliable and responsible middle-aged wife. *Ecclesiazusae* (c.391 BC) is one of Aristophanes's most interesting plays in terms of the present discussion. From the opening scene onward, the audience is invited to ponder such pertinent themes as the role of women in society and cross-dressing itself, a theme that in turn highlights the theatrical convention of cross-casting. In a scene reminiscent of Monty Python's stoning, Praxagora and her pioneering female companions (all, of course, originally played by male actors) disguise themselves as men and are equipped with false tie-on beards. Some of the coarser practicalities of cross-gender disguise are not eschewed as a number of the women claim deliberately to have allowed their body hair to grow so as, in the words of the second woman, "to get hairy all over and not look like a woman at all" (sc 1).[2] Similarly, they explore other aspects of cross-gender disguise as they practise speaking like men. The comic impact of this opening scene was undoubtedly enhanced by the fact that these female roles were portrayed by men: their cross-casting was successfully exploited for the comic irony it bestowed upon their words and actions. The convention of cross-casting is thus also employed as a device. This is supported by the inclusion of a number of lines that deliberately draw attention to the relationship between the performers and their audience: the theatrical illusion is thereby temporarily broken, or at least challenged, as the audience is invited to reflect on the complex relationship between illusion and reality in theatrical entertainment.

In *Ecclesiazusae*, the ultimate aim of the cross-cast, cross-dressed women is to gain access to, and control of, the Athenian Assembly and to reform it radically. They are successful in their enterprise and one of the new laws that is introduced stipulates that every attractive young man must, before making love to the attractive young woman of his choice, offer his services to a less attractive woman first. This rule forms the backdrop to the events of scene 3 in which three old hags, each uglier than the last, vie with an attractive young woman for the attentions of a handsome youth. The attractive young woman of *Ecclesiazusae* is, according to Jeffrey Henderson, "the first maiden with a speaking part in extant comedy,"[3] and this scene is of particular interest to our exploration as it juxtaposes an attractive female role with three highly unattractive ones, all played by male actors. The comedy of the scene lies principally in its outrageous subject matter and in the exaggerated grotesqueness of the succession of ugly old hags, whose monstrosity must have been well served by their cross-casting. For the scene to succeed, however, it is important that the attractive female role, also cross-cast, should be performed in a way that is sufficiently credible for her cross-casting to be accepted as a convention (at least to the extent that it should not detract from her supposed femininity). Here the distinction between representation and impersonation is crucial: there is no question of the Athenian actors passing as women on stage.

To a large extent their portrayal is verbal. One might expect the hags to be abusive and aggressive while the girl remains sweet and polite. The hags are certainly offensive and vulgar: the first vaunts her great sexual experience and calls the girl a "perverted little bitch" and a "hussy"; the girl, on the other hand, enjoys a more mixed idiom. She is antagonistic toward the first hag (the only one with whom she has a direct encounter) whom she calls, amongst other things, a "mouldering antique," a "repulsive hag," and a "randy old cat." On the other hand, she is romantically seductive, singing songs that begin "Oh why do you tarry, do you tarry, lover dear?" and "Oh come, my heart's delight." But both the hag and the girl express their strong sexual impulses in explicit terms: the hag's opening song begins "If love's ecstasy you seek, / Come and sample my technique," while the girl's final song continues in terms that, if more elegant, are similar in sexual purport: "Strange, passionate desires / Sweep through my body like a hundred fires." Both types of cross-cast female figure are thus overtly sexual beings. Their cross-casting does not desexualize them—perhaps, on the contrary, it is their very performance by men that allows these female characters to be so sexualized, for the sexuality of men has long been considered more acceptable and less threatening than its female counterpart. Where the hag's desire is ridiculous owing to her age and appearance, the young girl's is legitimate owing to hers; where the hag's portrayal is grotesque, the young girl's is, at one level, erotic. Clearly the hags are more overtly comic figures than the girl, but both types are comically outspoken and abusive, and they interact to great effect.

In *Ecclesiazusae*, we have seen that Aristophanes's actors portray three distinct types of women, each of them comic to a greater or lesser degree: the respectable wives who wear tie-on beards, the archetypal old hag with a voracious sexual appetite, and her rival, the young girl eager to consummate her love. The fact that he was writing for all-male casts clearly did not prevent Aristophanes from developing a variety of female roles for the theatre—although it would certainly have had some impact on the nature of those roles. It seems that male actors could portray women for whom sexual activity is not a prime concern (the wives) as well as those for whom it is (the hags and the young woman). Within this second group, they could portray women whose sexual desire is a source of ridicule and, equally, those whose sexual desire is understood to be natural and agreeable. There is no question of Aristophanes's audience mistaking the actors for real women or of desiring them sexually as women (although they may have desired them as men). Rather, the audience was always aware that they were watching a performance by an all-male cast, and this was a convention that allowed them to accept the performance of female roles by men. In the comic tradition in particular, this convention offered the additional benefit of potentially being exploited as a theatrical device, thereby producing comic irony, and enhancing the overall comic impact of the play.

In the tragic tradition, comic irony is evidently less desirable. One of the most important distinctions between the great French tragedies of the seventeenth century and those of Shakespeare pertains to the question of comic relief. Where the Shakespearean tradition allows for comic elements within tragedy, the dominant esthetic of grand tragedy in France precluded anything that was considered superfluous to or incongruent with its tragic core. Shakespeare's use of cross-dressing (i.e., disguise plots) in both tragedies *and* comedies highlights the convention of cross-casting in much the same way as Aristophanes's cross-cast, cross-dressed Athenian women do. But neither cross-dressing nor comedy is necessary for cross-casting to be highlighted, and thereby exploited, as a device. Much has been made, for example, of the seemingly self-reflexive words of the eponymous Cleopatra

who, in the final scene of Shakespeare's play, anticipates being mocked
on the Roman stage, saying,

> . . . I shall see
> Some squeaking Cleopatra boy my greatness
> I' the posture of a whore. (*Antony and Cleopatra*, 5.2.219–21)

These lines have been widely understood to refer to the use of boy
actors in Renaissance England and specifically (and ironically) to
Cleopatra's own portrayal by a boy actor. Marvin Rosenberg has
recently argued, however, that *adult* male actors took Shakespeare's
great female roles, including that of Cleopatra.[4] Whatever the case,
Cleopatra's words draw the audience's attention to the familiar convention of cross-casting, thereby creating dramatic irony as she comments
indirectly on the deficiencies of that same convention. The same audience that tacitly accepts the convention of an all-male public theatre
is here temporarily invited to reflect on the peculiarities of that very
convention. Cross-casting is a convention that is always potentially
also a device.

To the important but fraught distinction between a theatrical
convention and a deliberate theatrical device one might usefully add
a third category: discrepant elements that *inadvertently* draw the
audience's attention to some aspect of the production or that invite a
certain response or reaction without necessarily seeking to do so. We
might call it a "trigger." Time and again we are reminded that audiences do not always respond in the way anticipated by the producer
or playwright, and this is especially common in modern attempts at
"authentic" productions of early theatre. Audience response is, of
course, notoriously difficult to pin down even at the best of times, as
it is so heavily dependent on the individual and on the expectations
that he or she brings to each performance at a particular moment in
time. Typically, one of the most problematic responses to cross-casting
among modern interpreters is to assume that it must have something
to do with homosexuality or homoeroticism (or, at the very least,
with camp). Corinne E. Blackmer and Patricia Juliana Smith, for
example, understand the phenomenon of a cross-cast woman (playing
a man) singing to a woman (playing a woman) to be an example of
"homoerotic vocal dynamics," and suggest that the operatic stage
was one of the few places where women were free to express their
lesbian desires in public.[5] However, such an interpretation radically
overlooks one of the fundamental tenets of the theatre: that the

performer is not the same as his/her role (although Plato, of course, famously warned of the dangers of imitation, for both imitator and spectator).[6] Blackmer's and Smith's overstated claim that baroque opera is "a very evidently *queer* art form" and that any analysis of Handel's *Serse* that is not queer is "somewhat far-fetched" (*En travesti*, 8 and 9) is, well, somewhat farfetched and too partisan to be credible as it stands.

Queer readings of cross-casting are not restricted to modern critics. While Blackmer and Smith gladly reclaim baroque opera on behalf of the lesbian and gay community, critics of the theatre have for centuries expressed their anxiety regarding what they considered to be the pernicious homoerotic impulse of cross-casting. Many of the antitheatricalists made little or no distinction between cross-dressing as a private or social activity and cross-casting on the public stage. For them, the latter (being public) was simply a more threatening and dangerous variety of a practice strictly prohibited by Deuteronomic law according to which "a woman must not wear men's clothing, nor a man wear women's clothing" (*Deuteronomy* 22.5). As they saw it, cross-dressing and its public theatrical counterpart posed a threat to sexual morality and in particular promoted homoerotic desire among actors and audiences alike, and it was therefore liable to lead to sodomy.[7] Once again, the crucial, but admittedly troubled, distinction between an actor and his performance on stage must be acknowledged. If a man wears what is understood to be feminine clothing for the purposes of playing a female role in the theatre, this does not alter his own sexuality, just as his donning of a crown does not turn him into a king. For the purposes of the theatrical performance, his clothes act as signifiers of his adopted sex, gender, rank, and so on, and the convention of costume as an external signifier of role is widely understood and accepted by the theatre audience. In the absence of any theatrical device that deliberately draws the audience's attention to the conflicting signifiers of sex and gender embodied by the cross-cast actor, it may yet be the case that the convention acts as a trigger, prompting the audience to reflect on, for example, the stability of the supposed correspondence between sex (which is biological and generally thought to be immutable) and gender (which is socially constructed and potentially highly mutable).

Writing about "drag, cross-dressing, and the sexual stylization of butch/femme identities," Judith Butler has demonstrated that what is at stake is not simply the discrepancy between the biological sex of the person in question (for our purposes, the actor) and the external signs of his/her gender (his costume). She writes that

> the performance of drag plays upon the distinction between the anatomy of the performer and the gender that is being performed. But we are actually in the presence of three contingent dimensions of significant corporeality: anatomical sex, gender identity, and gender performance. If the anatomy of the performer is already distinct from the gender of the performer, and both of those are distinct from the gender of the performance, then the performance suggests a dissonance not only between sex and performance, but sex and gender, and gender and performance. . . . *In imitating gender, drag implicitly reveals the imitative structure of gender itself—as well as its contingency.*[8] (Butler's emphasis)

Similarly, the cross-cast actor embodies, in addition to the inherent tension between his own sex and gender, a tension between the sex and gender identities of his person and his adopted role on stage. As Butler suggests, such a figure tacitly challenges the assumed correlation between sex and gender, thereby calling into question the binary opposition between male and female on which western patriarchal society rests.

One of the most interesting aspects of the cross-cast actor (and, indeed, the cross-dresser) is that s/he resists easy classification. In her seminal book on transvestism, Marjorie Garber recalls Freud's "third sex" when she asserts that the transvestite figure can be categorized as neither male nor female but constitutes a "third term" and that s/he thereby implicitly poses a challenge to the convenient simplicity of other binary pairs such as high/low, good/bad, public/private, and so on.[9] In the theatre, the cross-cast actor is particularly challenging as he embodies the tensions not only between male and female, sex and gender, but also between truth and falsehood, fact and fiction. In this way, the ambiguous identity of the cross-cast actor cleverly parallels the ambiguity of the theatrical illusion to which he owes his very existence.

Approaching it from a different direction, cross-casting cannot be separated from the question of the actress. Cross-casting came about as a theatrical convention precisely because women were excluded from the public stage. The fact that what was deemed acceptable for men was deemed unacceptable for women is an age-old and fascinating phenomenon in itself. For many centuries and in many countries and cultures, the cross-cast male actor was considered infinitely preferable to his obvious alternative: the actress. As Elizabeth Howe has demonstrated, the arrival of the professional actress on the English stage after the Restoration exerted a strong influence on the types of drama being written.[10] Among other aspects, Howe notes a resurgence of plays involving disguise plots that required the female characters (now played by women) to dress in men's clothing within the performance. The principal attraction of disguise plots in Restoration drama was the fact that men's clothing revealed the actresses' alluring legs — the leg being a site of intense eroticism at a time when this part of the female body was generally hidden from view by long skirts. The shift from female roles being played by adolescent boys (and possibly, sometimes, by adult men) to their portrayal by young women after the reopening of public theatres radically altered the nature and reception of these roles. Prior to the Civil War, female roles were, for the target audience (which was of course understood to be male and heterosexual), a site of gender ambiguity and possible anxiety. With the Restoration actress, they became a site of intense erotic interest and, for the critics of the theatre, a continued site of potential sexual immorality (albeit now of a thoroughly heterosexual variety).

This book is about cross-casting and related gender issues during the heyday of French theatre: the second half of the seventeenth century, the age of Molière, Racine, and the young Louis XIV.[11] Under Louis XIV, cross-casting, while no longer standard practice in the public theatre, persisted in a variety of forms, and instances of it are all the more interesting for the fact that they remained something of an anomaly. The majority of my examples are drawn from the period spanning the early ballets of Louis XIV (from 1651) to Lully's operas (written in the 1670s and 1680s), and Racine's sacred plays of 1689 and 1691. The three major types of theatre that flourished during this period are examined in turn: spoken drama, French court ballet, and opera. This tight focus is nonetheless far-reaching in terms of its bearing on theatre studies in its broadest sense, for casting practices are central to the study of theatrical performance and its reception. Despite the recent upsurge of interest in the all-male theatre of Shakespeare,[12] no book-length study has been made of casting practices in early-modern France (nor, to my knowledge, of any other European country). The all-male stage of Renaissance England was, as Stephen Orgel reminds us, anomalous within a European context (*Impersonations*, 2). In contrast with the formal exclusion of women actors and with a thriving all-male stage in England, other European countries permitted women to act in public throughout most of the

Renaissance. By the second half of the seventeenth century, it was typically the case that in Continental Europe female roles were played by female actors in spoken drama.

An examination of attitudes toward cross-casting and toward the actress in spoken drama in France, and an analysis of the rare (and therefore highly significant) examples of cross-casting in French comedy (we know of no examples from tragedy), is the focus of chapter I. Here we see that cross-casting was exploited as a comic device and performed by secondary actors, partly owing to the fact that French actresses were reluctant to perform unglamorous female roles. Their portrayal by male actors rendered these parts more grotesque than they might otherwise have been. Cross-casting was a necessity (rather than a choice) in school drama in France as elsewhere, and the issues that arose from this custom, both in Jesuit schools for boys and the girls' school at Saint-Cyr, are the subject of chapter II. For the Jesuits, cross-casting was considered less harmful than the inclusion of love plots, while the problem of female beauty and its effect on the male spectator ultimately inhibited the development of school drama at Saint-Cyr. In French ballet, which promoted female beauty, it was still common practice for men to dance female roles, and Louis XIV himself performed a number of female parts. The ballet programs often draw the audience's attention to instances of cross-casting, which are sometimes (but not systematically) exploited to comic or grotesque effect. This tradition, and its gradual erosion as the female ballet dancer emerged, is the subject of chapters III and IV. The arrival of women on the ballet stage brought about a considerable change in the nature of its female roles and brought into greater relief the question of male-female relations at the court of Louis XIV. In chapter V, I am concerned with the new genre of French opera, and with its striking rejection of the ambiguously gendered, ambiguously sexed, and frequently cross-cast Italian castrato, as well as its sparse use of cross-casting as a means of characterizing unfeminine roles. In the course of my study, it will be seen that the nature of cross-casting, its deployment and responses to it, varied widely according to theatrical genre. I hope to demonstrate that casting practices are crucial not only to our understanding of this period of French theatre history, but also to our understanding of theatre in general.

CHAPTER I

UNATTRACTIVE WOMEN: CROSS-CASTING IN COMEDY

The Early Actress

Cross-casting in seventeenth-century French drama cannot be properly understood without first examining the rise of the actress on the French stage. Her story is the single most important reason behind the striking scarcity of cross-cast roles in this period in general, and the use of cross-casting only in comic drama. It also constitutes one of the primary reasons why the attitudes of the French toward both cross-casting and female actors differed so much from those of the English. In England, puritan antitheatricalists raged against the immorality of the theatre, singling out the practice of having boys playing female roles for particular condemnation, while the French were far less vociferous in their denunciation of the same practice.[1] The French who did complain, however, used arguments similar to those employed across the channel. Inspired partly by the negative view dating back to Ancient Rome, actors were perceived by their detractors to be the very essence of the theatre's corruption.[2] Opponents of the theatre took as their foundation the precepts of the Church Fathers, in particular of Tertullian who had written with disapproval of "celui qui altère mensongèrement la voix de son sexe" (*he who falsely alters the voice of his own sex*).[3] Similarly, they objected to cross-dressed men who wanted to "sortir du rang où [leur] Créateur [les] a mis" (*to depart from their divinely appointed rank*).[4] For them as for the English antitheatricalists, to cross-dress was to violate the divinely created order. But ultimately, different attitudes held sway in the two countries: in England the dominant puritan ideology of the mid–seventeenth century rejected the theatre, whereas in France it was considered by the monarchy as both an instrument of state and an enjoyable and legitimate pastime. This difference is illustrated by a telling comparison: the closure of all public theatres in England was decreed in 1642, one year after Louis XIII, prompted by Richelieu, had published an edict according to which actors in France were absolved from their former charges of infamy. Where the English moved to abolish the public theatre, the French sought to improve it. In a similar way, the sudden appearance of the professional actress on the English stage after the Restoration provoked far more powerful reactions than in France where she was introduced more gradually and aroused comparatively little comment. The Restoration actress was met with great alarm by Puritans and with prurient fascination and delight by theatre audiences. While for antitheatricalists the appearance of women on stage was considered at least as dangerous and sinful as that of cross-dressed boys, the theatregoing public enjoyed the new spectacle of the female form and demanded scenarios that would exploit this new phenomenon as much as possible.[5]

Although Lynette Muir has documented a number of examples of female actors performing in early sixteenth-century Passion plays and Saints plays in France, these instances remain exceptional.[6] It was not until the mid–sixteenth century that actresses began to appear with any regularity on the French stage. This practice was stimulated by the appearance of visiting Italian actresses.[7] As early as 1548, Italian actors had given a performance in Lyons in honor of Henry II and Catherine de Medici of the *Calandria*, featuring "de plus excellens comediens et comedientes d'Italie" (*some of the most excellent actors and actresses from Italy*).[8] The first professional Italian actress to have left her mark in the annals of history is the Roman girl, Flaminia, whose talent was recognized by contemporary commentators as early as 1565 (Gilder, 57–58). Before long, every significant acting troupe in Italy boasted among its number an actress, enlisted to play the role of the attractive young heroine. Despite the relatively rapid development of the professional Italian actress at this time, she remained a controversial figure among certain groups, especially in Rome where women were banned from performing on stage.[9] The actor Nicolo Barbieri (known as Beltrame), who played in France in 1624 and 1625,[10] was among those who rebelled against the papal ban, requiring that women's roles in his troupe be played only by women.[11] Meanwhile, in less censorious circles, the actress was beginning to shed her image as a fallen woman and to establish a more respectable reputation. The actress who is thought to have contributed more than any of her contemporaries to this happy development was Isabella Andreini (1562–1604).

Isabella Andreini was described by Tomaso Garzoni as an "honneur de la scène, ornement ·du théâtre, exemple admirable de vertu et de beauté" (*honor of the stage, ornament of the theatre, admirable example of virtue and beauty*).[12] The wife of the celebrated actor, Francesco Andreini, Isabella performed with the Gelosi troupe and lent her name to what was to become one of the stock characters of the *commedia dell'arte*: the beautiful young heroine, Isabella. The Gelosi troupe was one of the first to bring Italian actresses to France. On May 19, 1577, for example, they played at the Hôtel de Bourgogne where, according to S. Wilma Deierkauf-Holsboer, their popular success was assured "surtout grâce aux femmes élégantes qui interprétaient les rôles féminins" (*above all owing to the elegant women who played the female roles*).[13] A quarter of a century later, the same troupe played in Paris at the Hôtel de Bourgogne in the winter of 1603–04 (Deierkauf-Holsboer, I, 60–61). The French poet, Isaac Du Ryer wrote about Isabella's departure from Paris, a lament that amply testifies to the impact she had had on her French audience:

> Je ne crois point qu'Isabelle
> Soit une femme mortelle,
> C'est plutôt quelqu'un des Dieux
> Qui s'est déguisé en femme,
> Afin de nous ravir l'âme
> Par l'oreille et par les yeux.
>
> . . .
>
> Divin esprit dont la France
> Adorera l'excellence
> Mille ans après ton trépas
> (Paris vaut bien l'Italie)
> L'assistance te supplie
> Que tu ne t'en ailles pas.[14]

> *I cannot believe that Isabella*
> *Is indeed a mortal woman.*
> *Rather she has come from the gods*
> *Clothed in human form to tempt us,*
> *To steal away our souls,*
> *As we listen and watch.*
>
> *Divine spirit whose perfections*
> *All of France will continue to adore*
> *A thousand years after your death—*
> *(Paris is the equal of Italy!)*
> *Your admirers implore you,*
> *Do not leave us here bereft!*

We notice that Du Ryer focuses particularly on Isabella's sexual attractiveness rather than on her acting talents, and this was undoubtedly a significant part of the actress's appeal for the contemporary French audience (considered, as an entity, to be male and heterosexual) accustomed to viewing adolescent boys in female roles. What is remarkable about French responses to the emerging actress, in comparison with responses to the same phenomenon in Restoration England, however, is the relative lack of prurient interest in her. While many male members of the French theatre audience were indubitably attracted to the beautiful actresses they beheld, the expression of their passions was more muted than across the channel—to some extent, no doubt, a result of their more gradual introduction to the public stage.

While visiting Italian troupes brought actresses to the Parisian stage on a fairly regular basis, provincial France was cultivating her own brand of actress. Léopold Lacour notes the existence of isolated documents, dated 1545, 1580 and 1592, that mention French actresses performing in the provinces and remarks that actresses in fact appeared in provincial troupes some considerable time before they appeared in Parisian theatres.[15] The first known document to have recorded the existence of a professional French actress is a contract between the actress Marie Fairet and her manager, Antoine l'Espéronnière, signed at Bourges in 1545 (Gilder, 86–87). At a time when more and more provincial troupes were including actresses among their number, female roles at the Hôtel de Bourgogne theatre in Paris continued to be played by cross-dressed male actors wearing masks (Lacour, 6).

Marie Venier, known as Laporte and introduced to the Parisian stage by the pioneering actor-manager Valleran, is the first French actress known to have performed in the French capital. Deierkauf-Holsboer surmises that she was probably performing in Paris by 1607, for in the "Acte d'association d'une troupe de comédiens du Roi sous la direction de Valleran Le Conte" (*act of membership of a troupe of the King's actors, under the direction of Valleran Le Conte*) of that year, mention is made of "une autre commedienne et aussy led. Gasteau de Rachel Trepeau aussy comedienne" (Deierkauf-Holsboer, I, 66 and 186) (*another actress* [probably Marie Venier] *and also the aforementioned Rachel Trepeau, also an actress*). From this time on, more and more actresses were hired as mixed troupes gradually came to be the norm in Paris as well as in the provinces. In his *Comédie des Comédiens*, which was performed at the Hôtel de Bourgogne c.1630–31 and published in 1633, Gougenot refers to no fewer than five actresses in the troupe, and by 1637 (the year of Corneille's *Le Cid*), most acting troupes included at least two actresses (Deierkauf-Holsboer, I, 148 and II, 17). Marie Venier, then, marked the first in a series of seventeenth-century French actresses who came to be celebrated by the theatregoing public, culminating most famously, later in the century, in the figure of La Champmeslé, mistress of Racine and creator of many of his most celebrated female roles.

The French actress appears to have inspired more comment in France than her predecessor, the boy-actor (although her impact on dramatic subjects and texts was, as we have observed, a less striking and a considerably less sexual one than in England). Inspired once again by the Church Fathers, French moralists warned of the dangers of actresses appearing on the public stage, but their remonstrations appear to have had little effect in practice.[16] For strict moralists such as Bossuet, the possibility of excluding female characters from the public theatre (and thereby eliminating the undesirable practice of cross-casting) is discussed, but ultimately dismissed. He writes in his *Maximes et réflexions sur la comédie* of

> les personnages de femme[s], qu'on exclut absolument de la comédie pour plusieurs raisons, et entre autres pour éviter les déguisements que nous avons vu condamnés, ... la réduisent à si peu de sujets, qui encore se trouveraient infiniment éloignés de l'esprit des comédies d'aujourd'hui, qu'elles tomberaient d'elles-mêmes, si on les renfermait dans de telles règles.[17]

> *female characters, which are entirely excluded from the [Jesuit] theatre for a number of reasons, among them in order to avoid the kind of disguise that we have seen condemned. . . . This reduces it to such a small number of topics, which, moreover, are so infinitely distant from the spirit of today's [public] drama, that the theatre would collapse of its own accord if we were to restrict it within such rules.*

For Bossuet, then, no reform can render the public theatre morally acceptable. That the acting profession should be considered particularly unbecoming for a woman rests partly on received assumptions regarding the condition of the female sex. Coustel complained that actresses offended against "la pudeur du sexe" (*the modesty of the female sex*) and against "l'honneur de la virginité" (*the honor of their virginity*) when they performed the role of "une femme passionnée, coquette, effrontée, emportée ou furieuse selon les diverses passions qu'exige son rollet" (*a passionate, coquettish, insolent, fiery or violent woman according to the various passions required by her role*).[18] Not only, the moralists claim, is the actress's behavior inherently unseemly, but also she inspires immoral, lustful thoughts among her (male, heterosexual) audience. As one of the letters in Voisin's treatise reads,

la nudité de son sein, son visage couvert de peinture et de mouches, ses œillades lascives, ses paroles amoureuses, ses ornemens affetez, et tout cet attirail de lubricité, sont des filets où les plus resolus se trouvent pris.[19]

the nudity of her breast, her face covered with paint and with beauty spots, her lascivious winking, her amorous talk, her mannered adornments and all this lubricious paraphernalia are the nets in which even the most resolute find themselves caught.

Since the French theatre audience was tacitly assumed to be male and heterosexual, clearly the spectacle of attractive women on stage was more likely to arouse dangerous libidinous passions than that of their male counterparts.

On the one hand, the very appearance of a woman on stage was perceived to be morally dangerous, both to her and to those who beheld her. On the other hand, her personal morality offstage was also called into question in a way reminiscent of, but less virulent than, the English notion of the actress as prostitute. Jan Clarke reminds us that "there are innumerable reports of the disruption caused by the hordes of followers they [the actresses] attracted backstage, together with expressions of real or mock outrage at the apparent fashion for members of the Court to take actresses and opera singers as their mistresses."[20] The Comédie Française actress, Mlle Raisin, for example, famously bore the Dauphin a child.[21]

As one would reasonably expect, dramatic theorists leapt to the defense of the personal morality of actors, and in particular of actresses. Their most ardent champion was Samuel Chappuzeau, whose *Théatre François* (1674) is essentially a defense against all charges of immorality in the theatre. Chappuzeau is keen to assert the personal morality of actors as exhibited in their alleged sober behavior offstage, their almsgiving, and their attendance at church whenever possible.[22] Dramatists too defended the respectability of actors in metatheatrical pieces such as Gougenot's *Comédie des comédiens* and Scudéry's 1635 play of the same name. In I, 3, of Scudéry's work, for example, la Beau Soleil speaks out in a relatively lengthy speech in response to one of the most commonly held beliefs regarding the personal morality of actresses:

> C'est une erreur où tombe presque tout le monde, pour ce qui regarde les femmes de nostre profession, car ils pensent que la farce est l'image de nostre vie, et que nous ne faisons que representer ce que nous pratiquons en effect. Ils croient que la femme d'un de vous autres, l'est indubitablement de toute la troupe.
>
> *It is a mistake that nearly everybody makes regarding the women of our profession, because they think that the play is an image of our lives and that we are merely representing what we do in real life. They think that the wife of one of you must necessarily also be the wife of the whole troupe.*

There is no doubt that some French actresses *were* promiscuous, but as a collective group, they tended to be less flagrant about it than their English counterparts. As we have seen, the figure of the actress constituted something of an obsession for the English, whereas the French treated her arrival with considerably more equanimity. The collective response to the boy-actor among Puritan antitheatricalists in England had been nothing short of hysterical. Moreover, the Puritans succeeded in putting a stop to (just about) all public theatre for eighteen years — a more radical response than anything that could realistically have been envisaged by the antitheatricalists in France. It is all the more ironic, although perhaps inevitable, then, that the arrival of the actress in England promptly led to an epidemic of new plays in which the much-feared sexuality of women was exploited in all its richness for the entertainment of the public. In the 1660s in France, the heyday of Molière, the plays performed in the mainstream public theatre included virtually no comment on the actresses as explicitly sexual beings, even if their personal morality off-stage continued to be called into question. What is most strikingly different is that in England the sudden arrival of the actress (and of Charles II on the throne) had a strong and direct impact on both the form and content of new plays, as bawdy and explicit comedies were written alongside some surprisingly provocative tragedies. In that sense, Father Courbeville may have been correct when he asserted that French theatre was not quite as immoral as its English counterpart.[23]

Pierre Corneille

The rise of the French actress coincided with the emergence of one of France's greatest playwrights: Pierre Corneille (1606–1684). Corneille is most famous for his tragedies, but his comic theatre is important in its own right and as a forerunner to that of Molière. As women became established as stage performers, it is clear that changes took place in the dramatic output of playwrights, as an examination of the development of the *nourrice* (nurse) figure into that of the *suivante* (lady in waiting) in Corneille's comic theatre will illustrate. Corneille's first two comedies, *Mélite* (c. 1629) and *La Veuve* (c. 1632), include an unnamed *nourrice* figure who was traditionally performed by a cross-dressed male actor wearing a grotesque mask.[24] The purpose of the mask was not, in this instance, to conceal the sex of the performer beneath in order that he might pass more successfully as a member of the opposite sex, but rather to emphasize the grotesque nature of the character being portrayed. The cross-cast nurse was certainly not a sophisticated figure and Henry Lyonnet, for instance, expresses his strong disapproval of "cet usage ridicule consistant à faire tenir par un homme masqué, déguisé en femme, des propos plus ou moins libres pour complaire au public de bas étage" (*this ridiculous custom of having a masked man, dressed as a woman, uttering words of a more or less vulgar nature to please the lower ranking members of the public*) and praises Corneille for his decision to eliminate such a figure from his own theatre.[25] It is likely that Corneille's *nourrices* were played by an actor known by his stage name, Alizon (his real name is unknown), who specialized in such roles and who was a member of the Marais troupe at the time the plays were premiered.[26] The origins of the *nourrice* are to be found in farce, where the character is typically a lively, excessive, rather vulgar (in all senses of the term) figure of dubious morality and whose bawdiness would have been a reliable source of easy humor.[27] Corneille offered a more sophisticated form of comedy, however, and the excesses of his *nourrices* are somewhat more muted than their farcical forerunners.

It is a matter of some debate whether Corneille's comedies may be deemed comic at all, and many of those critics who maintain that they are comic qualify this notion with the understanding that "Corneille's is a discreet, charming conception of comedy which is intended to arouse not laughter but a knowing, compassionate smile."[28] While it is true that Corneille's is a gentler form of comedy than, for example, Molière's, in so far as it involves far fewer overtly comic protagonists, it is clear that the *nourrices* in both *Mélite* and *La Veuve* are comic characters, in the sense that they would have made their audience laugh. In his perceptive analysis of *Mélite*, Jonathan Mallinson rightly draws our attention to the more overtly comic parts of the play, although he does not comment on the fact of the nurse's cross-casting (Mallinson, 40–42).[29] Louis Rivaille, on the other hand, is sensitive to the fact that having the nurse played by a male actor intensifies her impact as a grotesque and highly comic character.[30]

In *Mélite*, the most powerful comic moment in the play is when a delirious Éraste mistakes the *nourrice* for the beautiful Mélite and this is wittily anticipated by the nurse who, on hearing that Éraste has mistaken Cliton for the ferryman, Charon, quips "Et moi, quand je devrais passer pour Proserpine, / Je veux voir à quel point sa fureur le domine" (5.1.1611–12) (*And when I must pass for Proserpine, I shall see the extent to which his madness has overcome him*). The comic potential of the scene that follows, in which a frenzied young suitor takes an aged, unattractive, and grotesque nurse for his beautiful and youthful mistress, is evident and is underlined by the contrast between Éraste's use of the conventional language of gallant love and the *nourrice*'s less refined idiom. He remarks, for example, "c'est lui, qui n'a plus d'autre envie / Que d'épandre à vos pieds son sang avec sa vie" (5.2.1675–76) (*It is he who has no other desire but to offer at your feet his blood and his life*), while she commands him to "Dessillez la paupière" (5.2.1684) (*unstick your eyelids*). The comic impact of this scene must have been heightened by the fact that this highly unsuitable woman was played by a man. There is no question of even a passing homoeroticism, but only of the comic absurdity of a young man pronouncing such words to an older man wearing a dress.

The climax of the scene is Éraste's gradual recognition of the "true" identity of the woman before him, culminating in his horrified exclamation at the point of full realization:

> . . . plus je vous contemple, et plus sur ce visage
> Je m'étonne de voir un autre air, un autre âge,
> Je ne reconnais plus aucun de vos attraits,
> Jadis votre nourrice avait ainsi les traits,
> Le front ainsi ridé, la couleur ainsi blême,
> Le poil ainsi grison, ô Dieux! c'est elle-même.

> *The more I look at you, the more in your face*
> *I am surprised to see another appearance, another age:*
> *I no longer recognize any of your appeal.*
> *Before, your nurse looked like this,*
> *With her wrinkled brow, her pallid complexion,*
> *And her graying hair. O gods, it is her!*

The nurse's cross-casting serves to exaggerate certain traits that are inherent to this type: in direct contrast to the beautiful young heroine, the *nourrice* is sexually unattractive, postmenopausal, and experienced. In other words, she is unfeminine. Her lack of femininity was clearly enhanced to the point of grotesqueness by her costume and mask, and by the way the role was performed, particularly, of course, because no effort was made to conceal the fact that she was played by a man. In this context, Tircis's mocking suggestion to the nurse that she offer herself "pour maîtresse à Philandre" (5.6.1808) (*as Philandre's lover*) becomes, as Joseph Harris has observed, a playful parody of the typical marriage ending of comedy (*Hidden Agendas*, 78). What had at one time been a necessity (men playing female roles on stage) here becomes a means of enhancing the comic impact of a particular role.

In *La Veuve* too, the quick-witted *nourrice* is an important source of comedy, although allusions to her unattractiveness (and by implication to the man beneath the costume) are less overt than in *Mélite*. In addition to the gentle comedy of her cunning scheming (a trait not limited to the nurse, although she is particularly good at it), her lively enthusiasm and apparent skill as an actor are delightful and, as Mallinson has suggested, provide a comic focus at the heart of the play (Mallinson, 56). In Act III, for example, after her mistress, Clarice, is kidnapped (an event engineered by the nurse herself), she comments directly upon the need for convincing play acting: "Sortons de pâmoison, reprenons la parole, / Il nous faut à grands cris jouer un autre rôle" (3.10.1167–68) (*I must stop my swooning now and recover my speech, with much shouting I must play another role*). She (over)plays the role with repeated exclamation and emotive exaggeration:

> Aux armes, aux voleurs, on m'égorge, on me tue,
> On enlève Madame, amis, secourez-nous,
> A la force, aux brigands, au meurtre, accourez tous,
> Doraste, Polimas, Listor. (3.10.1176–79)
>
> *To arms! There's a thief! They're cutting my throat and killing me!*
> *Madame is being kidnapped! Friends, help us!*
> *Help, help! There are brigands! There are murderers! Come quickly*
>   *all of you,*
> *Doraste, Polymas, Listor!*

Of course, it is in the nurse's wild and hypocritical overstatement of events that the comedy lies, and one has no difficulty imagining her words being accompanied by equally wild and exaggerated gestures on stage. Nor must the additional comic element afforded by the fact that she is played by a male actor be overlooked. It is no coincidence that the comic focus of Corneille's two comedies that include a cross-cast nurse lies precisely with that figure, for the comedy of the elderly scheming female character is fruitfully enhanced by her cross-casting in a manner not dissimilar to that of the modern pantomime dame. Like Corneille's nurses, the pantomime dame occupies the ambiguous position of being secondary in terms of the central love plot (the mainstay of comedy), but of primary importance in terms of comic impact. In pantomime, comic impact is of primary importance and, for most audience members, the pantomime dame is therefore the star of the show. In Corneille's comedy on the other hand (for the majority of critics, both modern and contemporary), the love plot takes precedence and the nurse's more overtly comic antics provide a distracting, if entertaining, diversion from the central scenario. Partly for this reason, no doubt, her cross-cast exuberance was curbed as she was refashioned into the figure of the *suivante* in his next comedy, *La Galerie du Palais* (c. 1632).

Corneille himself commented directly on this transformation from *nourrice* to *suivante* in his 1660 *Examen* of *La Galerie du Palais*:

> Le Personnage de Nourrice, qui est de la vieille Comédie, et que le manque d'Actrices sur nos Théâtres y avait conservé jusqu'alors, afin qu'un homme le pût représenter sous le masque, se trouve ici métamorphosé en celui de Suivante, qu'une femme représente sur son visage.

> *The figure of the nurse, who is from old comedy and who, owing to the lack of actresses, had been kept on stage until now in order that a man could play her part with a mask is here metamorphosed into the figure of the* suivante, *who is played by a woman with no mask.*

Here, Corneille draws our attention to two significant (and related) details: first, that male actors might be able to perform in a manner that was acceptable to contemporary audiences only certain types of female role, and second, that the advent of actresses affected the nature of female roles written for the stage. By this point in French theatre history, cross-cast roles in professional acting troupes were limited to the occasional postmenopausal and sexually unattractive woman whose comic traits could be productively enhanced by the fact of her cross-casting. Cross-casting in professional theatre was thus in decline and something that Corneille chose to eliminate from his own compositions at a relatively early stage in his career.

The emergence of the actress in professional troupes in Paris and the ensuing rapid increase in the number of actresses in these troupes no doubt further advanced the decline of cross-casting in French theatre: it was no longer necessary, nor was it desirable.

The *suivante* in *La Galerie du Palais*, Florice, is not the nameless masked type from which she evolved, although she still displays many of the attributes that characterized the Cornelian *nourrice*. She is of an older generation than her mistress, and she is both cunning and experienced in life, but she is not grotesque, and any humor with which she is associated is therefore of a different kind from that of her predecessors: it is gentler, more discreet and focuses on her wily scheming. The evolution is completed in Corneille's next comedy, tellingly entitled *La Suivante* (c. 1633). The most significant change in the *suivante* figure at this point is that she is now young, sexually attractive, and in love. This is a far cry from the postmenopausal, grotesque figure of the early *nourrices*. Although she cannot in the end compete with her in terms of suitors, Amarante forms a credible, if temporary, rival to her mistress. She is finally rejected owing to her lack of money and inferior social status, but it is clear that, were such matters of no concern, she would have had no difficulty maintaining a line of eligible suitors. As Théante explains to Damon:

> Quelques puissants appas que possède Amarante,
> Je treuve [*sic*] qu'après tout ce n'est qu'une Suivante,
> Et je ne puis songer à sa condition
> Que mon amour ne cède à mon ambition.
> Ainsi malgré l'ardeur qui pour elle me presse
> A la fin j'ai levé mes yeux sur sa maîtresse. (1.1.9–14)

> *Whatever strong attractions Amarante possesses,*
> *I find that, at the end of the day, she is only a* suivante
> *And I cannot think of her status*
> *Without my love giving way to my ambition.*
> *Thus, despite the ardor that draws me to her*
> *In the end I have set my sights on her mistress.*

Amarante is the victim of a world in which station is more important than love. In its defiant bitterness, her concluding monologue in the final scene of the play (5.9) is reminiscent of the comparable monologue for the *nourrice* in *Mélite*. The apparent harshness of the *nourrice*'s monologue would have been tempered by her comic-grotesque portrayal by Alizon, whereas Amarante's monologue has more serious implications. The cross-cast actor concludes Corneille's first comedy on a note of farce; the straight-cast actress of his fourth comedy concludes on a note of apparent acrimony. That is not to say that *La Suivante* should be interpreted as a bitter play, but rather that Corneille, in the development of his comic theatre, has come down firmly on the side of nonfarcical comedy—precisely on the side of comedy that, as so many critics have commented, makes the audience smile rather than laugh. The cross-cast comic *nourrice* figure is a source of overt laughter, whereas the straight-cast *suivante* character inspires a wry smile. In this sense, the *suivante* fits more comfortably in the world of Corneille's comedy in general than does the *nourrice*: the farcical *nourrice* was an anomaly in Corneille's comic universe, a misfit from a different comic tradition; the *suivante*, although socially inferior to the other young lovers, belongs to the same, broad tradition as the other characters on stage. While the *nourrice* offers useful material for those critics who wish to assert that Corneille's early comedies did provoke laughter among the theatre audience, the *suivante* on the other hand contributes to the dramatic unity—and one might argue, integrity—of her play.

One of the most significant differences between Corneille's *nourrices* and his *suivantes* is, as we have seen, their age. The implication is that while men might successfully portray older female characters, actresses might more usefully play younger women. Indeed, there is evidence to suggest that actresses insisted on playing only younger female parts. Chappuzeau wrote in his *Théatre François*,

Comme il n'y en a pas vne [femme] qui ne soit bien aise de passer toûjours pour jeune, elles ne s'empressent pas beaucoup à representer des Sisigambis. Il est de l'art du Poëte de ne produire des meres que dans vn bel âge, & de ne leur pas donner des fils qui puissent les conuaincre d'auoir plus de quarante ans. . . . Il y a de la peine à regler les femmes, & les hommes en donnent moins. (Chappuzeau, 85)

Since there is not one woman who does not always want to appear young, they are not eager to play the role of the old shrew. It is the art of the playwright to produce only mothers who are still in bloom, and not to give them sons who could make them think that they must be older than forty. . . . It is very difficult to please the women, but the men are easier to accomodate.

The number of postmenopausal women on the stage was thus reduced not only because roles that could be performed by men were no longer required, but also because actresses were reluctant to perform such unglamorous roles. As early as the 1650s, in correspondence with Chapelle, Molière expressed his displeasure with regard to his three principal actresses (Madeleine Béjart, Magdelon, and Menou) and the problems they posed with regard to casting.[31] Each of them wished to play the glamorous female lead, a desire that suggests some kind of blurring of the distinction between person and persona, between actor and role. Actresses seem to have believed that, by playing glamorous roles on stage, they were somehow enforcing their own offstage glamour and attractiveness. Much has been made of the fact that Molière and his much younger wife, Armande, often portrayed husband and wife teams on stage. This has led to considerable (and in my view unhelpful) speculation with regard to parallels between their onstage and offstage relationships. What is important for the current discussion, however, is not any similarity between life and art, but rather the fact that the male lead in Molière's plays (usually played by Molière himself) needed to play opposite a young, attractive wife (often, therefore, from a second marriage) because his actresses did not wish to play anything else. That his real wife happened also to be much younger than him is, in this context, irrelevant. What is relevant is the fact that the same reluctance to play older characters does not appear to have extended in the same way to *male* actors and their roles.

This blurring of person and persona was also a feature of audience response as suggested by Corneille who, during the *Querelle du* Cid in his "Discours à Cliton," commented on audience members who attended theatre performances not for the drama or for an interest in the characters depicted, but in order to witness their favorite performers:

> Ne venant au Théâtre que pour se divertir, ils sont aussi contents d'ouyr de beaux vers, et de voir faire la Beaupré ou la Devilliers, que d'admirer telle ou telle Héroine qui leur estoit promise et à laquelle ils ne pensent plus.[32]

> *Only coming to the theatre to be entertained, they are just as happy to hear beautiful poetry and to see La Beaupré or La Devilliers, as they are to admire this or that heroine who had been promised them and whom they have already forgotten.*

So, while actresses identified with the glamorous roles they insisted on playing (their personae), audiences enjoyed the spectacle of attractive and talented women on stage (their persons).[33]

Roger Herzel reminds us that actors (and actresses) tended to keep their roles throughout their acting career, so that actresses who had premiered the role of the young heroine at a more suitable age would continue to play that role into middle age and sometimes beyond. The result was that, having avoided playing roles for which they considered themselves unsuited when young, they ended up sometimes playing roles for which they were clearly unsuited at the end of their career. An extreme example of this is a well-known anecdote about Mlle de Brie playing Agnès in *L'École des Femmes* when she was sixty-five years old at the insistence of the public (who objected to her having been replaced by Mlle Du Croisy).[34] This particular episode has more to do with continuity, conservatism, and the popularity of an established actress than it does with the spectacle of attractive female roles played by attractive female actors. Such type-casting also affected the performance of cross-cast roles in Molière's theatre, to which we now turn.

Molière

Jean-Baptiste Poquelin de Molière (1622–1673) remains France's most famous and most popular comic playwright to this day. By the time of Molière's return to Paris in 1658 (following his early training in the provinces), Parisian audiences were fully accustomed to watching women perform female roles in the theatre, and cross-casting had become a relatively rare phenomenon that persisted in the occasional portrayal of older female characters. Molière, who wrote specifically for his own troupe and with each actor's specific talents in mind, composed a small number of older female roles to be played by cross-cast men. Two members of his troupe made something of a specialty of cross-cast roles: Louis Béjart (an original member of Molière's troupe, who retired in 1670) and later André Hubert (who joined in 1664 and retired in 1685). Louis Béjart is famous principally for having had a pronounced limp (from a sword wound) that gave him a certain cult status and which Molière sometimes wrote into his parts (most famously in the part of La Flèche in *L'Avare*). Hubert was a more versatile actor, although Herzel observes in all his roles "a note of high-pitched nervousness," which was manifest "in characters as various as old men and women, excitable sons, doctors, and a Theban general" (Herzel, *The Original Casting*, 86). That their cross-cast parts were noteworthy at the time is made clear by the *Mercure galant* that commented in April 1685 (on the occasion of

Hubert's retirement) that

> jamais Acteur n'a porté si loin les rôles d'homme en femme. Celui qu'il représentoit dans les *Femmes sçavantes;* Madame Jourdain, dans *le Bourgeois Gentilhomme*, & Madame Jobin, dans *la Devineresse*, lui ont attiré l'applaudissement de tout Paris.[35]

> *No other actor has taken the role of a man dressed as a woman to such heights. The one that he played in* Les Femmes Savantes, *Mme Jourdain in* Le Bourgeois Gentilhomme *and Mme Jobin in* La Devineresse *were applauded by the whole of Paris.*

In addition to a number of cross-cast dancing parts in the *comédies-ballets* and some minor bit-parts, Molière's principal cross-cast roles are Mme de Sotenville in *George Dandin* (1668), Mme Pernelle in *Le Tartuffe* (1669), Mme Jourdain in *Le Bourgeois gentilhomme* (1670), and Philaminte in *Les Femmes savantes* (1672). Mme de Sotenville and Mme Pernelle were premiered by Béjart.[36] Following Béjart's retirement at Easter in 1670, Hubert abandoned his male role of Damis in *Le Tartuffe* to play instead the female role of Mme Pernelle. Having thereby proven himself as a cross-cast actor, Hubert subsequently premiered the roles of Mme Jourdain and Philaminte (Herzel, *The Original Casting*, 28). As Herzel asserts, "these were the roles that established Hubert's reputation" (*The Original Casting*, 55). It is interesting to note that in the 1685 season of the relatively young Comédie Française (founded in 1680), for which we have detailed cast lists — these roles were still being performed by male actors.[37] As was customary, Hubert continued to play the roles he had created (Mme Jourdain and Philaminte), Mme Pernelle was to be played by Hubert, with Brecourt as his understudy, and Mme de Sotenville by Beauval, understudied by Mlle La Grange (Hubert had almost certainly taken the role of M. de Sotenville in 1668 and he kept it in 1685).[38] In addition to these parts by Molière, the Repertory informs us that Hubert played two other cross-cast roles in the 1685 season: the old woman, Thérèse, in Thomas Corneille's *Le Festin de Pierre* (a 1677 verse version of Molière's 1665 work, *Dom Juan*) and the wife of Hierosme in Champmelé's *Le Parisien* (1682) (Lancaster, *Actors' Roles*, 52 and 68). That an actress, Mlle La Grange, was Beauval's understudy for the part of Mme de Sotenville does not necessarily represent a deliberate move away from cross-casting. As Herzel puts it, "after 1673 Mlle La Grange seems to have taken absolutely any role she could lay hands on; this is vividly illustrated by the fact that in 1685 she served as understudy to a female impersonator" (*The Original Casting*, 67).

That cross-casting in the spoken theatre of the second half of the seventeenth century in France was sporadic renders these isolated examples all the more interesting and worthy of examination. It is not enough to dismiss them simply as lingering examples of an obsolete theatrical tradition according to which women were excluded from the public stage (although this is indeed part of the story). The fact that an apparently anachronistic tradition was preserved in these isolated instances (and by such a key playwright as Molière) raises a number of important questions regarding the development of that tradition. We have already seen how the advent of the professional actress led to an increase in the number of glamorous and attractive female roles in the theatre and that actresses were generally disinclined to play older, unattractive women. One wonders how, in Molière's case at least, the foreknowledge that such parts would be performed by male actors shaped the writing of them and what effect this cross-casting had in performance.

Richard Parish rightly notes that the principal effect of (and reason for) these examples of cross-casting is "to enhance the audience's comic appreciation of the roles by the fact of their being cross-dressed."[39] Unlike the numerous examples of disguise within seventeenth-century plays (Parish gives the example of the bearded, eponymous Pourceaugnac who dresses as a woman in 3.2), the adopted sex of Mme Pernelle and her associates is fully accepted by the other characters on stage. The comedy of the cross-casting is therefore largely communicated directly from the male actor to the audience and not via the other characters on stage. Having said that, there is little doubt that, in performance, although not explicitly stated in the text, part of the comic effect of such characters was derived from the very fact that a female part, conspicuously played by a man, was apparently accepted as a woman by his/her coperformers. The scope for dramatic (and comic) irony in this situation is great: there is direct complicity between actor and audience and there is a subtler complicity between the actor, his coperformers, and the audience. One is reminded again of the figure of the pantomime dame: she is supposedly accepted as a female character according to the narrative of the play, but much of the humor surrounding that figure is related to the fact that she is so obviously not a woman and that this is, in reality, as obvious to her coperformers as it is to the audience. His/her coperformers do not step beyond the fiction of the performance (in which she is a woman), but they sometimes tread a very fine line between that fiction and the reality of the male performer wearing the dress.

In terms of how these roles were played, René Bray writes that the actors performed "masqués et faisant entendre une voix de fausset" (*masked and speaking in falsetto*).[40] Unfortunately, Bray provides no support for these assertions and they remain a matter of some conjecture. Masks were seldom used by Molière's troupe—a fact that is not in itself proof that they were not used for these cross-cast roles (given that both cross-casting and masks were something of an anachronism, it is perfectly possible that the two were combined in these instances). The use of a falsetto voice persists to great effect in pantomime, and it is quite likely that, as Bray claims, this method was exploited for its comic potential in the performances of Molière's works too.

Mme Pernelle is probably the most famous example of a cross-cast role in Molière's theatre, although her cross-casting is still overlooked more often than not by commentators or at best given very short shrift. In a brief note at the end of his article, Parish gives details of some interesting discussion points that emerged when he first presented his work at a conference.[41] It was observed that by casting Mme Pernelle with a man "placed her/him in the same gender group, as well as the same ideological sub-set, as the variously fanatic Orgon and Tartuffe" (Parish, 58n). I would like to suggest, however, that the alignment is not so much a triple one between Mme Pernelle, Orgon, and Tartuffe as one between Orgon and his mother, who share a number of characteristics, including willfulness, selfishness, and gullibility. Orgon is very much his mother's son and in this sense it seems appropriate that they should both be played by male actors. Tartuffe, on the other hand, is a different character altogether. More interesting, perhaps, is the way in which Mme Pernelle's cross-casting serves both Molière's comic purpose and his more controversial satirical one. One of Molière's principal lines of argument in defending *Le Tartuffe* (and in submitting his request that the ban on public performances be lifted) concerns the extent to which the hypocrite, Tartuffe, is distinct from his genuine counterparts. Molière wrote in his preface, for example, "j'ai mis tout l'art et tous les soins qu'il m'a été possible pour bien distinguer le personnage de l'hypocrite d'avec celui du vrai dévot" (*I have used all the skill and all the care possible to make the distinction clear between the character of the hypocrite and that of the genuinely religious person*). He continues: "j'ai employé pour cela deux actes entiers à préparer la venue de mon scélérat" (*in order to do that I spent two whole acts preparing for the arrival of my villain*). Mme Pernelle plays a crucial part in preparing the audience for Tartuffe's arrival.

Both in the 1660s and in more recent literary criticism, the debate regarding Molière's most famous play has focused overwhelmingly on its eponymous villain. As Molière himself reminds us, however, Tartuffe does not appear on stage until Act III, by which time the theatre audience will have already formed an opinion of him. As early as the opening scene, Tartuffe is being characterized as he is discussed by the other members of the cast. His hypocritical nature rapidly becomes apparent, owing largely to Mme Pernelle's praise of him combined with her own ridiculous portrayal, itself enhanced by the fact that she is played by a male actor. The play opens with a frenetic Mme Pernelle dashing about and complaining. In a highly comic sequence that establishes her as a caricature of the bad tempered old woman, Mme Pernelle interrupts and insults each of her companions in turn. She even has words of criticism for the eminently reasonable Cléante, remarking that "je vous estime fort, vous aime, et vous révère; / Mais . . ." (1.1.34–35) (*I have a very high opinion of you, I like you and I esteem you, but . . .*). That she was originally played by a man in a dress, probably speaking falsetto, further enhances both her comical and ridiculous status in the play. Under other circumstances, Mme Pernelle might have been a wise and venerable matriarch. Played by Béjart, her views are conspicuously misguided and not to be taken seriously. Crucially, the fact that Mme Pernelle is an ardent admirer of Tartuffe dispels any doubt that might have existed regarding his status as a hypocrite and charlatan. When the notion of his hypocrisy is introduced directly into the discussion by Dorine, who comments that "Il passe pour un saint dans votre fantaisie: / Tout son fait, croyez-moi, n'est rien qu'hypocrisie" (1.1.69–70) (*In your imagination he is a saint, but believe me he is in reality nothing more than a hypocrite*),[42] Mme Pernelle responds with an outraged "Voyez la langue!" (1.1.71) (*listen to her talk!*). In her closing speech at the end of the scene, Mme Pernelle, in true comic fashion, complains about the noise and chatter of those around her, while remaining oblivious to her own prattling and, having struck her servant Flipote, speaks to her in a vulgar, disrespectful, and aggressive way.

There is nothing feminine about Mme Pernelle. Just as she does not make a credible woman, so is there nothing credible about her admiration for Tartuffe. In this sense, Mme Pernelle paradoxically fulfils, through different methods, the same function as the *raisonneur* figure. Just as we understand Cléante to offer a levelheaded view of Tartuffe, so we understand that Mme Pernelle's view of Tartuffe is equally reliable in its inaccuracy. Each of them thus guides the audience toward an awareness of Tartuffe's hypocrisy (and of Orgon's duping). Mme Pernelle offers the additional advantage of being a highly comical character, and so her comical function and her serious function are in fact intimately linked.

It is a well-known fact that *Le Tartuffe* underwent extensive revision between its first performance at court on May 12, 1664 (after which public performances of the play were banned), its single public performance on August 6, 1667 (which led to a renewal of the ban), and subsequent public performances from February 5, 1669. Opinion is divided concerning the exact nature of these revisions (and elaborate theories have been devised to ascertain them), but it seems likely, given the difficulties Molière encountered in having the play performed at all, that many of them served to distinguish still further Tartuffe from a *vrai dévot* (a sincerely devout person). Indeed, Molière alludes to some of these changes in his preface and in his petitions to the king. There is some evidence to suggest that the role of Mme Pernelle may not have formed part of the original version of the play at all and that it was added with precisely this purpose in mind. Stephen Dock notes that a costume for Mme Pernelle was bought on August 24, 1664, over three months after the play had been premièred, and concludes that her role must postdate the première, having been added "to lend comic relief to the play" (though as we have seen, in view of her serious function detailed above, it is clearly more than just comic relief that Mme Pernelle contributes to *Le Tartuffe*).[43] Her costume was clearly considered an important part of her impact, for, as La Thorillière's *Second Registre* informs us, it was chosen by Molière himself and was moreover "the first Molière bought for a speaking role" (Dock, 148). We do not have a detailed description of Mme Pernelle's costume, but, as Dock suggests, it seems likely that it was ridiculously old-fashioned, a view supported by the author of the *Lettre sur la comédie de l'Imposteur* who comments on her predilection for "l'austérité ridicule du temps passé" (Dock, 148) (*ridiculous old-fashioned austerity*). The fact that the *Lettre sur la comédie de l'Imposteur* begins with a detailed commentary asserting the ridiculousness of Mme Pernelle is not simply a result of the anonymous author's chronological approach to his analysis of the play. It also underlines how crucial Mme Pernelle is to Molière's attempts to render his play acceptable for performance. There is no doubt that her cross-casting, which would have been apparent from the moment she appeared on stage, played a large part in her characterization as an old fool whose opinions were not to be taken seriously.[44]

The second of Molière's cross-cast roles created for Béjart was the part of Mme de Sotenville in *George Dandin*.[45] Originally a *comédie-ballet* written to entertain Louis XIV and his court as part of the *Grand Divertissement Royal de Versailles* in 1668 (a celebration of the conquest of the Franche-Comté, followed by the peace of Aix-la-Chapelle, signed on May 2), the farcical *George Dandin* remains one of Molière's lesser-known works. Mme de Sotenville is denied the serious function of Mme Pernelle, but she makes a wonderful comic caricature of the mother-in-law figure and contributes in no small way to the farcical spirit of the play.[46] The very name "Sotenville" (literally "idiot in town") conjures up images of ridiculous behavior, and the comic potential of a married couple who always appear on stage together and who are both played by men is evident. From the moment she first arrives on stage, Mme de Sotenville's verbalizing is hysterical as she employs a large number of exclamations and questions (her first utterance is "Mon Dieu!" as she is outraged by her son-in-law's failure to employ the correct forms of address for a member of the bourgeoisie addressing the aristocracy). She is pretentious, pompous, proud, and thoroughly ridiculous. Her maiden name "Prudoterie" with its suggestions of prudishness, combined with the fact that she frequently holds herself up as an example of ideal feminine behavior, evokes a specifically *female* form of prudishness that is all the more comical thanks to her embodiment by a male actor.

As is the case for all of Molière's cross-cast roles, there is nothing bawdy about Mme de Sotenville's portrayal. When she appears in her nightdress in 3.7, the humorous potential of the scene lies in the comical absurdity of her appearance rather than in any homoerotic overtones or sexual innuendo. Similarly, Monsieur de Sotenville's final rejoinder to his wife at the end of the same scene— "Et nous, mamour, allons nous mettre au lit" (3.7) (*As for us, my dear, let's go back to bed*)—is comical owing to his use of affectionate (and therefore highly inappropriate) language and to its tacit implication that they are an ordinary, cohabiting couple. It is unlikely that any innuendo is intended although clearly the role invites other interpretations and could, in a modern production, be successfully camped up. Brissart's engraving for the 1682 *Œuvres de Monsieur de Molière* (figure 1.1) is based on this penultimate scene of *George Dandin* and reminds us of how unreliable such illustrations can be, for Mme de Sotenville appears neither in her nightgown nor is she played by a man. She is, however, given a face that is conspicuously less attractive than those of Brissart's younger women, including Angélique who features in the same image.

Figure 1.1   Engraving by Pierre Brissart of *George Dandin* (1682).

Source: Beinecke Rare Books and Manuscripts Library, Yale University.

The first cross-cast role that Molière wrote for Hubert was that of Mme Jourdain in *Le Bourgeois gentilhomme* (in which he also played the part of the Maître de Musique). As Gaston Hall, following Antoine Adam's lead, has noted,

> we know how Hubert must have looked in this role from a reference in *Araspe et Simandre* (1672), the author of which is reminded of Mme Jourdain by "une grande femme maigre entre deux âges, vêtue d'un manteau feuille morte qui assortissait à merveille la couleur de son teint" (*a tall, thin women, neither exactly old nor young, dressed in a coat the color of dead leaves that went perfectly with the color of her skin*).[47]

Mme Jourdain is an interesting example of the cross-cast role because she is not the straightforward, ridiculous old shrew in the manner of Mme Pernelle or Mme de Sotenville. For many commentators who have ignored her cross-casting and its implications, she functions as a voice of reason in the Jourdain household, a rational foil to M. Jourdain's madness. Roland Bruyelle, for example, describes Mme Jourdain as "la vivante antithèse de son mari" (*the very antithesis of her husband*) and remarks that "autant celui-ci est 'fou', autant elle est 'sage' " (*to the extent that he is mad, so she is wise*).[48] These normative readings of Mme Jourdain tend to focus on her responses to the eccentric behavior of her social-climbing husband. But, as Parish has noted, "the view of Madame Jourdain as a 'normative' character was challenged by her casting, in early performances, as a cross-dressed one" (Parish, 58n) and our knowledge of this early performance practice must inform our reading of Mme Jourdain even today. It is of course the case that Mme Jourdain does, at the level of language, offer a commonsense view of her husband's increasingly madcap world, a view that she expresses in earthy, sometimes even rather crude, terms. Objectively, his behavior *is* ridiculous and her assertion that Jourdain is being duped by Dorante is equally justified, as is her gradual awareness of his intended infidelity with Dorimène. Textually, Mme Jourdain *is* the reasonable wife, exasperated by her ridiculous (but good-natured) husband. The fact that she was originally played by a man, and that the role was written specifically with a male actor in mind, however, must modify our view of her. That she is cross-cast need not necessarily render her apparently reasonable comments unreasonable: her desire that her daughter should marry someone of similar rank because "les alliances avec plus grand que soi sont sujettes toujours à de fâcheux inconvénients" (3.12) (*marrying above one's station always ends in tears*), for example, is based on good principles. Rather, her cross-casting adds an *extra* comic dimension to her character. She may offer a voice of objective reason, but that voice is itself made ridiculous, owing to an incongruity between the views expressed and the man-in-a-dress expressing them. Mme Jourdain thus literally embodies a comic tension between language and physical appearance. Moreover, this insight shifts greater emphasis onto her more hysterical outbursts as in 5.1 when she exclaims, on seeing Jourdain dressed as a Mamamouchi:

> Ah! mon Dieu! miséricorde! Qu'est-ce que c'est donc que cela? Quelle figure! Est-ce un momon que vous allez porter; et est-il temps d'aller en masque? Parlez donc, qu'est-ce que c'est que ceci? Qui vous a fagoté comme cela?
>
> *Oh, my God! Mercy upon us! What on earth is that? What a sight! Is that a costume that you're going to wear for the carnival, and is it time to go? Speak to me and tell me what's going on? Who has dressed you up like that?*

A number of critics have commented on the carnivalesque nature of *Le Bourgeois gentilhomme*, whereby the follies of the principal deviant character (Jourdain) are ultimately indulged (in the Turkish ceremony) rather than corrected.[49] Mme Jourdain herself complains that:

> Je ne sais plus ce que c'est que notre maison: on dirait qu'il est céans carême-prenant tous les jours; et dès le matin, de peur d'y manquer, on y entend des vacarmes de violons et de chanteurs, dont tout le voisinage se trouve incommodé. (3.3)
>
> *I don't know what's going on in our house anymore: you'd think it were Carnival time every day here and, from first thing in the morning, for fear of missing out on anything, the place is filled with a racket of violins and singing. It's disturbing the whole neighborhood.*

But Mme Jourdain is herself part of this carnivalesque atmosphere. She and M. Jourdain are a carnivalesque couple; they bicker continually in the manner of the traditional comic couple, but neither one of them offers an attractive and sensible solution to the problems they face. Mme Jourdain cannot be taken seriously as a wife figure, and her husband's folly ultimately offers a more appealing alternative than her burlesque common sense. One of the few critics to have addressed the character of Mme Jourdain in the light of her cross-casting is

David Whitton who concludes that "rather than a socially realistic voice of opposition to her husband, she is intended to produce a dramatic clash of opposites in a burlesque pantomime register."[50] These encounters do not form, then, a balance between an eccentric, unreasonable, comical husband and his much put-upon, sensible (but uncomical) wife; rather they provide a further imbalance between an eccentric, unreasonable, comical husband and his more subtly comical wife. To modify Whitton's observation, the comedy of their scenes lies not so much in a clash of opposites, the reasonable character highlighting the unreasonable behavior of her counterpart, as rather in a clash of two different forms of comedy that interact to greater, more carnivalesque, effect. An example of this may be found in Mme Jourdain's attitude toward clothing and costume: in both 3.3 and 5.1, she openly mocks her husband's appearance, first when he appears in a new outfit made especially for him by his master tailor, and then in his mamamouchi costume (mentioned above). While M. Jourdain is undoubtedly supposed to look ridiculous, the comic irony of such observations being made by a man in a dress would not have been lost on Molière's audience.

The only scene in which any verbal reference to Mme Jourdain's cross-casting may perhaps be detected is in 3.5 when an awkward conversation takes place between Mme Jourdain and Dorante. In true courtly fashion, Dorante emphasizes traditional gender roles by politely and gallantly inquiring about her daughter Lucile's health and then inviting Lucile and her mother to "le ballet et la comédie que l'on fait chez le Roi" (*the ballet and comedy that are being performed at court*). Mme Jourdain is unreceptive to his gender-based civility partly owing to her class, but partly also owing to her own ambiguous gender. Dorante's subsequent compliment is certainly an ambiguous one:

Je pense, Madame Jourdain, que vous avez eu bien des amants dans votre jeune âge, belle et d'agréable humeur comme vous étiez.

I imagine, Mme Jourdain, that you must have had a good number of suitors when you were younger, beautiful, and good-humored as you were then.

Whatever the nuances of Dorante's conversational gambit, it is clear that the discrepancy between the youthful, beautiful, and charming Mme Jourdain he imagines and the unfeminine incarnation with which he finds himself is a source of humor whose impact is undoubtedly strengthened by Mme Jourdain's portrayal by a male actor.

Similarly, as the textual part of the *comédie-ballet* draws to an end in 5.6 (there is still the extensive Ballet des Nations to follow) and an array of betrothed couples is established, Monsieur Jourdain's final comic flourish reminds us one last time of Mme Jourdain's lack of feminine charms as he offers "ma femme à qui la voudra" (*my wife to anyone who wants her*).

Hubert also premiered the role of the fanatical Philaminte in *Les Femmes Savantes*, although there is some evidence to suggest that the role was not originally conceived with him in mind. Drawing on his intimate knowledge of the history and talents of Molière's actors, Herzel has suggested that, at the time when the play was first conceived (prior to spring 1670), Molière would not have allocated such an important role to Louis Béjart (whose acting talents were limited) or to Hubert (who had not yet established himself as a cross-cast actor).[51] Herzel concludes, fascinatingly, that the role of Philaminte was destined to be played by Madeleine Béjart, "an actress with excellent credentials in both tragedy and comedy who had just passed her fiftieth birthday," but who did not live to perform it (Herzel, "Problems in the Original Casting," 226). Herzel's hypothesis may hold the key to why Philaminte is so different from Molière's other cross-cast roles. However, as Herzel also observes, it is likely that Molière in due course adapted the play for the cast that eventually performed it in 1672 (Herzel, "Problems in the Original Casting," 229). What we are left with is a role probably inspired by a female actor but whose performance by a male actor endowed it with different nuances that enhance both the comic message of the play and especially its commentary on gender roles.

Philaminte is Molière's only cross-cast role in a play in which the calling in to question of gender roles is a central theme, and this adds some particularly interesting dynamics to her portrayal by a man. This is all the more appropriate given the fact that in comedy the father is more frequently the parent who poses an obstacle to the daughter's marriage. Even before she appears on stage, Philaminte's domineering (and therefore masculine) personality is established. A marriage in which the wife dominates her husband, thereby subverting traditional gender roles, is a mainstay of comic theatre, and Philaminte's marriage to Chrysale is a particularly forceful example of the genre. Their daughter, Henriette, comments on the power relations between her parents in a revealing way when advising her lover Clitandre on how he should attempt to win their favor:

Le plus sûr est de gagner ma mère:
Mon père est d'une humeur à consentir à tout,

Mais il met peu de poids aux choses qu'il résout;
Il a reçu du Ciel certaine bonté d'âme,
Qui le soumet d'abord à ce que veut sa femme;
C'est elle qui gouverne, et d'un ton absolu
Elle dicte pour loi ce qu'elle a résolu. (1.3.204–210)

The best way is to win over my mother:
My father will agree to anything,
But he never follows through the things that he's decided
He has received from heaven an easygoing nature
Which makes him submit to his wife's wishes
It is she who is in charge and, with a voice of authority,
Whatever she has decided is set in stone.

Chrysale's weakness is a source of comedy in the same way that Philaminte's strength is, and the comic impact of their relationship as a married couple is further enhanced by Philaminte's cross-casting: she is so masculine in her domineering behavior that she is perhaps best played by a man. Philaminte is masculine in other respects too. Her intellectual leanings are masculine in themselves: as Harris reminds us, Guez de Balzac had condemned women intellectuals as mental transvestites, as women "qui se travestissent par l'esprit."[52] Similarly, her lack of interest in being an object of male desire makes of Philaminte the type of woman whom La Bruyère later described as having "de leur sexe que les habits" (*of their sex only the clothing*).[53]

Philaminte's masculinity further emasculates Chrysale who struggles in the course of the play to assert himself over his overbearing and ridiculous wife. Where M. Jourdain was unreasonable and engaging in his eccentricity, Chrysale is reasonable and weak. The role of Chrysale is undoubtedly a humorous one, but it is strongly dependent, both in terms of the comic fiction and for its comic effect, on Philaminte, and as such is an unusual one for Molière himself to have played. The actor-playwright almost without exception took the principal comic lead in his plays, but here he is somewhat upstaged by a number of comic characters, including most notably the powerfully comic Philaminte, distinguished by her cross-casting. None of Molière's other cross-cast roles is as central to the play as Philaminte: her powerful status is owing to her dominant position in her own household, to her extreme embodiment of the satirized *femme savante* figure (including her lack of discernment with regard to the famously ridiculous poet, Trissotin), and to the distinctively comical aspect bestowed upon her by virtue of being played by a man in a play in which the many remaining female characters (some of whom are also *femmes savantes*) are all played by women.[54] Bray suggests that Philaminte is younger than Molière's other cross-cast roles, that she is "encore en pleine maturité" (Bray, 81) (*still in the ripeness of middle age*).[55] Her age is not clear from the text, but in the 1685 Répertoire she is clearly labeled as "philaminte, vieille" (Lancaster, *Actors' Roles*, 40) (*Philaminte, old woman*). It is possible that the role of Philaminte aged as Hubert did, but it is more likely that she was always perceived as menopausal or postmenopausal—an age that is somehow desexualized.

The combination of Philaminte's declared interest in female education and her cross-casting offers ample scope for comic irony when gender roles are discussed. Chrysale, even more than his daughter Henriette, holds an extreme traditional view of such things:

> Il n'est pas bien honnête, et pour beaucoup de causes,
> Qu'une femme étudie et sache tant de choses.
> Former aux bonnes mœurs l'esprit de ses enfants,
> Faire aller son ménage, avoir l'œil sur ses gens,
> Et régler la dépense avec économie,
> Doit être son étude et sa philosophie. (2.7.571–576)

> *There are many reasons why it's really not seemly*
> *For a woman to study and know so many things.*
> *Developing good morals in the minds of her children*
> *Running her household, keeping an eye on the servants,*
> *And overseeing the domestic expenditure with prudence:*
> *That's what she should study and what her philosophy should be.*

Philaminte on the other hand complains about:

> . . . cette indigne classe où nous rangent les hommes,
> De borner nos talents à des futilités,
> Et nous fermer la porte aux sublimes clartés. (3.2.854–856)

> *This inferior class to which men reduce us*
> *Restricting our talents to futile pursuits,*
> *And shutting us out from advanced learning.*

What might in a different context be read as a commendable proto-feminist protest is challenged on at least two counts, both of them comic. First, Philaminte and her companions are exaggerated parodies of educated women and not the genuine article, and second, their most ardent advocate, Philaminte, is conspicuously male beneath his/her costume. This second point is highlighted when Martine comments to Chrysale on the dangers of a woman "wearing the trousers":

> Et nous voyons que d'un homme on se gausse
> Quand sa femme chez lui porte le haut-de-chausse. (5.3.1645–1646)
> *And we see that a man is mocked*
> *When it's his wife who wears the trousers in his home.*

The irony of this statement operates simultaneously on a number of levels. First, it highlights the fact that the addressee, Chrysale, finds himself in exactly the situation being described; second, it highlights the fact that Philaminte is a woman who wears the metaphorical trousers and at the same time a man who is wearing a real dress. Philaminte thus dramatically, and on two different levels, calls into question the supposed correspondence between traditional signifiers of gender and sex and supposedly related gender roles. The fact that Philaminte's plea for women's education is in reality pronounced by a man might under less comic circumstances be understood to subvert the female cause. It is an interesting question whether the fact that the actor pronouncing a text that advocates women's rights and education is a man invalidates or supports those views.[56]

Ultimately, Molière's cross-cast characters are not fundamentally subversive either of traditional gender roles or of conventional sexuality. Mme Pernelle, Mme de Sotenville, and Mme Jourdain are strong characters but in the end they have little influence on the people around them. Philaminte is the strongest of the four and is seen to exert a great deal of power over her husband. In her deluded admiration for Trissotin, however, she represents the deviant character who is eventually brought back into line at the end of the play. She remains an unreformed *femme savante*, but she has seen Trissotin's true colors and the mismatched marriage between him and Henriette is avoided. The lack of femininity of these four women is highlighted (and in part created) by their cross-casting that serves as a pertinent reminder to masculine women that such behavior is not welcome. Although Molière includes passing allusions to the fact that they are not sexually attractive (to heterosexual men), there is no suggestion of homo-eroticism. Neither is their portrayal bawdy or vulgar in a sexual way.

The principal purpose of Molière's cross-cast women remains a comic one, as we are reminded of the enduring comic appeal of a man wearing a dress and speaking in falsetto. They also represent a self-conscious celebration of comic theatre and theatricality. The comic cross-cast figure makes no attempt to disguise herself convincingly as a woman; rather, the jarring coexistence of female signifiers (her clothes) and the reality of the male body beneath them is essential to his/her comic impact. The cross-cast female character rejoices in this discrepancy and deliberately draws the audience's attention to the fragile nature of the theatrical illusion. This is probably best illustrated in *Le Bourgeois gentilhomme*, which with its ample musical and dancing episodes (including most notably the gloriously over-stated Turkish Ceremony at the end of Act IV), is a highly and self-consciously theatrical work. It is probably no coincidence that none of Molière's works to include a cross-cast figure is a straightfor-ward piece of prose writing: the two that are in prose were originally *comédies-ballets: George Dandin* was composed in a strong spirit of court *fête*, while *Le Bourgeois gentilhomme* is arguably Molière's most carnivalesque work. *Le Tartuffe* and *Les Femmes savantes* are composed in rhyming Alexandrine couplets that lend them an air of gravity, but also of artificiality, of self-conscious theatricality. Earlier in the cen-tury, Corneille had inherited the tradition of the cross-cast nurse, a tradition that was comically successful, but increasingly less desirable in view of the emergence of the professional actress and of Corneille's own development of the comic genre. The cross-cast characters in Molière's theatre thus constitute further examples of an increasingly outmoded tradition, but one whose comic and theatrical potential was successfully exploited by France's greatest comic playwright.

A Tradition in Decline: *La Devineresse*

Additional examples of cross-cast parts in mainstream spoken theatre of this period in France are few and far between. We noticed above that Hubert was singled out by the *Mercure galant* not only for having played Mme Jourdain and Philaminte, but also Mme Jobin in *La Devineresse*, a comedy by Donneau de Visé and Thomas Corneille (the younger brother of Pierre Corneille). First performed by the Guénégaud troupe on November 19, 1679 (and published in February 1680), *La Devineresse* was, in terms of box-office receipts, the most popular play of its time.[57] Its popularity was owing not to the quality of the dramatic writing (which verges on substandard at times) but to the topicality of its subject. The play coincided with a series of high-profile witch trials in France and with the arrest of a certain Mme Voisin on whom its protagonist Mme Jobin is thought to have been based. A number of suspected witches were executed around this time and Mme Voisin herself was burned in February 1680.

La Devineresse cleverly combines a widely publicized and frightening news story with the agreeable genre of comedy. Drawing on the heightened anxieties and interest of the theatregoing public, the play temporarily replaces the frightening figure of the female witch with the reassuring spectacle of a distinctly masculine woman who is nothing more dangerous than a charlatan. As will be seen, an important factor in establishing Mme Jobin as nonthreatening is her comic portrayal by a man.

This is a particularly interesting example of cross-casting for a number of additional reasons: it was one of the last (possibly *the* last) cross-cast roles played by Hubert, who was himself one of the last actors to specialize in such roles. Moreover, the eponymous figure of Mme Jobin is an unusually significant (i.e., central) cross-cast role in what was a very popular and successful play. There is no doubt that Mme Jobin's cross-casting would have been exploited for many of the same basic effects that we saw in Molière's cross-cast parts. There is a certain irony in the fact that she knows "des Secrets tous merveilleux pour conserver la beauté" (3.9) (*wonderful secrets for preserving beauty*) and, perhaps, in the fact that, when clients meet her for the first time, they tend to appear uncertain regarding her identity: "Est-ce vous qui sçavez tout, & qui s'appelle Mme Jobin?" (2.5) (*is it you who know everything and who are called Mme Jobin?*) asks the Paysanne, for example; "N'estes-vous pas Mme Jobin" (*are you not Mme Jobin?*), asks Mme Des Roches who then addresses Mme Jobin with words that draw attention to the *devineresse*'s unusual appearance "Si vostre visage m'est inconnu, vostre réputation m'est bien connuë" (3.9) (*if your face is unknown to me, I know your reputation well*). The greatest ironic exploitation of Mme Jobin's cross-casting, however, is in 5.3 when she encounters a certain Mme de Troufignac who, it is indicated in the text, is disguised as a man. This encounter between a cross-cast man and a cross-dressed woman is a highly entertaining one, particularly in view of the fact that Mme de Troufignac has come to ask Mme Jobin to turn her into a man so that she can marry a delightful woman with whom she is in love. Mme Jobin herself comments on the comedy of the situation, saying "Je vous écoute pour rire avec vous, car vous estes trop éclairée pour me parler serieusement" (*I'm listening so that I can laugh with you, for you are too enlightened to be talking to me seriously*). Mme de Troufignac's cross-dressing is noteworthy for another reason: unlike the other examples of cross-casting that we have examined, here the play *does* touch, even if only briefly, upon issues of homosexual love—in this case between women. But homosexuality is not what

Mme Jobin is about: she is neither an object nor a subject of sexual desire, as her cross-casting reminds us. Clearly such a role would not have appealed to actresses anxious to uphold their femininity on stage; equally, it seems appropriate for the purposes of characterization that such an unfeminine figure should be played by a man.

In addition to this, as I suggested above, Mme Jobin's cross-casting appears to have served a more important function: to defuse the potentially explosive role of the seer or witch. This is achieved partly by the fact that she is presented quite clearly as a charlatan (and a self-confessed one at that) from the opening speech of the play onward (though, as Molière found to his cost, with *Le Tartuffe* and then *Dom Juan*, even self-confessed hypocrites can be (mis)interpreted as sinister or controversial). The contemporary witch trials that inspired her creation were truly sinister, but the same cannot be said about Mme Jobin, played by a man in a dress, probably speaking in falsetto. She thus becomes a highly comical character, a fact that no doubt helped avert any scandal that the play might otherwise have provoked. Mme Jobin is not a mysterious witch possessed of alarming and puzzling occult powers. Rather, she is a cunning, scheming, but ultimately nonthreatening charlatan who successfully plays on the credulity (and occasionally the scepticism) of her clients. She is in no way taken in by her own successes (although she happily rejoices in them) and, as is fitting in comedy, she is finally exposed for what she really is at the end of the play. Mme Jobin therefore represents at once some kind of apotheosis of the cross-cast female figure and her demise. As Reynier writes of Hubert's portrayal of Mme Jobin, "Après sa retraite, en 1685, on renonça à cette espèce de mascarade, et il fallut bien trouver des actrices qui consentissent à se vieillir" (*after his retirement in 1685 this kind of mascarade was abandoned and actresses had to be found who agreed to grow old*).[58]

CHAPTER II

BOYS WILL BE GIRLS: CROSS-CASTING IN SCHOOL DRAMA

Although as we have seen, cross-casting was only rarely a feature of traditional theatre in seventeenth-century France, it persisted out of necessity in the school drama of the period.[1] Drawing on the great theatrical tradition of the Jesuits at the Collège de Clermont in Paris (which became the Collège Louis-le-Grand in 1683) and on the performance history of Racine's two plays written for Saint-Cyr, I shall examine how the question of cross-casting was received in these two very different performance contexts. It will be seen that the all-male productions at the Collège de Clermont provoked quite different responses from the all-female productions at Saint-Cyr. In Jesuit drama, cross-casting was inextricably bound up with debates regarding the inclusion of female roles and love plots in their drama, while the performances at Saint-Cyr highlighted wider questions regarding the role of women in society.

The Jesuits

Many of the leading lights of early modern Europe were educated in Jesuit schools, among them Pierre Corneille (in Rouen) and Molière (in Paris). The Jesuits offered a system of education that combined a humanist approach to learning with an emphasis on religious and moral instruction. One of the most successful features of Jesuit education was the importance given to developing a symbiotic relationship between duty and discipline on the one hand and pleasure on the other. The performance of Latin plays was, in theory at least, concordant with both their humanist and their religious principles, for it offered the scope for the development of a number of personal skills (including language, rhetoric, poise, and public speaking) and also for spiritual development and edification.

The Jesuits' commitment to school drama is demonstrated by a long and varied history of theatrical productions. Jesuit plays evolved in the mid–sixteenth century from the performance of Latin dialogs, simple rhetorical exercises employed to develop students' articulacy, declamation, poise, bearing, and memory. Latin plays were typically performed for the annual school prize-giving in August, and often to celebrate carnival and various church festivals, or on the occasion of a special visit to the school by a member of the royalty or high nobility. The majority of these plays were written by the resident poetry teacher. They were composed specifically for performance within this very particular context and very few Jesuit plays were ever published. Our most useful sources are therefore eyewitness accounts that are for the most part tantalizingly scant in detail, and the programs, many of which have survived and give us a good idea of the subject matter of these plays as well as the names of many of the students who performed in them. Their casts were, of course, all male, as Robinet observed when describing a production at a prize-giving at the Collège de Clermont:

> Ains [*sic*] que c'estoyent toutes merveilles
> Pour les Yeux, & pour les Oreilles,
> Quoi que le beau Séxe enchanteur,
> Qui plaît le plus au Spectateur,
> Et qui fait qu'on est Idolâtre,
> La pluspart du Temps, du Théatre,
> N'agisse ni peu, ni prou là,
> Dedans ces beaux Spectacles là. (August 8, 1671)[2]

> *Thus there were all these marvels*
> *For the eye and for the ear*
> *Even though the enchanting fair sex,*
> *Which pleases the spectator most*
> *And which means that most of the time*
> *We worship the theatre,*
> *Does not participate at all*
> *In these beautiful spectacles.*

The subject matter of early Jesuit plays tended to be historical, religious, or both, including scenes from the Old Testament, from Ancient History, the history of the Church, and even contemporary history. Plays were composed and performed in Latin and were generally, although not always, restricted to the tragic genre (comedy being thought unfit for the didactic purposes of such productions). However, theatre productions in Jesuit schools became so popular with their students and audiences (which included friends and relations of the student actors, patrons and supporters of the school, members of the clergy, and visiting nobles) that expansion and development rapidly followed. What had originated as modest productions became more and more elaborate, with increased importance being accorded to such spectacular elements as décor, costume, stage machinery, and so on. Jesuit schools in seventeenth-century France (notably at the Collège de Clermont in Paris) are famous for having cultivated ballet on the school stage. As opera emerged in the later part of the century, the Jesuits came to include more and more singing in their productions as well. As the second half of the century drew on, it was increasingly the case that the balletic and musical portions of Jesuit productions were of prime importance to the entertainment, to the point where they overshadowed the traditional Latin tragedy. Occasionally, even, professional dancers and dancing masters, musicians, and composers from the Paris Opéra were brought in to Jesuit schools to assist the schoolboys in their performances.[3] In this chapter, however, I shall focus on responses to the spoken plays, for it is on those that most of the contemporary commentators themselves focus.

Unavoidable associations with secular theatre helped to make Jesuit drama and responses to it the bundle of contradictions that it was. Tensions emerged between the theory of edifying school drama (which was itself open to question) and its practice. Jesuit drama in particular, being the most prominent form of school drama in France (at least until Racine's *Esther* was performed at Saint-Cyr) became bound up in the *querelle du théâtre* (the ongoing controversy surrounding the theatre) in which the morality of theatre was called into question and heavily debated. The Jesuits were no fools and, in order to guard against potential and probable criticisms from various opposing quarters (and also to uphold the morality of their theatrical endeavors), the central authorities in Rome set down a number of guidelines for dramatic productions being performed in their schools throughout Europe.

One of the earliest extant documents dealing with school tragedy in France is the *Ratio docendi et discendi* (published in 1585) by the Jesuit schoolmaster and playwright, Père Jouvancy. He wrote,

> La tragédie doit servir à former les mœurs. . . . Quelque sujet que l'on choisisse, il faut le traiter de telle façon qu'il ne s'y rencontre rien qui ne soit sérieux, grave et digne d'un poète chrétien. Que l'on s'abstienne

donc de tout amour profane, même chaste, et de tout personnage de femme, de quelque costume qu'on le revête. On ne peut toucher sans danger au feu, même sous la cendre, et les tisons, même éteints, s'ils ne brûlent pas, du moins salissent. Le maître religieux trouvera, dans cette precaution, l'avantage qu'il n'aura pas besoin de lire certains poètes en langue vulgaire qui ont fait à l'amour la part la plus large dans leurs œuvres.[4]

Tragedy must be used to develop personal morals. . . . Whatever subject is chosen, it must be dealt with in such a way that nothing is found in it that is not serious, solemn, and worthy of a Christian poet. All profane love, even when it is chaste, must be excluded, as must any female character, whatever costume she might wear. One cannot play with fire or even with its embers without running a risk, for even when the fire is extinguished the pokers will still tarnish even if they do not burn. The religious teacher will find in this precaution the advantage of not having to read certain vernacular poets who have made love the most important part of their work.

In a single paragraph, Jouvancy raises the principal problematic issues facing religious school drama at the time: its didactic purpose, the question of secular (i.e., erotic) love, female characters, cross-dressing, and use of the vernacular. As will be seen, the question of cross-casting in school drama is inseparable from these other concerns, each of which is itself ultimately linked with the question of what is appropriate to the moral and spiritual development of young men in such an educational establishment.

With this dilemma in mind, an official committee, established in 1584 in Rome under the supervision of Père Aquaviva, composed the *Ratio Atque Institutio Studiorum* (commonly referred to as the *Ratio Studiorum*) in which the Jesuit authorities set down their educational policy. The first version of the *Ratio* appeared in 1586, and it underwent a number of revisions in the years that followed. The question of women and female roles in plays was first raised in the 1591 edition of the *Ratio Studiorum* in which it was deemed that no women were to be admitted as spectators and that no female clothing was to be used on the stage, with the notable caveat that, if it were unavoidable, it should be decorous and dignified (McCabe, 13). By the time of the definitive 1599 edition of the *Ratio Studiorum*, the caveat was removed and the more rigorous stricture was put in its place whereby *no* female characters or costumes were to be used.[5] This was not the end of the matter, however. McCabe records that when this edition of the *Ratio* was sent out for comment to a number of Jesuit regions, this was one of the issues that provoked criticism (McCabe, 180). Playwrights and others responded with the complaint that such a severe restriction would inevitably limit—and therefore damage—the quality of drama being produced in their schools. As Henri Fouqeray has noted, their complaints were met with a certain degree of indulgence on the part of the authorities in Rome who allowed the French Jesuit fathers to "présenter sur la scène, mais rarement, des personnages de femmes dont le rôle serait très sérieux" (*to present on stage, but only seldom, female characters whose roles would be very serious*).[6]

The most straightforward way for playwrights to avoid controversy in this regard was to write plays with all-male plots. The Jesuit repertoire does offer a number of examples of these, among them *Constantinus* performed at Louis-le-Grand on August 6, 1681.[7] *Constantinus* features the struggle between Constantine and Maximius, the latter having been proclaimed emperor of Rome. After a series of long negotiations and intrigues, Constantine in Act IV finds himself in a critical situation, having been betrayed by his best generals. He realizes that he has put too much faith in human support and implores the help of Jesus Christ. The miraculous cross bearing the inscription *Hoc signo vinces* appears before him and gives him courage. He emerges victorious from battle and the Roman consuls bring him the head of Maximius, who, when retreating, had drowned in the Tiber.

All-male plots are, however, inevitably limited in scope and variety. For those playwrights and producers who wanted to remain technically within the guidelines but who also wanted to feature occasional female characters, there were a number of ways to proceed. The most common and the most straightforward of these was to allude to female characters who thus formed part of the dramatic action but who never appeared on stage; theirs was an invisible presence. More curiously, female characters sometimes appeared on stage but disguised as men. It is interesting that this type of double impersonation should have been deemed more acceptable than a standard male-to-female disguise. Most intriguingly of all, the Italian Jesuit Saverio Bettinelli (1718–1808) narrates how in his latest play "je fais jouer un grand rôle dans une tragédie . . . à une Reine, comme mère et épouse en même temps; mais après sa mort. C'est son tombeau, qui la représentera" (*I have a Queen play a large part in a tragedy, as both a wife and mother; but after her death. It is her tomb that represents her*). He claims, not without a little humor, that such a ploy will be successful because "mes Aristotes ne sont pas jaloux des femmes trépassées, quoiqu'ils craignent peut-être les revenans" (*My critics are not jealous of women who are dead, even if they are perhaps afraid of ghosts*).[8]

Another means of negotiating the all-male ideal was, of course, to ignore it. Some of the female characters who appeared on stage are, as we might expect, of relatively minor importance to the drama, featuring as wives, mothers, and sisters of the male hero. Others, however, figure in their own right as motivators of the plot and, more importantly still, as a means for the transmission of the didactic message of the play. Many of them are Christian martyrs such as the eponymous Suzanne in the Père Jourdain's tragedy performed (with ballet) on August 4, 1653, or the jealous Alexandra who, as a result of divine inspiration and the example of the eponymous hero, converts to Christianity during the play and is martyred with him in *Andronicus martyr*, performed on August 11, 1667 (also with ballet). In the Père Lucas's tragedy, *Catharina*, performed on August 3, 1672 (with ballet), closet Christian Catherine is martyred for her faith, while the Père Lejay's first play, *Eustachius martyr* (given with the *tragédie en musique*, *Eustache* on February 14, 1684), features Eustache's pagan wife who converts toward the end of the play and seeks her own martyrdom as well as that of her husband.

Given the morally didactic and inspirational importance ascribed to dramatic accounts of Christian martyrdom in the Jesuit theatre repertoire, the fact that several of the models offered to the schoolboys are female is compelling evidence that women's parts in Jesuit school drama were not restricted to matters of secondary moral purpose. It is clear that the Jesuit masters involved in such productions were content to countenance the exemplary behavior of *exceptional* women. In this context, biological sex is no obstacle to the Christian ideal. Moreover, it would appear that the fact that these parts were cross-cast was similarly of little or no consequence when dealing with such significant, spiritual matters. If prominent female figures were to be included on the Jesuit stage, then they had to exemplify certain *masculine* qualities that could be emulated, or at least admired, by the young, male *collégiens*. That this masculine agenda is present even within female roles is crucial to our understanding of the function of female characters on the Jesuit stage.

The type of female character who will arouse an appropriate response in the audience is discussed by the Jesuit playwright the Père Lejay who poses the rhetorical question, with regard to the work of Corneille:

A-t-il jamais présenté sur la scène de plus nobles caractères de femmes que ceux de Cornélie dans *Pompée*, de Cléopâtre dans *Rodogune*, l'une

tout entière à sa vengeance, l'autre à son ambition, toutes deux igno-
rant les tendres mouvements de l'amour? (Boysse, 95)

*Has he ever presented on stage a more noble female character than Cornélie
in* Pompée, Cléopâtre *in* Rodogune, *the one wholly committed to
her vengeance, the other to her ambition, both of them oblivious to feelings
of love?*

To equate the notion of the noble female character with the qualities
of unalleviated vengeance and ambition may first appear surprising.
Corneille's Cléopâtre is a particularly unexpected model, an abhor-
rent character, who is void of any morally redeeming feature, and who
dies unrepentant, having killed one of her sons and attempted to take
the life of the other. But, as Corneille himself was at pains to point
out in his *Discours de l'utilité et des parties du poème dramatique* (1660),
there is yet something admirable about her:

Cléopâtre dans *Rodogune* est très méchante, il n'y a point de parricide
qui lui fasse horreur, pourvu qu'il la puisse conserver sur un trône
qu'elle préfère à toutes choses, tant son attachement à la domination
est violent; mais tous ses crimes sont accompagnés d'une grandeur
d'âme, qui a quelque chose de si haut, qu'en même temps qu'on déteste
ses actions, on admire la source dont elles partent.[9]

Cléopâtre in Rodogune *is very wicked; there is no parricide that horrifies
her, as long as it can keep her on a throne that she values above everything
else—such is the violence of her attachment to power. But all her crimes are
accompanied by a greatness of soul that has something so distinguished about it
that, while we hate her actions, we admire their inspiration.*

The purpose of tragedy, then, even in a religious educational context, is not limited to the depiction of exemplary moral behavior,
Christian or otherwise. Effective tragedy is also about the arousal of
certain powerful emotions. While we are horrified by Cléopâtre, we
also marvel at her—and this is a legitimate response. Lejay goes on to
argue that what Racine is really revered for is not his depiction of passionate love, but rather his characters who do *not* display such passions:

Je préférerais la malheureuse Andromaque, tantôt regrettant son
Hector, tantôt craignant pour les jours d'Astyanax, brûlant enfin du
désir de les venger l'un et l'autre, aux plaintes fastidieuses d'Hermione
et d'Oreste. De grands applaudissements ont accueilli au théâtre
Agamemnon rongé de soucis, accablé de douleurs, lorsqu'il se voit
forcé d'immoler sa fille; Clytemnestre gémissant et s'indignant quand

on arrache Iphigénie de ses bras; Iphigénie elle-même, au milieu des pleurs de ses parents, se dévouant pour le bien commun, et montrant un courage au-dessus de son âge et de son sexe. On aurait préféré un Achille ardent, intrépide à un Achille amoureux et soupirant. On admira l'âme invaincue de Porus au milieu de ses revers; on a moins loué Alexandre brûlant pour Axiane d'un amour indigne de lui. (Boysse, 96)

I would prefer the unhappy Andromaque—sometimes missing her Hector, sometimes fearing for Astyanax's life, finally burning with the desire to avenge them both—to the tedious laments of Hermione and Oreste. Those who were met with great applause in the theatre were Agamemnon, eaten away by worry and overwhelmed with pain when he finds himself forced to sacrifice his daughter; Clytemnestra groaning and furious when Iphigénie is taken from her arms; Iphigénie herself, in the midst of her parents' tears, sacrificing herself for the common good and displaying a courage well above her age and sex. One would have preferred an ardent, intrepid Achille to the sighing, lovesick Achille. One admired the unvanquished soul of Porus in the middle of his setbacks; but Alexandre burning for Axiane with a love unworthy of him inspired less praise.

What is most interesting about Lejay's remarks is the fact that he admires the same qualities in women as in men. He admires women who are, by ordinary standards, unfeminine—as he himself suggests with the words "au-dessus de . . . son sexe." Men and women who suffer for acceptable reasons are an inspiration to students at Jesuit colleges. Those who suffer for erotic love, on the other hand, are not.

Nevertheless, many Jesuit plays did debate love, including the Père La Rue's *Cyrus* (performed on August 17, 1679 with the *Ballet de la paix*) that features Cyrus asking Palmyre to marry him. Palmyre resists at first but finally agrees. She is quick to assert that what she loves about Cyrus is his passion for honor, justice, virtue, and above all his *gloire*. She states specifically that the qualities she loves in Cyrus are the same qualities that have brought him "l'admiration des hommes et des dieux" (*the admiration of both men and gods*). Not only that, these qualities have inspired the admiration of even his enemies and rivals. Here there is nothing therefore specifically sexual about Palmyre's description of her love for Cyrus. He, on the other hand, uses a more sexual language, telling her that "c'est votre présence qui rend mon visage joyeux" (*it is your presence that makes my face joyful*) speaking of "le flambeau de notre hymen" (*the flame of our marriage*) and, particularly, urging her to "cessez de retarder une union tant désirée" (*stop delaying a union that is so strongly desired*). To her father, Palmyre explains that "j'aime

Cyrus parce que vous m'avez ordonné de l'aimer" (*I love Cyrus because you have ordered me to love him*), and yet she also talks about "cette flamme [qui] m'a pénétrée" (*this flame that has penetrated me*) and "les feux que vous avez allumés" (*the fires that you have lit*), as though a genuine and powerful sexual love can be developed by the power of the will.[10]

René Rapin complains, however, that "c'est degrader la Tragedie de cet air de majesté qui luy est propre, que d'y mêler de l'amour, qui est d'un caractere toûjours badin & peu conforme à la gravité" (*to include love, which is always lighthearted and hardly appropriate for a serious genre, is to detract from tragedy's rightfully majestic tone*).[11] For such critics, the feminine softness of tender loving emotion of this kind is opposed to the masculine power of true tragedy.[12] Interestingly, this supposed feminization—or effeminization—of tragic drama (a tendency prevalent in the secular, public theatre) is attributed by Rapin to a desire to please the female spectator. He complains,

> Car en effet les passions qu'on represente deviennent fades & de nul goust, si elles ne sont fondées sur des sentiments conformes à ceux du spectateur. C'est ce qui oblige nos Poëtes à privilegier si fort la galanterie sur le theatre, & à tourner tous leurs sujets sur des tendresses outrées, pour plaire davantage aux femmes, qui se sont érigées en arbitres de ces divertissemens, & qui ont usurpé le droit d'en decider. (Rapin, 183–84)
>
> *Because it is the case that the passions depicted become dull and tasteless if they are not based on feelings that correspond to those of the spectators. It is this that compels our authors to favor gallantry so much on the stage and to focus their subjects on excessive tenderness in order to please the women who have made themselves arbiters of these entertainments and who have usurped the right to judge them.*

Here Rapin is of course writing about the public theatre to which women were freely admitted, but the question of the presence of female spectators at Jesuit productions was also a matter of some debate.

We remember that the Jesuits were not keen on admitting women to their theatre productions, either on stage or in the audience. There is ample proof, however, that women were present at many Jesuit productions in France, as members of the royal party, and as mothers of the performers. In 1653, for example, Loret comments in his *Muse historique* on a number of court beauties attending another performance at the Collège de Clermont, alongside a dazzling array of dignitaries (including Louis XIV, his brother, the Queen, Mazarin, Charles II of England, and the Duke of Gloucester):

> Enfin, jétant partout les yeux,
> Je vis briller en pluzieurs lieux
> Des beautez tant blondes que brunes. (August 9, 1653)
>
> *Looking around,*
> *I saw, radiating in many places,*
> *A host of beauties, both blonds and brunettes.*

It could be argued however, that women were partially excluded from these productions in a different and subtler way. Jesuit plays were written in Latin and, while most male members of the audience would have been able to follow the development of the action without too much difficulty, the majority of women would not.[13] This fact further enforces the notion of Jesuit drama as a masculine genre whose intended audience is emphatically male.

One of the few guidelines mentioned above that appears to have been adhered to is that of having all-male casts. This conformity, however, inevitably led to the inclusion of cross-cast roles as the complete absence of female characters proved to be too restrictive for the majority of Jesuit playwrights. What was the effect of these roles in performance? On several occasions, Loret comments on them. He recorded, for example, his and the audience's response to the performance of a female role by a young man in the following terms:

> Cyané, fort jeune princesse,
> Par son esprit et son adresse,
> Bonne grace et naïveté,
> Charma des cœurs en quantité;
> On la trouva jolie et belle,
> Et l'on fit cent éloges d'elle.
> De l'aimable Enfant destiné
> A ce Rollet de Cyané,
> Dézinant fort le nom apprendre
> Quelque voizin me fit entendre
> Que c'était Hubert de Servien,
> Qui, sans mentir, mérite bien
> D'avoir place dans notre Histoire,
> Car il aquit honneur et gloire. (August 19, 1656)
>
> *Cyané, a very young princess,*
> *By her wit and her skill,*
> *Her good grace and simplicity,*

Won over a good number of hearts.
She was thought to be pretty and beautiful,
And was praised one hundred times.

Of the lovely child chosen
To play the role of Cyané,
Ardently wishing to find out the name,
One of my neighbors informed me
That it was Hubert de Servien,
Who, in truth, fully deserves
To have a place in our history
For he has gained honor and glory.

Cross-dressed Hubert de Servien clearly made quite an impression on his audience. It seems that he made a convincingly pleasing female figure, so much so that Loret and other members of the audience seem to have been attracted to him. Alongside the homoeroticism of Loret's account, we note a perceived close correspondence between feminine attractiveness and male youthfulness: boys, like women, are not men; like women, boys are attractive. Similarly, Loret comments on how the boy actor playing the eponymous heroine in *Le martyre de sainte Suzanne* (1653) takes this a stage further by wearing beauty spots—adornments that clearly have more in common with contemporary views of women's fashion and beauty than with the way a female saint might have dressed:

Une vierge, jeune et sage,
Dont le cœur étoit pur et saint,
Avoit des mouches sur son teint
De formes rondes et longuettes,
Ainsi qu'on en void aux coquettes,
Que, mesme à l'heure du trêpas,
Ladite sainte n'ôta pas: car, quand d'une sanglante épée,
Sa belle teste fut coupée
Pour n'adorer pas les faux Dieux,
J'aperçus de mes propres yeux
Ces mouches, de couleur de more
Qui sur sa joüe, étoient encore. (August 9, 1653)

A young and wise virgin,
Of pure and holy heart,
Had beauty spots on her skin,
In the long, curvaceous shapes
Of a coquette,
Such that even at the moment of death

> *The aforementioned Saint did not remove them. For, when, with a*
> *bloody sword*
> *She had her head cut off*
> *Because she refused to worship false gods,*
> *I noticed with my own eyes*
> *That these beauty spots, the color of a Moor,*
> *Were still on her cheek.*

Loret's accounts reveal that, in practice, cross-casting did sometimes challenge the sexual response of the theatre audience, as well as the integrity of the tragic genre, and its impact in performance. For this reason and others, Jesuit school drama, although thriving, always remained controversial. As Henry Phillips has demonstrated, much of the controversy stemmed from the tension between the church's acceptance of theatrical productions in schools and its concurrent condemnation of the public theatre.[14] Inevitably, comparisons and cross-references were made between these two distinct varieties, culminating in 1694 in Caffaro's misguided attempt at defending professional actors with reference to the supposed existence of blameless school drama. But the argument can work both ways: if the purity of school drama can support the notion of the propriety of secular public theatre, so too can the immorality of the public theatre taint the reputation of its theatrical counterparts in schools. For this reason, other defenders of school drama were keen to assert the *differences* between that and the public theatre, not only in terms of repertoire, but, above all, in terms of aim and context: school drama is instructive, while the principal purpose of the public theatre is to entertain.[15]

Bossuet, one of the fiercest critics of the public theatre, strongly defends school drama in his rejoinder to Caffaro:

> On voit en effet des représentations innocentes; qui sera assez rigoureux pour condamner dans les collèges celles d'une jeunesse réglée, à qui ses maîtres proposent de tels exercices pour leur aider à former ou leur style ou leur action, et en tout cas leur donner, surtout à la fin de leur année, quelque honnête relâchement? (Bossuet, 266)
>
> *Blameless performances do exist. Who would be so rigorous as to condemn those given in schools by a well-ordered youth, whose masters devise for them such exercises in order to help them develop their style or their behavior and anyway to give them, especially at the end of the year, some decent recreation?*

Students in Jesuit schools, it was argued, were not making a profession of acting. Rather they were involved in drama as a means of developing

skills that would be useful to them later in their worthy adult profes-
sions and, moreover, as a method of spiritual and moral instruction—all
within a highly regulated environment. On the question of female
roles, we note that Bossuet recalls the precepts of the *Ratio Studiorum*
according to which female characters were to be excluded from the
Jesuit stage, while conveniently failing to acknowledge the fact that
this guideline was not strictly adhered to.
Other critics eagerly engaged with the question of cross-casting.
Joseph de Voisin, for example, bemoaning the inclusion of female
characters on the school stage, wonders rhetorically:

> S'il est juste & raisonnable que les Payens n'ayent peu souffrir que leurs
> enfants contrefissent la voix de femme, & que des Chrestiens permet-
> tent que leurs enfants se déguisent en filles & femmes, qu'on leur couvre
> le visage de mouches, & qu'on les pare de tous les ornemens & de tout
> l'attirail du luxe, & de l'affeterie, qu'on leur apprenne à imiter des œil-
> lades & les paroles des femmes qui vivent selon l'esprit du monde.[16]

> *If it is right and good, given that the pagans did not allow their children to
> mimic the voice of a woman, that the Christians should allow their children
> to disguise themselves as women and girls, that they should cover their faces
> with beauty spots and dress them in adornments with all the trappings of
> luxury and of affectation, and to teach them to bat their eyelids and to imitate
> the speech of worldly women.*

Recalling Deuteronomic law, he suggests that the adoption of the
clothing traditionally worn by members of the opposite sex is fundamentally opposed to good Christian behavior. In addition, he alerts
his audience to the risks associated with replicating the artifices of
worldly women. Even Chappuzeau, in his decidedly pro-theatrical
Théatre François, invites the reader to ponder the respective merits of
allowing women on the school stage as opposed to the custom of
cross-casting:

> Mais, me dira-t-on encore, on ne void point de femmes sur le Theatre
> dans les Comedies qui se representent aux Colleges . . . . Ie ne sçais s'il
> est moins blâmable de voir des hommes trauestis en femmes & pren-
> dre l'habit d'vn autre sexe que le leur, ce qui hors de pareilles occasions, &
> des tems ácordez aux rejouissances publiques, est punissable & defendu
> par les Loix. (Chappuzeau, 28–29)

> *But, people will say to me, we see no women on the stage in the plays that
> are performed in schools . . . . I do not know whether it is any less blameworthy*

to have men dress as women and wear the clothes of a sex other than their own,
something that is, apart from on such occasions and at times of public festivity,
liable to punishment and prohibited by law.

With regard to the question of the morality of school drama, however, he is in no doubt: "les spectacles qui se donnent aux Colleges sont tres loüables" (Chappuzeau, 29) (*the performances put on in schools are most commendable*).

In 1698, Guy, Bishop of Arras published a mandate on the regulation of theatre productions in the schools of his diocese.[17] One of the most significant elements of the mandate is its ban on the operas and dances between the acts of tragedies that had grown rapidly in frequency, duration, and importance during the second half of the seventeenth century. Once more recalling the final edition of the *Ratio Studiorum*, Guy reiterates the requirement that the performances must all be in Latin, and "que l'on n'y introduise aucun personnage de femme, ni jamais l'habit de ce sexe" (Gofflot, 191n) (*that no female role should be included, nor should any female clothing be worn*). Gofflot, however, records how a stricter adherence to the guidelines of the definitive *Ratio Studiorum* led to a decline in the tradition of school drama in France—a decline owing in no small part to the omission of female roles. He notes how even chefs d'œuvre from the secular theatre came to be arranged in such a way as to be acceptable to the stricter Jesuit precepts:

L'arrangement consistait à supprimer les rôles de femmes, à enlever les scènes où figurait l'amour; ainsi *expurgata*, la pièce était jouée. Les meilleures productions de Corneille, de Racine, de Molière même, furent de la sorte passées au crible et figurèrent ensuite sur les scènes scolaires. Bien accueillies au début, elles finirent par lasser, car elles n'étaient plus qu'une expression lointaine du génie qui les avait enfantées. (Gofflot, 202)

The procedure consisted of eliminating all the female roles, of omitting any love scenes. Thus expurgata, *the play was performed. Even the masterpieces of Corneille, Racine, and Molière himself were scrutinized in this way and then performed on the school stage. Well received to begin with, they became tiresome, for they were only a pale shadow of the genius that had created them.*

If the guidelines set out in the *Ratio Studiorum* were closely followed, it was at the expense of dramatic integrity. It seems that the tensions inherent in the notion of a form of school drama that is morally irreproachable and simultaneously dramatically effective had rendered that notion untenable, at least in the climate of late seventeenth-century France. Similar tensions were to afflict the efforts of the young ladies at Saint-Cyr, whose experiences offer a fascinating counterpoint to those of the Jesuits.

Saint-Cyr

The pupils at Saint-Cyr were not the first females to perform (or to be cross-cast) in private, religious theatrical productions in France. Lynette Muir notes, for example, that women had played in Latin Liturgical plays in convents since the thirteenth century.[18] Saint-Cyr was, however, the first educational institution for girls whose theatrical productions reached a relatively wide public and which, as a consequence, provoked strong and diverse responses. Saint-Cyr was itself something of a pioneering educational establishment: founded in 1686 by Louis XIV to provide an education for the daughters of impoverished noblemen (particularly those who had died in the king's service or who had spent their personal fortune serving the state), Saint-Cyr was set up under the direction of the austere, morganatic wife of Louis XIV—Mme de Maintenon. The girls were educated by members of the religious order known as the Dames de Saint Louis. The significance of the direct involvement of the king and his wife, in both the establishment of Saint-Cyr and in its management, should not be underestimated. Neither should Saint-Cyr's geographical proximity to the court, for the school was situated within the great park of Versailles. As will be seen, the influence of the French court on theatrical productions at Saint-Cyr was to prove strong.

We read in the letters patent that Saint-Cyr was to offer the girls "toutes les instructions qui peuvent convenir à leur naissance et à leur sexe" (*all the instruction that befits their birth and their sex*).[19] This phrase is a revealing one, for the history of dramatic productions at Saint-Cyr is inextricably and necessarily bound up with the notion of women's education, of what was suitable for the nurturing of young girls.[20] What was considered appropriate for the education of young women was itself based on a certain understanding of the nature of women and on a number of assumptions with regard to the roles of women in society. One of the most influential documents in this regard was Fénelon's *Traité de l'Education des Filles*, published in 1687, in which the education of women is perceived primarily as a means to social order. Significantly, Fénelon's treatise includes a chapter entitled

"Remarques sur plusieurs défauts des filles" (*Remarks on certain faults found in girls*). For Fénelon and Mme de Maintenon, who followed in his wake, educationalists must be aware of the "faults" that are inherent in the female sex, and these tendencies must be brought under control for the benefit of society. Fénelon wrote, for example,

> Mais ne craignez rien tant que la vanité dans les filles; elles naissent avec un désir violent de plaire: les chemins qui conduisent les hommes à l'autorité et à la gloire leur étant fermés, elles tâchent de se dédommager par les agréments de l'esprit et du corps, de là vient leur conversation douce et insinuante; de là vient qu'elles aspirent tant à la beauté et à toutes les grâces extérieures, et qu'elles sont si passionnées pour les ajustements; une coiffe, un bout de ruban, une boucle de cheveux plus haut ou plus bas, le choix d'une couleur, ce sont pour elles autant d'affaires importantes.[21]

> *But beware above all of the vanity of girls: they are born with a strong desire to please. The paths that lead men to authority and glory being closed to women, they try to make up for this by the charms of their body and their wit. This is the source of their sweet, insinuating conversation, of their great aspirations to beauty and to all the external graces, and of their obsession with physical detail: a headdress, a piece of ribbon, a curl of hair placed higher or lower, the choice of color, all these are for them matters of utmost importance.*

His words about beauty and external graces resonate particularly strongly with the phenomenon of the young women of Saint-Cyr appearing on stage, a place where such qualities are inevitably brought to light, and we shall return to this question in our examination of the impact of the performances of Racine's *Esther* below.

Saint-Cyr's early repertoire consisted mainly of old martyr plays and saints' plays, as well as some new compositions by the First Superior, Mme de Brinon. These were, by all accounts, thoroughly uninspiring, and so Mme de Maintenon looked instead toward the tragedies of Corneille and Racine "choisissant seulement celles où il y auroit le moins d'amour" (*choosing only those which were the least concerned with matters of love*)[22] and occasionally plays by other authors. One such was Tristan l'Hermite's *Marianne* (given alongside Corneille's *Polyeucte*), for which Manseau mentions particularly Mme de Maintenon's efforts with regard to costumes:

> Polyeucte et Marianne se répétoient. Le mois de décembre estant arrivé, le théâtre fut dressé, et Mme de Maintenon fit apporter de

Versailles des habits pour toutes les actrices. Les gardesrobes de Messeigneurs les ducs du Maine et le comte de Toulouse qui estoient alors de l'âge de la plupart des jeunes demoiselles en fournirent beaucoup, ce qui décora extrêmement ces troupes.[23]

Polyeucte and Marianne *were being rehearsed. The theatre was erected early in December and Mme de Maintenon had clothes brought from Versailles for all the actresses. The wardrobes of Messeigneurs the Duke[s] of Maine and the Count of Toulouse, who were then the same age as the majority of the young ladies, provided many of them, and so the troupes were extremely well adorned.*

The use of lavish costumes was to prove to be one of the principal attractions of theatrical productions at Saint-Cyr, as well as one of their most dangerous components. It is significant that Mme de Maintenon went to such lengths to provide decorative attire for the actresses and that its source was, precisely, authentic court dress from Versailles. What is also interesting is the fact that Mme de Maintenon made use of the wardrobes of several boys. Given the age of the boys in question (around fifteen years), this was not the unisex/feminine clothing worn by boys in early childhood; rather, it was masculine clothing that was borrowed to be worn by the cross-cast actresses playing the male roles in *Polyeucte* and *Marianne* (the straight-cast actresses also wore clothes brought in from Versailles). We notice no sense of shock in Manseau's account of this cross-dressing, his only personal observation being that the young men's clothing formed a pleasing embellishment on the bodies of the young women ("qui décora extrêmement ces troupes.")

The substitution of some of these mainstream canonical works in place of the old, safe repertoire was met with some degree of concern. Mme de Maintenon famously wrote to Racine after one of these performances: "Nos petites filles viennent de jouer *Andromaque*, et l'ont si bien jouée qu'elles ne la joueront plus, ni aucune de vos pieces" (Caylus, 97) (*Our little girls have just performed* Andromaque *and they performed it so well that they will not perform it, nor any other of your plays, ever again*). It seems that the girls were becoming too adept at their portrayal of the passion of Racine's secular drama and that the promotion of such passion was not appropriate to their education. It is certainly ironic that the girls, who were understood to be more fragile and emotional than boys, boasted a theatrical repertoire in French, including passionate, secular tragedy, that necessitated a good deal of cross-casting—a repertoire more audacious in many respects than that of the Jesuit boys. Ultimately, however, as the history of Racine's *Esther* and *Athalie* will demonstrate, the performance context at Saint-Cyr was to prove the most vexed question with regard to Mme de Maintenon's search for morally acceptable school drama.

Mme de Maintenon's request to Racine for "quelque espèce de poëme moral ou historique dont l'amour fût entièrement banni" (*some kind of moral or historical play from which love was completely absent*) in order to "divertir les demoiselles de Saint-Cyr en les instruisant" (*entertain the girls of Saint-Cyr while instructing them*) was precisely a request for a piece of theatre that, even when performed by young women, would be morally acceptable to audience and performers alike (Caylus, 96). Racine, in his preface to the published edition of *Esther*, records how he was asked:

> Si je ne pourrais pas faire sur quelque sujet de piété et de morale une espèce de Poème, où le chant fût mêlé avec le récit; le tout lié par une action qui rendît la chose plus vive et moins capable d'ennuyer.
>
> *If I could write a kind of poem on a pious and moral subject in which song and the spoken word would be mixed, and the whole thing held together by a lively plot that would make it less likely to be boring.*

We should remember that Racine was by this time no longer a professional playwright. He had renounced the theatre after the publication of his great masterpiece, *Phèdre* (1677) and had subsequently strengthened his associations with the Jansenists at Port-Royal. His current position was that of *Historiographe du Roi* (Royal Historiographer) a post he took up in 1677. Mme de Maintenon's request put Racine in a difficult position on a number of levels: first, she was inviting him to take up his playwright's pen again after a hiatus of more than a decade and with a distinguished reputation to uphold; moreover, her request was for a move away from Racine's hitherto preferred genre of secular tragedy in favor of its sacred counterpart, and one featuring a substantial amount of music. But the most challenging feature of Mme de Maintenon's request was all that is contained within the slippery and exacting notion of a morally impeccable, educational, and entertaining drama, fit for performance by a cast of teenage girls.

In terms of writing a play for an all-female cast, the story of Esther, with its female protagonist, is clearly a good choice, and the reworking of the plight of the Israelites into a chorus of young girls is an inspired way of including a large number of young women in the production and of giving it a strong female bias. The daughters of Sion as such are absent from the biblical account, although they are congruent with the story and with its dramatic rendering. In certain other ways, however, Racine's choice is more surprising. Chapters One and, particularly, Two, of the Book of Esther are laden with references to female sexual beauty, the king's harem, Esther's beauty treatments, sexual attractiveness, and so on. While Racine was expected to eliminate such sexual content from his version of the story, female beauty and attractiveness would nonetheless remain an issue both in his text and especially in its performance context. The way the female chorus is introduced within the play, for example, sheds some interesting light on our investigation. In the opening scene, Esther relates to Elise,

Cependant mon amour pour notre nation
A rempli ce Palais de filles de Sion,
Jeunes et tendres fleurs, par le sort agitées,
Sous un ciel étranger comme moi transplantées. (1.1.101–104)

However, my love for our nation
Has filled this palace with the daughters of Sion,
Young and tender flowers, tossed about by fate
And transplanted like me beneath a foreign sky.

And Elise later comments,

Ciel! quel nombreux essaim d'innocentes beautés
S'offre à mes yeux en foule, et sort de tous côtés!
Quelle aimable pudeur sur leur visage est peinte! (1.2.122–124)

Heavens, what a great swarm of innocent beauties
Crowds before my eyes and appears from all sides!
What lovely innocence is painted on their faces!

Racine's daughters of Sion are firmly established in his text as youthful, innocent, vulnerable, and physically attractive—an assortment of qualities that resonates with the actresses' genuine condition and that is likely to appeal not only to the male sexual drive but also to the male desire to protect and dominate. Sure enough, for certain members of the audience, this was to prove something of a potent combination.

Esther does also include several key male characters and Racine comments precisely on the question of cross-casting in his preface to the published version of the play:

> Je crois qu'il est bon d'avertir ici, que bien qu'il y ait dans *Esther* des per-
> sonnages d'hommes, ces personnages n'ont pas laissé d'être représentés
> par des Filles avec toute la bienséance de leur sexe. La chose leur a été
> d'autant plus aisée, qu'anciennement les habits des Persans et des Juifs
> étaient de longues robes qui tombaient jusqu'à terre.

> *I think it is right to remark here that, although there are male characters
> in* Esther, *these characters are nonetheless played by the girls with all the
> propriety of their sex. The task was made easier by the fact that, in times
> gone by, the clothes of the Persians and Jews were long robes that fell to the
> ground.*

Racine stresses the fact that cross-casting, in this instance at least,
proved not to be incompatible with the decorum required of the
female sex (largely thanks to the fact that the girls' legs were covered).
The fact that the cross-cast actresses wore long robes would certainly,
as he suggests, have rendered the cross-dressing significantly less open
to criticism, just as it left the girls' bodies significantly less exposed to
the desiring gaze of the men in the audience. Racine's account of
these long, Persian-style robes is perhaps a little disingenuous, however, for it is clear from several contemporary eyewitness accounts
that the costumes for *Esther* were very lavish and very expensive.
They were designed by Jean Bérain (who also designed the sets), a
well-established *décorateur* who had in his time contributed to many
extravagant court productions. Manseau recorded in his memoirs
that Mme de Maintenon "fit habiller toutes les actrices d'habits mag-
nifiques faits proportionnément aux personnes et au sujet" (*dressed the
actresses in magnificent clothes in keeping with their character and their
subject*).[24] While the Dames de Saint Louis recorded simply that "elle
avoit fait faire des habits Persans pour toutes les Dlles qui devoient
paroître sur le Théatre" (*she had had the Persian costumes made for all the
girls who were to appear on stage*),[25] the writers of the *Nouvelles ecclésias-
tiques* (in February 1689) commented that "les actrices font des mer-
veilles avec des habits tout unis de taffetas blanc ou rouge" (*the
actresses are doing great things with their taffeta clothes colored in white or
red*).[26] Moreover, Louis XIV donated a host of expensive diamonds
and pearls that had previously been used for his sumptuous court
ballets during the early part of the reign. It is clear that these
costumes were not intended, in the end, to function as anything
approaching authentic dress, or even as costumes as distinct from the

girls' ordinary clothes; rather, they were fulfilling a more basic desire: to make the girls look pretty, feminine, and attractive.[27] *Esther* was first performed on January 26, 1689 in the presence of the king, his entourage, and a number of eminent ecclesiastics, including Bossuet.[28] The production met with a good deal of acclaim, and news of this and subsequent performances spread rapidly from the inner circles of the court of Versailles to a wider circle of affiliated outsiders, including Mme de Sévigné. Racine records in his preface.

A dire vrai, je ne pensais guère que la chose dût être aussi publique qu'elle l'a été. Mais les grandes vérités de l'Ecriture, et la manière sublime dont elles y sont énoncées, pour peu qu'on les présente, même imparfaitement, aux yeux des hommes, sont si propres à les frapper; et d'ailleurs ces jeunes Demoiselles ont déclamé et chanté cet Ouvrage avec tant de grâce, tant de modestie, et tant de piété, qu'il n'a pas été possible qu'il demeurât renfermé dans le secret de leur Maison. De sorte qu'un divertissement d'Enfants est devenu le sujet de l'empressement de toute la Cour.

In truth, I had hardly thought that it would be as public a spectacle as it was. But the great truths of scripture and the sublime way in which they are stated, if one only presents them, however imperfectly, before an audience, are so disposed to make a great impact; and, moreover, these young ladies declaimed and sang this work with such grace, such modesty, and such piety, that it was not possible that it should remain enclosed in the seclusion of their house. In this way, a children's entertainment has become the subject of the enthusiasm of the whole court.

He modestly attributes the success of his play to its sacred sources and subject, but also to the impact of the performance by the group of young girls. Mme de Sévigné's account of her conversation with Louis XIV, after she had attended a performance of *Esther*, neatly makes a distinction between the playwright's input and that of the performers:

Le Roi me dit: *Racine a bien de l'esprit.* Je lui dis: *Sire, il en a beaucoup, mais en vérité ces jeunes personnes en ont beaucoup aussi; elles entrent dans le sujet comme si elles n'avaient jamais fait autre chose.* Il me dit: *Ah! pour cela, il est vrai.* (February 21, 1689)

The King said to me: Racine is very talented. *I said to him*: Sire, he is, but, in truth, these young people are very talented as well: they enter into the subject as though they had never done anything else. *He said to me*: Ah, that is true!

A similar account commenting, somewhat naïvely, on this agreeable combination of blameless subject matter performed by attractive girls is given in the *Mémoires de Dames de Saint Louis*:

Tout le monde convint que l'Opéra et la Comédie n'approchaient pas de ce spectacle. D'un côté on voyait, sur le théâtre, de jeunes demoiselles bien faites, fort jolies, qui représentaient parfaitement bien, qui ne disaient que des choses capables d'inspirer des sentiments honnêtes et vertueux, et dont l'air noble et modeste, sans affectation ne donnait aux spectateurs que l'idée de la plus grande innocence. Si l'on tournait la tête de l'autre côté, on voyait cette multitude de demoiselles, rangées pour ainsi dire, en pyramides, très proprement mises dans leurs habits de Saint-Cyr, qui, avec les rubans de chaque couleur qu'elles portent, faisait une diversité agréable. (Piéjus, 608)

Everyone agreed that the Opéra and the Comédie did not come close to this spectacle. On the one hand, you saw on stage very pretty and attractive young ladies who acted perfectly, who said only things that were capable of inspiring honest and virtuous thoughts, and whose noble and modest manner, without affectation, only inspired in the spectators the idea of the greatest innocence. If you turned your head the other way, you saw this multitude of young ladies, arranged, as it were, in pyramids, most neatly dressed in their school uniforms and who, with their multicolored ribbons, created a delightful diversity.

The girls of Saint-Cyr, both performers and audience members alike, are established as objects of the external audience's gaze, to be observed and admired for their physical qualities. The description of the performers as "fort jolies" and especially "bien faites" sits uneasily with the notion of innocence and virtue that the Dames are so eager to uphold. It may indeed be the case that they said only things that were capable of inspiring honest and virtuous thoughts, for that is a question of text or script. What is more doubtful is the indication that their noble and modest manner only inspired in the spectators the idea of the greatest innocence.

Paradoxically, of course, their appearance of innocence may have formed part precisely of their sexual appeal for some of the audience members (see below). It does seem that the girls formed a refreshing and welcome alternative to the figure of the professional actress. Dangeau commented that "toutes les petites filles jouèrent et chantèrent très-bien, et Madame de Caylus fit le prologue mieux que n'auroit pu faire la Champmeslé" (Piéjus, 537) (*all the little girls acted and danced very well, and Mme de Caylus performed the prologue better than la Champmêlé could have done).* Similarly, Mme de Sévigné wrote on March 21, 1689 that

> Il est fort vrai qu'il fallait des personnes innocentes pour chanter les malheurs de Sion; la Champmeslé vous aurait fait mal au cœur. C'est cette convenance qui charmait dans cette pièce.
>
> *It is absolutely true that innocent people were needed to sing the laments of Sion. La Champmêlé would have been wrong. It is this suitability that worked very well in this play.*

Further emphasis is given to the distinction between adult professional female performers and their younger amateur counterparts in an account of the fourth performance of *Esther*, given for James II of England, on February 5, 1689. The *Mémoires de Saint-Cyr* inform us that

> Le Roi avoit donné, pour ce jour-là, quelques-unes de ses musiciennes des plus sages et des plus habiles, pour mêler avec les Demoiselles, afin de fortifier le chœur des Israélites: on les habilla comme elles à la persane, ce qui auroit dû les confondre avec les autres; mais ceux qui ne les connoissoient pas pour être de la musique du Roi les distinguoient fort bien pour n'être pas de nos Demoiselles, en qui on remarquoit une certaine modestie et une noble simplicité bien plus aimable que les airs affectés que se donnent les filles de cette sorte. (Taphanel, 87)
>
> *For this particular day, the king had provided a few of his most well-behaved and skillful female singers to blend in with the young ladies in order to reinforce the chorus of Israelites. They were dressed like the others with Persian robes, which should have enabled them to blend in with the rest. But those who did not know that they were from the king's music were easily able to identify them as not being among our young ladies, in whom we noticed a certain modesty and noble simplicity that was far more pleasant than the affectations adopted by girls of this kind.*

It is likely that professional singers did have a bearing different from the teenage girls; they were probably also older and taller.

On a different level, *Esther* (together with *Athalie*, Racine's other sacred play, also written for Saint-Cyr) was praised by some because it was seen to open up in a very real and practical way the possibility of a successful reform of the public theatre, something that many antitheatricalists, we remember, considered to be an impossibility. In 1694, P. Bardou, a critic of the public stage, in an enthusiastic letter to Racine, comments on the happy consequences of Racine's move away from secular drama in favor of a more edifying form of theatre:

> Tu voulus, dans les vers d'Esther et d'Athalie,
> Donner un nouveau lustre à la Scene avilie;
> Et par toy, dans saint Cyr, le théâtre ennobli
> Offre du vray sublime un modele accompli.[29]

> *You wanted, in the poetry of Esther and of Athalie,*
> *To give new credibility to the degraded stage;*
> *And by you, at Saint-Cyr, the stage ennobled*
> *Offers an accomplished example of the truly sublime.*

He continues,

> C'est là que la vertu peut tenir son école.
> L'acteur innocemment peut y joüer son rôle.
> Là, mettant à profit les heures du loisir,
> Le parterre chrétien s'instruit avec plaisir. (Bardou, 282)

> *It is there that virtue can learn*
> *And that the actor can play his role innocently.*
> *There, putting their leisure time to good use,*
> *The Christian audience can enjoy learning.*

Bardou also praises Racine's handling of the vexed question of love in *Esther*:

> Si de la belle Esther un Prince est enchanté,
> C'est sa vertu qu'il vante et non pas sa beauté.
> Rien du profane amour n'y ressent la licence;
> "*Tout respire en Esther la paix et l'innocence.*" (Bardou, 282)

> *If the prince is enchanted by the beautiful Esther*
> *It is her virtue that he praises and not her beauty.*
> *There is no hint of the license of profane love:*
> "*Everything in Esther exudes peace and innocence.*"

The problem with *Esther*, as it turned out, had little to do with Racine's text. As even the enemy of the theatre, A. Arnauld, wrote on March 21, 1689 in a letter to Ruth d'Ans, "c'est une fort belle pièce et fort chrétienne" (*it is a most beautiful and a most Christian play*).[30] Rather, the difficulty lay with the performance context of the piece, as Quesnel was quick to observe. In a letter to the Père du Breuil, he comments that "si on s'était contenté de la mettre sur le papier, j'en serais encore plus content" (*if they had been content to leave it on paper, I would be all the more content*), and in another letter to the Abbé Nicaise, he writes, "Je voudrais qu'elle ne fût que sur le papier" (*I wish that it existed only on paper*).[31] Mme de Sévigné's account of a performance she attended in February 1689 also reminds us of the question of performance practice:

> On continuera à représenter *Esther*. Mme de Caylus, qui en était la Champmeslé, ne joue plus. Elle faisait trop bien, elle était trop touchante. On ne veut plus que la simplicité toute pure de ces petites âmes innocentes. (February 11, 1689)

> *Esther will continue to be performed. Madame de Caylus, who was its Champmêlé, no longer takes part in it: she was too good, too touching. What is wanted now is only the purest simplicity of these innocent little souls.*

Her words recall Mme de Maintenon's earlier objections to the girls' excessively touching performances of *Andromaque*. These had been attributed primarily to Racine's emphasis in his text on the passions, and in particular on passionate erotic love. But, as it turns out, this was not a problem that could be solved simply with a skillful change in repertoire.

As we have seen, the strongest criticisms of school drama in general were focused on the effect such performances would have on the performers themselves. François Hébert, vicar of Versailles and later Bishop of Agen, for instance, insists on the harmful effect of the girls being

> à la vue de toute sorte de personnes de la Cour. On leur ôte par ce moyen cette honte modeste qui les retient dans leur devoir, car une fille qui a fait un personnage dans une comédie aura beaucoup moins de peine de parler tête à tête à un homme, ayant pris sur elle de paraître tête levée devant plusieurs.[32]

> *viewed by all kinds of people from the court. In this way their modest reserve that keeps them in check is removed, for a girl who has performed a role in a play will find it much less difficult to speak with a man, having already learned to appear with her head held high before an audience of many.*

Participation in dramatic productions before the court, he claims, gives young girls the confidence to become acquainted with men, something that he clearly considers to be fundamentally improper.[33]

Moreover it promotes the girls' vanity "qui est le vice dominant de leur sexe" (*which is the principal vice of their sex*).[34] Quesnel in a wonderfully hyperbolic reaction voices his fear that "l'exemple de cette maison ne porte l'amour de la comédie dans tous les monastères qui prennent des pensionnaires, qu'on n'en fasse des comédiennes, et que les religieuses même ne montent sur le theatre" (*the example of this house will send this type of drama to all the monasteries that have boarders, that they will become actresses, and that the nuns themselves will appear on stage*).[35]

Mme de Maintenon herself comments on the adverse aftereffects of having produced *Esther* at Saint-Cyr:

Dix mois après les grandes journées de février, l'effervescence n'était pas encore calmée, et les pensionnaires n'étaient pas revenues à leur ancienne discipline: elles étaient entêtées de théâtre, et les exercices religieux en souffraient.[36]

Ten months after the great days of February, the excitement still had not calmed down and the boarders had not returned to their former discipline. They were obsessed with the theatre, and their religious exercises suffered as a result.

It does seem to be the case that the excitement of *Esther* had a disruptive effect on the girls of Saint-Cyr and that, in this sense, such productions were seen in practice to be opposed to the ends of female education. As François Hébert declares,

Le principal soin qu'on doit avoir et la fin la plus raisonnable qu'on se doit proposer dans l'instruction des jeunes filles, est de les porter à une très grande pureté de mœurs, à conserver leur pudeur en toutes occasions et les éloigner de tout ce qui peut y être tant soit peu contraire.[37]

The principal concern that one must have and the most reasonable aim regarding the education of young girls is to direct them toward a very deep purity of morals, to conserve their modesty at all times and to keep them away from anything that might represent the slightest threat to that.

Not only was the presence of men in the audience thought to pose a threat to the vulnerable young girls; more intriguingly, the sight of the performing girls was also thought by many to pose a substantial threat to the men. A. Rivet was of the opinion that the performances of young girls and women "ne sont pas seulement capables d'esmouvoir une populace, mais aussi d'attirer et arrester les yeux des hommes, qui sont d'ailleurs graves et prudents" (*are not only capable of moving the people, but also of attracting and holding the attention of men, whose eyes are otherwise serious and prudent*).[38] For him, even the strongest and most virtuous men are at risk. In a similar vein, François Hébert asks rhetorically,

> Croyez-vous d'ailleurs qu'il soit fort décent à des personnes de notre caractère d'assister à une tragédie représentée par des jeunes filles fort bien faites, et qu'on ne peut, pour lors, se défendre de regarder pendant des heures entières? N'est-ce pas s'exposer à des tentations, et le peut-on en conscience?[39]

> *Moreover, do you believe that it is appropriate for people of our standing to witness a tragedy performed by attractive young girls whom one cannot prevent oneself from looking at for hours on end? Is it not to expose oneself to temptation, and can we in all good conscience do so?*

He acknowledges the physical attractions of the girls of Saint-Cyr in surprisingly frank terms ("fort bien faites") and professes the immense dangers for men of gazing upon them. Vulnerability and weakness are clearly not limited to the female sex, whatever the educationalists had to say about the specific defects of women. However exaggerated Hébert's fears might sound, they were, he claims, borne out by the testimony of a number of courtiers who admitted to him:

> que la vue de ces jeunes demoiselles faisant de très vives impressions sur leurs cœurs, que, sachant qu'elles étaient sages, ils en étaient incomparablement plus touchés, que de la vue des comédiennes qui ne laissaient pas que d'être pour eux des occasions de chute, quoiqu'ils ne doutassent point que souvent elles étaient d'une vie très déréglée.[40]

> *that the sight of these young ladies made a very strong impression in their hearts and the fact of knowing that they were innocent touched them infinitely more than the sight of actresses who nonetheless still represented an opportunity for them to fall into sin, even though they never doubted that they often led a dissolute life.*

This account also confirms the notion that the innocence of the girls was precisely part of their appeal, rather than protection against male interest.[41]

A number of other objections were raised to Saint-Cyr's *Esther*. Much has been made of a supposed allegorical meaning behind the play, according to which there was a correspondence between

Mme de Maintenon and the eponymous heroine, and between the girls of Saint-Cyr and the daughters of Sion. As Mme de La Fayette wrote, "tout le monde crut toujours que cette comédie était allégorique" (Orcibal, 23n) (*everyone always thought that this play was an allegory*). Certainly there are resonances between the two that may even have been pleasing to Mme de Maintenon, but a fully fledged allegory becomes more problematical as well as more provocative. If Esther corresponds to Mme de Maintenon and Assuérus to Louis XIV, then the spurned wife Vasthi must be linked with the Marquise de Montespan and Aman perhaps with Louvois—at which point the associations become decidedly more uncomfortable. Still more uncomfortable interpretations have been made according to which Racine was using *Esther* to put forward a Jansenist agenda, implicitly likening the Dames de Saint Louis with the Filles de l'Enfance in Toulouse, whose order had been abolished in response to their complaints about Jesuitical casuistry. As Molière had discovered to his cost with *Le Tartuffe*, the stage was not thought to be an appropriate venue for the discussion of serious, contentious, religious issues.

Her private correspondence reveals that, even from the time of the early performances of *Esther*, Mme de Maintenon herself had ambivalent feelings about the production. She wrote to her confessor, the abbé Gobelin, on February 14, 1689 in the following terms:

> La représentation d'Esther m'empêche de les voir [les dames de Saint-Cyr] aussi souvent que je voudrois. Je n'en puis plus soutenir la fatigue, & j'ai résolu de ne plus faire jouer pour le public que demain. Je ferai dire que nos Actrices sont malades; & elles ne joueront plus que pour nous en particulier, ou pour le Roi, s'il l'ordonne.[42]

> *The performances of* Esther *prevent me from seeing them [the ladies of Saint-Cyr] as often as I would wish. I can no longer endure the fatigue and I have resolved to perform for the public tomorrow only. I will say that our actresses are ill and they will only perform for us in private, or for the king if he commands it.*

Her resolution was not acted upon at this early stage, but, as the controversy surrounding *Esther* came swiftly to overshadow its acclaim, performances were officially terminated in 1690.

Despite the growing controversy surrounding performances of *Esther*, Racine received a royal request for a second play on a similar theme to be performed the following year. *Athalie*, also based on biblical sources and featuring a mixed cast and an all-female chorus, was finished toward the end of 1690. Preparations at Saint-Cyr went ahead for a production on a scale similar to that of *Esther*, with new lavish sets and expensive costume designs by Bérain, as well as music by Moreau. But no such performance was ever given, as Mme de Maintenon yielded instead to the mounting pressure upon her and agreed to a ban on public performances of the play.

Three private performance-rehearsals of *Athalie* were given before Louis XIV, Mme de Maintenon, and a select group of other guests in January and February 1691 (members of the audience at the third of these performances included the exiled King and Queen of England as well as a number of prominent ecclesiastics, among them the Père de la Chaise and Fénelon). In addition to the tightly restricted audience, the principal difference between these performance-rehearsals and the anticipated performances of *Athalie* lies in the decision not to use any of the specially designed costumes and sets.[43] Manseau wrote in January 1691 of one of these performances,

> Le théâtre et les habits qui avoient servi à la représentation d'Esther furent supprimés . . . et quoyque cela se fist avec les habits ordinaires, les chants ny la bonne grâce des demoiselles n'en reçurent pas moins d'acclamations.[44]
>
> *The stage and the clothes that had been used for the performances of* Esther *were done away with . . . and although it was performed with ordinary clothes, neither the songs nor the good grace of the girls was greeted with any less acclaim.*

Boileau attended a performance of *Athalie* and afterward, echoing Manseau, wrote politely to Racine that "quoique les élèves n'eussent que leurs habits ordinaires, tout a été le mieux du monde et a produit un grand effet" (Gofflot, 226) (*although the students wore only their usual clothes, everything was wonderful and created a great effect*). Just as the décor and, particularly the costumes, had formed an important part of the spectacle of *Esther*, so their elimination (or moderation) formed an important part of Mme de Maintenon's attempt to render the private performances of *Athalie* acceptable. It is interesting to note that the engraved frontispiece for the first edition of the play (as had been the case for the frontispiece for *Esther*) depicts the production not as it was originally intended, nor as it was ultimately performed, but rather as it might have been presented in the professional, adult theatre, or even as a stand-alone engraving (see figure 2.1). Not only does the engraving feature elaborate costumes and décor, it

I.B. Corneille inv.   *I. Mariette Sculp.*

Figure 2.1   Frontispiece to the first edition of Racine's *Athalie* (1691).
Source: Beinecke Rare Books and Manuscripts Library, Yale University.

also depicts a whole gamut of roles, ranging from the elderly, bearded Joad to adult men and women, and to the diminutive and youthful Joas on his throne.

Like *Esther*, *Athalie* was open to interpretation along dangerous religious lines, the most obvious reading of the play being its supposed indictment of Louis XIV's persecution of the Jansenist base at Port-Royal. The now familiar arguments concerning the pernicious effects of such productions on the audience, above all on the girls of Saint-Cyr, continued to be voiced, often with great vehemence. Mme de Maintenon, who had always had some qualms regarding these productions, seems to have felt increasingly wretched about them. Several months after the greatly toned down performance-rehearsals of *Athalie*, she wrote on September 20, 1691 to Mme de Fontaines, *maîtresse générale des classes*:

> La peine que j'ai sur les filles de Saint-Cyr ne se peut réparer que par le temps et par un changement entier de l'éducation que nous leur avons donnée jusqu'à cette heure; il est bien juste que j'en souffre, puisque j'y ai contribué plus que personne, et je serai bien heureuse si Dieu ne m'en punit pas plus sévèrement. Mon orgueil s'est répandu par toute la maison, et le fond en est si grand qu'il l'emporte même par-dessus mes bonnes intentions . . . . J'ai voulu que les filles eussent de l'esprit, qu'on élevât leur cœur, qu'on formât leur raison; j'ai réussi à ce dessein: elles ont de l'esprit et s'en servent contre nous; elles ont le cœur élevé, et sont plus fières et plus hautaines qu'il ne conviendroit de l'être aux plus grandes princesses; à parler même selon le monde, nous avons formé leur raison et les avons rendues discoureuses, présomptueuses, curieuses, hardies. (Taphanel, 117–18)

> *The trouble that I have regarding the girls of Saint-Cyr can only be put right by time and by a complete overhaul of the education that we have given them until now. It is right that I should suffer for it, for I have contributed more to it than anybody else and I would be very happy if God did not punish me any more severely. My pride has been spread about the whole house and there is so much of it that it has gone far beyond my good intentions . . . . I wanted the girls to have wit, I wanted their hearts to be uplifted, and their minds developed. I have succeeded in this enterprise: they have wit and use it against us; their hearts are uplifted and they are more proud and more conceited than the greatest princesses should be. Speaking in worldly terms, we have developed their minds and have made them talkative, presumptuous, inquisitive, and overconfident.*

Under her auspices, Saint-Cyr now embarked upon a period of heightened austerity, with particular attention being paid to the corrupting potential of the arts. Interestingly, Manseau notes in 1692 that one of the first measures taken by Mme de Maintenon in this regard was an intriguing reworking of the costumes and some of the jewelry that had been used for *Esther* and designed for *Athalie*:

> Pour mieux en perdre l'idée, les habits en furent défaits et convertis par ordre de Mme de Maintenon en une tapisserie pour le reposoir du Jeudi Saint, et partie des pierreries de la construction d'une niche pour l'exposition du Saint-Sacrement.[45]

> *In order to forget it more easily, the clothes from* Esther *were unstitched and reworked by order of Madame de Maintenon into a tapestry for the altar of repose for Maundy Thursday, and some of the precious stones were used in the construction of a niche to exhibit the Holy Sacrament.*

It seems that it was less problematic to convert exotic theatre costumes and jewelry into items of religious symbolism than it was to devise a suitable performance context for the presentation of drama by young girls.

From this point of extreme, Saint-Cyr moved slowly back to a more moderate position: drama began to be once again studied in class and modest performances were permitted. As the Dames de Saint Louis record,

> On ne jouoit plus du tout avec l'appareil qu'on avoit fait ci-devant à *Esther*, ni en autre habit que celui de Saint-Cyr, à quoi Madame de Maintenon ne vouloit pas qu'on ajoutât des ornements extraordinaires, disant qu'il ne falloit qu'un assortiment simple à un habit aussi simple qu'est celui des Demoiselles, et qu'il étoit de mauvais goût d'en user autrement. Cela n'empêche pas que quand elles ne jouent qu'entre elles ou devant la communauté, on leur souffre de se parer plus qu'à l'ordinaire, et de mettre les diamants qui sont restés de la tragédie d'*Esther*. Madame de Maintenon n'a pas désapprouvé qu'on eût cette complaisance pour leur jeunesse. (Taphanel, 134–35)

> *They no longer performed with all the trappings that they had used previously for* Esther, *nor in any clothes other than those of Saint-Cyr, to which Madame de Maintenon did not want them to add any superfluous decorations, saying that only a simple adornment was suitable to go with the young ladies' simple uniforms and that it was in bad taste to do anything else. This did not prevent them, when they were performing among themselves or in front of the community, from adorning themselves more than usual and from putting on the diamonds that were left over from* Esther. *Madame de Maintenon did not mind our indulging their youth in this way.*

Mme de Maintenon's attitude toward drama at Saint-Cyr is fraught with contradictions, and reflects the complex nature of school drama at this time. This account of her allowing the girls to dress up a little, and even to wear expensive jewelry for these private performances is not, however, as inconsistent as it might first appear. Rather, it reminds us of where the underlying problem lay with the earlier performances of *Esther* that had provided an environment in which (heterosexual) men were invited to gaze upon a large number of attractive and talented young women, dressed in all their finery. Any didactic purpose was thus rapidly subordinated to a more basic instinct. For this reason, Madame de Maintenon warned Mme du Pérou in a letter dated February 24, 1701 with regard to the girls:

Renfermez-les dans votre maison: ne les faites point paraître à la grille sous quel prétexte que ce soit. Il sera toujours dangereux de montrer à des hommes des filles bien faites, & qui ajoutent aux agréments de leur personne le talent de se passionner dans leur rôle, & d'attendrir. N'y souffrez donc aucun homme, ni pauvre, ni riche, ni vieux, ni jeune, ni Prêtre, ni Laïque, je dis même un Saint, s'il en est un sur la terre. (Maintenon, *Mémoires et lettres*, IX, 167)[46]

Keep them within the confines of your house. Do not let them appear at the gates for any reason. It will always be dangerous to allow men to gaze upon attractive girls who, in addition to the qualities of their person, display the talent of their enthusiasm for the role and their ability to move an audience. Do not allow any man in, neither a poor man, nor a rich one, neither an old one nor a young one, neither a priest nor a layman, nor even a saint, if there are any on this earth.

We have seen that cross-casting in school drama cannot be separated from other, related issues. For the girls of Saint-Cyr, cross-dressing was less of a concern than *dressing-up*, which itself became particularly dangerous only in the presence of desiring (heterosexual) men. The Jesuit schoolboys were to be protected from the harmful effects of contemplating and performing love of an erotic nature, albeit it of the most mild and modest kind, while the girls of Saint-Cyr were to be protected from their arousing this same love (or at least desire) among their audience. As Mme de Maintenon discovered, it was easier to exclude men from the audience by authorizing only private performances than it was to try to confront some of the natural consequences arising from the interaction of members of the opposite sex.

CHAPTER III

FEMALE ROLES IN COURT BALLET I: MEN PLAYING WOMEN

French Court Ballet

By the beginning of Louis XIV's reign, *ballet de cour* (French court ballet) was a well-established and popular feature of the French court, dating back to the late–sixteenth century. The first example of the genre is generally taken to be the *Balet Comique de la Royne*, written to celebrate the marriage of the Queen's sister, Mademoiselle de Vaudemont, to a favorite of Henri III, the Duc de Joyeuse, in 1581 and performed in the Great Hall of the Louvre as part of a long series of wedding festivities.[1] The *Balet Comique* is generally attributed to its principal creator and choreographer, Balthazar de Beaujoyeulx (d.1587), but any single attribution is inevitably misleading as French court ballet was a fundamentally collaborative genre, combining as it did the efforts of choreographers, composers, musicians, dancers, set designers, costume designers, and many others. Like the majority of its successors, the *Balet Comique* was embedded in a specific context of royal celebration, that is to say of entertainment (or *divertissement*—such events were often called *divertissements de cour*), but also, inevitably, of political display. Spectacular magnificence, exhibited in the extravagant costumes, décors, music and choreography, as well as in the sheer scale of the entertainment, was a persuasive means of demonstrating—or rather, performing—the power of the sovereign. The king was understood to be both the driving force behind all such performances and also its privileged spectator. In addition, both Louis XIII and Louis XIV appeared as dancers in a number of court ballets (some of Louis XIV's roles are examined below).

The content of Beaujoyeulx's *Balet comique* also alludes to a more specific political agenda as the evil enchantress, Circé, is opposed to a virtuous French king. Ultimately the king triumphs, thereby fulfilling and promoting the wider myth of the powerful French monarch who rights wrongs and brings peace to the troubled State. The *Balet comique* is, however, a more accurate reflection of a desired reality rather than of a lived one, a portrait of how things should be rather than of how they were. As Margaret McGowan has noted, "it is interesting to reflect on the fact that Henri III's reputation for justice and virtue, and his control over political events, were never more precarious than at the precise times when artists exerted themselves to present a picture of their King's merits and omnipotence" (*Le Balet Comique*, 36). *Ballet de cour* is thus tightly bound up with courtly politics and historical events, but its take on them is often more of an illusion than a reality.

This performance of hypothetical monarchical greatness extended beyond the duration of the ballet itself, as participants and spectators took away with them not only their memories of the event but often also the ballet programs (or *livrets*) that, as will be seen below, offered an acceptable guide to interpreting the spectacle. Official accounts of the great court festivals or *fêtes* in which ballets featured alongside feasts and fireworks, masquerades and mock combats, were written and judiciously distributed around the kingdom and throughout the courts of Europe. The *ballet de cour* was thus not only a means of performing the official history of the reign, but also of diffusing it. It is this broadly political dimension to ballet that explains the willingness of French courtiers (and their kings) to participate in such events. At one level, dance was considered a suitable aristocratic pastime, and a means of developing and then displaying one's elegance and refinement. At another level, to perform in a court ballet was to please its principal spectator, the king, and to perform alongside him was an even greater privilege and honor. That these amateur dancers were also spectators of French court ballet points to another important aspect of the genre: the porous relationship between audience members and performers, which in turn suggests a further blurring of reality and illusion.

Beaujoyeulx claimed (with a little poetic license) that his *Balet Comique* was the first court spectacle that consciously attempted to unite dance, poetry, and music in an integrated dramatic plot according to the principles of the Académie de Musique et de la Poésie (founded by Baïf in 1570). In its complex mélange of diverse theatrical components, French court ballet was, as Mark Franko has observed, "closer . . . to twentieth-century performance art than to classical ballet."[2] For all Beaujoyeulx's rhetorical emphasis on unity, the esthetic of the *ballet de cour* was thoroughly unclassical and fundamentally baroque. In stark contrast to the principles that came to govern spoken, classical tragedy (best exemplified by the work of Racine), ballet remained free to follow its own esthetic of spectacle and diversity. The seventeenth-century theorist Claude-François Ménestrier claimed that the pleasure of a ballet audience depended precisely on the work's diversity:

> Le Ballet qui ne se propose que le plaisir dans les Representations justes, sçavantes, & naïves, demande plus de varieté, & ne souffre pas ces contraintes.[3]
>
> *Ballet, which offers only pleasure in its agreeable, skillful, and innocent performances, requires more variety and is not subject to these constraints.*

A degree of unity was achieved by virtue of the fact that each ballet was organized around a central theme that could be interpreted in many varied ways within the work. Ballets include mythological and pastoral figures, characters from popular novels of the day, as well as interesting or exotic social groups such as gypsies, Spaniards, and other foreigners. Burlesque ballets, which were particularly popular during the reign of Louis XIII, incorporated such outlandish personages as drunkards, beggars, and peasants, as well as grotesque inventions, many of them not human. Some ballets were satirical and others displayed a clear political agenda, often through the use of allegory.[4] Richelieu was particularly keen to exploit the political potential of ballet, but under Louis XIV the emphasis in court ballets shifted instead toward the *galant*. Thus, where ballets under Louis XIII had tended to be either burlesque or political, ballets under Louis XIV emphasized male-female relations at court. It is in the light of this preoccupation with love and sex that cross-casting and female roles are examined in the following two chapters.

Although the *ballets de cour* under the Valois had included regular appearances by female members of the French court, the majority of ballets performed under Louis XIII included only male dancers, both professional and noble. The notable exceptions to this tendency were the *ballets de la Reine* (the queen's ballets) such as *Psyché* (1619) and *Le Ballet de Junon la Nopcière* (1623), in which the queen and female members of her entourage performed in the *grand ballet* at the close of the entertainment.[5] Thus, at the beginning of Louis XIV's reign, the ballet stage was essentially male, and the performance of female roles by male dancers was an established convention. Under Louis XIV, however, casting practices in ballet evolved rapidly to include more and more frequent appearances by both female courtiers and female professionals. The convention of male to female cross-casting was, during this time, challenged, then toyed with as a device, and ultimately replaced with the new convention of straight casting. A general shift in favor of greater participation on the part of female dancers in the *ballet de cour* is discernible, although the progression is not an entirely linear or consistent one.

That Louis XIV and his court should have inherited a theatrical genre of which cross-casting was a fundamental part is worthy of note, particularly at a time when women already appeared regularly on the professional public stage in France (see chapter I). A comparison with the contrasting situation in England is instructive. Just as women performed in private, courtly entertainments in England decades before professional actresses were permitted to appear on the public stage, so men continued to perform female roles in French court ballet even decades after actresses had become the norm in the professional theatre. This apparent paradox would suggest that potentially threatening casting practices (the appearance of sexually attractive women on stage in the case of England, and the appearance of the sexually ambiguous figure of the cross-dressed male in the case of France) were considered less dangerous, and more manageable, within the safer confines of the court than before the wider theatre-going public. While England and France approached the problem of how to perform female roles in the theatre in different ways, both countries acknowledged that the problem was different in the public and private spheres.

It is important to remember, however, that even in ballets that included an all-male dancing cast (and an all-male orchestra), women frequently participated as *singers*.[6] Indeed, certain female professional singers at Louis XIV's court (notably Mlles Hilaire, de la Barre, and Bergerotti) were granted star status, and their participation was clearly considered to be part of the attraction of the ballet genre. In *Le Ballet de la Galanterie du Temps* (1656), for example, in which all the female roles were danced by men, Mlle de la Barre sang the opening "Récit de Vénus."[7] More intriguingly, in the *Ballet de la Naissance de Vénus* (1665), which included only male dancers, the "Plaintes d'Ariadné" were sung by Mlle Hilaire, while the dancing Ariadné was performed cross-cast. While dancing was an integral part of participatory life at court, singing, it seems, was not; and any songs required for theatrical productions at court were left to the professionals. With very few exceptions, then, the singing roles of the *ballet de cour* are all straight cast, whereas the dancing roles are frequently cross-cast.

No attempt was ever made to conceal the convention of cross-casting either in the ballet programs (*livrets*) or in terms of the performers' costumes. Ménestrier comments on the most significant difference between ballet costumes for men and those for women:

> Que l'habit [de l'homme] ne soit point embarassant, & qu'il laisse le corps & la jambe bien libre pour danser. Les habits de femmes sont les moins propres, parce qu'ils doivent estre longs. (Ménestrier, *Des ballets*, 253)
>
> *The [man's] costume should not be at all restrictive. It should leave the body and the legs free to dance. Women's costumes are the least suitable because they have to be long.*

However, he fails to mention specifically the interesting case of male dancers cross-cast as women. The most significant difference between costumes for men playing female roles and those for women was precisely skirt length: women's costumes had full-length skirts, while men's skirts were much shorter. The biological sex of the performer (a man may reveal his legs) thus takes precedence over the gender of his assumed role (a woman may not), as his cross-dressed status is heralded by costumes that correspond neither exactly to traditional male ballet costumes, still less to female modes of dress. These cross-cast performers are not strictly men in women's clothing, but men in an adapted form of women's clothing: a third sartorial category.

The binary model of male and female is also challenged by the subject matter of many *ballets de cour*, particularly those that draw heavily on classical mythology. As Nicole Loraux remarks (with specific reference to Heracles) the mythological tradition is steeped in gender ambiguity:

> Myths give us . . . a systematic disruption of the "normal" distribution of the characteristics of man and woman, expressing the experience of the feminine lived out by man or the terrifying conquest of the masculine by woman.[8]

Figure 3.1 Louis XIV as Apollo. From Ballet "La nuit." Anonymous, 17th century. French School. Watercolor.

Source: Photo: Bulloz. Bibliotheque Nationale, Paris, France. © RMN-Grand Palais/Art Resource, NY

Classical sources provide us with mythological accounts not only of cross-dressing, but also of metamorphosis from one sex to another and of sexual ambiguity, notably in the figure of the Amazon whose embodiment of masculine virility and feminine chastity seems to have captured the imagination of a good number of seventeenth-century French writers. Metamorphosis and disguise are the inspiration behind Benserade's *Ballet des Amours déguisés* (1664), for example, while Talestris, Queen of the Amazons, and four lovesick Amazon women feature in the *Ballet de Psyché* (1656). The fact that these amazons were cross-cast in a ballet in which the majority of female roles were performed by women is particularly interesting: the male sex of the performers, combined with their third category costumes, neatly characterizes the amazons' sexual identity as ambiguous. The sexual indeterminacy of the amazon is also her defining characteristic, and the challenge she poses to the binary model of sexual identity is, in this instance, well served by a declining convention that is being used increasingly as a device.

Ballet Verses

At every performance, ballet *livrets* containing brief plot summaries, the names of the dancers for each *entrée* (entry or scene) and, most importantly, the *vers* (verses) for the courtly performers, were distributed to the audience. The *livrets* were intended not only as a souvenir of the event, but also as an essential guide to the performance. Contrary to what one might expect, the verses were not read aloud by the performer, but were intended rather to be read silently by the spectator as the performance unfolded. They were thus conceived as an integral part of the spectacle in performance and as a means of binding spectator and performer together in the wider theatre of the French court. In addition to the ambiguity of subject and the ambiguity associated with cross-casting, the ballet verses (which are my principal source for this chapter and chapter IV) deliberately draw attention to the different levels of theatrical illusion in the *ballet de cour*, including the layers of conflicting sexual identity present in certain roles. The fact that these verses are provided for the courtly dancers only (and not for the professionals) reveals the genre's preoccupation with life at court, which ultimately takes precedence over the fiction of the entertainment itself.

Just as the clear-cut distinction between spectator and performer in French ballet was undermined by the participation of dancing courtiers, so the distinction between a courtier's adopted role and his/her person was self-consciously manipulated in his/her verses.[9] The great writer of ballet verses under Louis XIV was the court poet, Isaac Benserade (1613–91), whose texts invite the spectator to respond to the performers in certain ways. We cannot know to what extent the spectators' genuine responses overlapped with Benserade's suggested response, but the verses are a wonderfully rich source and one from which we can learn a good deal about the author's attitude toward the performers and their roles. Benserade's verses are not quite official accounts of the reign but they may certainly be understood to represent a sanctioned and acceptable attitude toward the ballet in question (and some of the verses' content is surprising). Reading the verses was as much a part of what was entertaining about the ballets as were their music, dance, and costumes, as spectators were expected to take pleasure in reading witty accounts of their fellow courtiers.

In the *livrets*, the fact that the name of the performer always appears alongside that of his/her role indicates that the spectator is to keep both person and persona in mind simultaneously. In many theatrical genres, the actor is intended to disappear behind his/her role as the fiction of the drama takes precedence over the reality of the identity of the performers. In the *ballet de cour*, on the other hand, the performer is always double, appearing on stage as him/herself and in his/her role. In this way, the convention of theatrical disguise (including cross-casting) is used as a device to highlight and celebrate the theatrical illusion and to establish a close complicity between the courtly audience and the courtly performers (who, in any case, overlapped). The verses enforce this asymmetrical duality in a fascinating combination of fact and fiction, of person and persona, in which references to the adopted role are commonly used to comment on the person playing that role. To write successful verses, Benserade needed to know at least as much about court gossip and intrigue as he did about his literary and historical sources.

For all that Benserade's verses delight in playing with different levels of reality, their commentary on cross-casting and male-female relations is ultimately a normalizing one. In the *Ballet de l'Amour malade* (1657), for example, the verses for the Duc Damville playing the cross-cast bride comment precisely on the discrepancy between his person and his role:

> Faire ainsi l'Espousée, est fort peu conuenable
> Pour vn pauure Amoureux las de viure en garçon:
> Dieu vueille qu'on en voye vne bien veritable
> Qui soit de ma façon. (I, 380)

To impersonate the bride is most inappropriate
For a poor suitor tired of being a bachelor:
God willing, may a genuine one be seen
Who will suit me.

As Marie-Claude Canova-Green notes (I, 380n), the second line is a reference to the Duke's recently thwarted marriage. Not only is this an example of how Benserade's verses include direct references to the personal lives of his courtly performers, it also effects an important transition away from the homoerotic or otherwise threatening potential of the cross-cast role in favor of the more comfortable reality of the Duke's heterosexual pursuits. The verses thus draw the spectator's attention to the Duke's conflicting signals of gender only to reassert his sexual identity as resolutely masculine and heterosexual. In this sense, they do betray a degree of anxiety with regard to the practice of cross-casting, and part of the purpose of the verses is precisely to deal with that anxiety and to reassert what Monique Wittig has famously called the "straight mind," that is to say, the assumption that we are operating within a heterosexual model.

Similarly, the verses for the Marquis de Mirepoix playing Thisbe in the *Ballet des Muses* (1666) comment openly on his cross-casting:

Vous auez bonne mine, & ne prétendez pas
Que pour vostre beauté l'on souffre le trépas
Aussi la Fable ingénieuse & sage
Sur l'accident funeste ou Pyrasme est tombé
Quand elle parle de Thisbé
N'accuse que son voile, & non pas son visage. (II, 781)

You look well and do not claim
That anyone would die for your beauty.
Thus the ingenious and wise fable
About Pyramus's gloomy accident,
When it talks about Thisbe,
Accuses only her veil and not her face.

Here, the verses are not so much about reasserting the Marquis's own sexuality as they are a commentary on the convention of cross-casting. Benserade playfully refers to Thisbe's bloodstained scarf as a means of drawing the audience's attention to the discrepancy between the dancer's real identity as a man and his dancing role as a woman. Here cross-casting does not require a suspension of disbelief (as it did in serious school drama—see chapter II), rather the spectator's enjoyment stems from his/her participation in the supposed pretence. Far from abandoning his disbelief for the duration of the performance, the spectator is encouraged to derive part of his/her pleasure precisely from that disbelief, particularly when confronted by men playing female roles. At the same time, the spectator is reassured that life at court continues to operate within the anticipated heterosexual paradigm. More insidiously, the Marquis's verses also suggest that beauty, is a particularly female domain, indicating that it is specifically his lack of feminine beauty, rather than the simple fact that he is a man, that renders the Marquis's cross-casting so unconvincing. As will be seen below, the potentially deviant practice of cross-casting was used not only to affirm the traditional model of male-female sexual relations, it also served, paradoxically, to enforce the feminine ideal.

The relationship between performer and spectator in court ballets under Louis XIV is one of complicity, as seen in its repeated allusions to a base of common knowledge regarding the lives of the performers, and in its deliberate undermining of the theatrical illusion. In other regards, the relationship between performer and spectator is more challenging. Louis XIV inherited from his father a ballet stage that was essentially all-male, and in Benserade's all-male ballets (but less so in ballets that include female dancers) there is a discernible tendency toward identifying the audience (which was in fact always mixed) as officially female.[10] This privileging of the female spectator is demonstrated in the many *récits* that, in the *livrets*, are addressed specifically "Aux Dames" (to the ladies) and in many of the verses that clearly speak to the female members of the audience. The opening *récit* of the *Ballet de Cassandre* (1651), for example, is designated "Aux Dames" and reads as follows:

Belles qui venez dans ces lieux
Voir le Triomphe de Cassandre
Elle va descendre des Cieux:
Croyez sans vous méprendre
Que c'est pour vos beaux yeux.
Tous les coeurs seront sous vos Loix. (I, 42)

Beauties who have come here
To witness the triumph of Cassandra,
She is about to descend from the heavens:
Make no mistake,
It is for your beautiful eyes.
Every heart will be under your command.

The male spectator is overlooked, while the female spectator (to whom the *récit* and the whole ballet are dedicated) is equated with beauty from the very first word ("belles"). The ballet audience that is addressed is not just a group of women, but specifically a group of beautiful women who will gaze admiringly (with their own alluring eyes) upon the male performers.

The way in which the (female) spectator is to respond to the (male) dancer's performance becomes more explicit in the verses for the participants in the second entry of the same ballet (these are also designated "Aux Dames"):

> Belles dont les regards mettent nos coeurs en cendre,
> Quand nous aurons marqué le logis de cassandre
> Comme vous nous voyez fait d'esprit et de corps
> Aurez vous le coeur d'entreprendre
> De nous laisser coucher dehors? (I, 43)

> *Beauties, whose eyes burn our hearts to cinders,*
> *After we have set up Cassandra's dwelling,*
> *Given the quality of our bodies and our minds,*
> *Will you have the heart*
> *To leave us to sleep outside?*

The women of the audience are to gaze at the dancers and be so moved by their performance that they will invite them into their bed. In this sense, French court ballets may be understood not simply as entertainment, but as a potential means of seduction or, at the very least, as a forum for the discussion of male-female relations at court.

However, a seductive agenda as specific as the above was, for obvious reasons, more difficult to uphold when the dancers performed cross-cast. In my examination of the functioning of cross-casting, I shall draw particularly on the verses written for Louis XIV, his brother, Philippe d'Orléans, and the Marquis de Genlis (a courtier).

Louis XIV

Contrary to what has sometimes been assumed, Louis XIV did not dance only majestic and grandiose roles in court ballets. While he is most famous for his spectacular portrayal of the rising sun at the end of the *Ballet de la Nuit* (1653), he also performed a great variety of other roles, including a Spaniard, an Egyptian, a shepherd, a debauched man, and an iceman, as well as the female roles with which we are concerned here.[11] At first sight, the idea that the young Louis should have taken roles that so patently run counter to his official image as a (future) glorious and invincible king seems almost impossible to countenance. This is particularly the case for the female characters that, one might assume, must surely have jeopardized his all-important virility. In the light of what we have seen about the emphasis on the person of the performer rather than his adopted role, however, cross-cast roles for the young king, although not without their risks, become a more viable phenomenon.

Louis XIV performed his first cross-cast roles in the *Ballet des Fêtes de Bacchus* (1651) when he was only twelve years old. Before he reached full adult maturity, Louis's latent qualities were stressed in his verses and his future glory anticipated—and this is the case in both his straight-cast roles and in his cross-cast ones. The verses depicting him as the wine-loving *Bacchante*, for example, move from a description of his hyperactivity in the first stanza, to an allusion to his future susceptibility to love in the second. In the third and final stanza, we read,

De là ie quitte en peu de temps
Tous ces petits vins, & pretens
Aualer à longs traits du grand vin de la gloire,
Déja la Nature & les Cieux
En naissant m'en ont tant fait boire,
Qu'on voit qu'il me sort par les yeux. (I, 73)

From here, very soon, I shall leave behind me
All these little wines and will
Drink deeply of the great wine of glory.
Already, Nature and the skies
From my birth have made me drink so much of it
That it can be seen coming out of my eyes.

The bacchanalian imagery is here employed to describe Louis's future glory within the context of his God-given birthright. Even the phenomenon of the twelve-year-old Louis playing a seemingly inappropriate role in a court ballet can thus be manipulated, at least in his verses, to remind his audience (and perhaps also himself) of his official image. Later in the same ballet, when Louis reappears as one of the nine Muses (all of them played by male dancers) no mention is made of his cross-casting. Instead, he is given a set of verses addressed, interestingly, not "Aux Dames" but "Avx Poètes" (to the poets) in which his future exploits are anticipated:

> Ie medite vn hardy projet,
> Et vous prepare le sujet
> D'vn grand & beau Poëme heroïque. (I, 85)

> *I'm planning an audacious project*
> *And am preparing for you the subject*
> *Of a great and beautiful heroic poem.*

The story of the final cross-cast role written for Louis in this ballet suggests, however, that there are limits to the attenuating powers of Benserade's verses. The future king was to have played the role of a coquette in an entry that was eventually omitted (known as the "Entrée Supprimée.") We cannot be certain why this entry was excluded, but it is more than likely that the sexuality (specifically *female* sexuality) depicted in the role was the principal reason. Benserade's opening verses embrace Louis's cross-casting, writing of him in the feminine form:

> Ie doute qu'avec moy pas vne Demoiselle
> Entre en comparaison,
> Car ie suis belle enfin, ieune, spirituelle,
> Et de bonne maison. (I, 87)

> *I doubt that any young woman*
> *Can measure up to me,*
> *For I am beautiful, young, and lively,*
> *And from a good family.*

The assertion that the young Louis is unlike any other young woman may be read in various ways. As a man, he is, of course, set apart by virtue of his biological sex; the implication that to compare him with a young woman would be a comparison of different, unequal entities here seems to promote his position as unique and untouchable, owing to his kingly status. Although a correspondence between his youthful femininity and that of a young woman could be argued, the spectator is directed away from this interpretation by the deliberate emphasis on kingly (and therefore masculine) qualities. In the fourth stanza, the image of male suitors pursuing the female coquette is employed as a punning double-entendre to illustrate the power Louis already wields (and will wield) over the French court:

> Combien d'adorateurs marchent dessus mes traces,
> Et vont baisant mes pas,
> Et que de gens voudroient auoir mes bonnes graces
> Qui ne les auront pas. (I, 87)
>
> *How many admirers walk in my footsteps,*
> *And kiss my path,*
> *And how many people would like to receive my good graces*
> *Who will not do so.*

The seemingly conflicting forces of female seductress and future male monarch thus conspire to assert a more expedient image. Benserade's verses for Louis acknowledge that this combination is unusual: "L'on ne voit qu'en moy de la coquetterie, / Et de la Majesté" (*Only in me is found coquetry / And majesty*) and insist on the possible coexistence of a feminine appearance with a masculine, regal essence: "Ie sens que dans le corps d'vne ieune Mignonne / I'ay l'ame d'vn grand Roy" (I, 87–88) (*I feel that in the body of an attractive young woman / I have the soul of a great king*). Benserade's separation of Louis's coquettish female body from his masculine kingly soul evokes the notion of the king's two bodies and is strongly reminiscent of the reported separation of the female body of Elizabeth I from her kingly heart and stomach in her famous speech before her troops encamped at Tilbury in 1588.[12] But, where her dilemma was especially fraught as she confronted the reality of her biological sexual identity, Louis XIV at least had the advantage of being biologically male. There is of course a correspondence between youth and femininity, and in that sense it was more appropriate for Louis to play female roles before he reached full sexual maturity. And the contextual difference between a battleground and a court ballet is immense. Nonetheless, this entry's omission indicates that it was problematical. In turn, it also suggests that Louis XIV was not, as his propagandists would have had us believe, untouchable.[13]

Louis continued to play female roles into his early adulthood and at the beginning of his personal reign (after the death of Mazarin in March 1661). In the *Ballet des Saisons* (1661), for example, he played the corn goddess Cérès. His verses make no allusion to his cross-casting and refer no longer to his future exploits but link him directly with current events:

> Destin, vous le vouliez, par vostre ordre tout pur
> La Terre a dû souffrir qu'vn fer trenchant & dur

Luy déchirast le sein dans vne rude Guerre;
Maintenant s'en est fait, & de ma propre main
Je séme heureusement sur cette mesme Terre
Dequoy donner la vie à tout le genre Humain. (II, 545)

Destiny, you desired it, at your purest command
The earth has had to endure a sharp and hard sword
That tore it apart in a harsh war.
Now it is over and with my own hands
I happily sow on that same earth
Enough food to sustain the whole human race.

Written at a time of peace, these verses link Louis XIV's supposed
power to look after the French people with Cérès's power over
nature—specifically agriculture. The fact that she is a goddess (and
not a god) is apparently irrelevant.

In the lighthearted mascarade ballet, *Les Noces de village* (1663),
Louis XIV played a village girl and a (male) gypsy. The verses for the
royal village girl are as follows:

Sa grace n'est pas commune,
Et son moindre attachement
D'vn honneste homme aisement
Feroit la bonne fortune:
De tous ceux qu'elle void elle engage le coeur,
A quiconque la sert elle fait bon visage:
Mais jamais fille de vilage
N'eût tant de soin de son honneur. (II, 634)

Her grace is uncommon,
And the slightest attachment to her
Would easily make the good fortune
Of an honest man.
She engages the hearts of all whom she sees
She looks kindly upon whoever serves her.
But never has a village girl
Taken so much care of her honor.

The idiom commonly used to describe the qualities of attractive
women is here punningly applied to the king, and the power of
women to attract admiring men is assimilated to the power he exerts
over his (male) courtiers. Just as the men of the court were supposed
to be devoted to the women they were trying to seduce, so should
they be even more devoted to the king whose power over them is far
greater. Benserade's mildly risqué reference to the village girl's honor

(i.e., her virginity) moves rapidly away from any suggestion of innuendo toward a punning reminder of the king's official image as a man of honor.

Louis XIV's final cross-cast role was that of a nymph in the *Ballet des Muses* (in which he also played four male roles). His verses are divided into two contrasting stanzas. In the first, the nymph-king is referred to by feminine pronouns and is hailed as "la Nymphe merueilleuse agreable & terrible" (*marvelous, agreeable, and terrible nymph*) who "des Ours & des Lyons médite vn meurtre horrible" (II, 798) (*is planning the horrible murder of the bears and the lions*). The imposing qualities of the nymph are stressed within the context of the Anglo-Dutch war that France had recently entered. In the first stanza, then, the image of a ferocious nymph is used to depict the king as a formidable enemy; in the second, Benserade focuses on the king himself, now employing the masculine pronoun, and anticipating a positive outcome of the war that will earn Louis manifold praise. Thus, when Louis XIV performed cross-cast within the relatively safe confines of court ballet, Benserade was able to fashion his appearances into something appropriate and seemly. What the unofficial and genuine response really was to these and other indecorous roles we can unfortunately never know. The suppression of the entry in which Louis was to have appeared as a coquette suggests, however, that his appearances in ballet had the potential to threaten the official image that he was so keen to uphold.

Philippe d'Orléans

Benserade's gloss on the cross-cast roles of Louis's younger brother, Philippe d'Orléans (known as "Monsieur"), differs from that given to the king in some interesting ways.[14] In the *Ballet des Fêtes de Bacchus* (1651), Philippe d'Orléans took the part of a girl possessed by a demon and his verses begin "I'estois vn fort joly garcon" (I, 61) (*I was a very pretty boy*). This account of him is reminiscent of the Abbé de Choisy (himself a cross-dresser in real life), who once described Philippe as "la plus jolie créature de France" (*the prettiest creature in France*).[15] At the time of the performance of the *Ballet des Fêtes de Bacchus*, Philippe d'Orléans was only eleven years old and he is known to have worn children's dresses until a later age than was customary for boys, even at the time.[16] The description of him as a pretty boy may be factually correct, but it brings with it some uncomfortable suggestions regarding the stability of gender (and even, perhaps, biological sex). His verses inform us that Monsieur's youthful and feminine good looks, when combined with the company of women and the donning of female clothing, are enough to turn him into a woman (or rather, a girl):

Quand à force de m'attacher
Au beau sexe qui m'est si cher,
En m'habillant comme il s'habille
Ie suis enfin deuenu fille. (I, 61)

When, by dint of my attachment
To the fair sex that is so dear to me,
By dressing as members of the fair sex do,
I eventually became a girl.

Coupled with the familiar notion that a lover will come to resemble his loved one, is the more alarming suggestion that gender is unstable and that if it can happen to him, it could happen to us too. However, at this critical moment, Monsieur chooses to revert to his original sex in order that he may enjoy normal heterosexual relations with women:

Mais je sens bien que je ne puis
Seruir ce sexe quand j'en suis,
Et je commence à recognoistre
Pour l'aymer qu'il n'en faut pas estre;
C'est pourquoy je serois d'auis
De reprendre auec mes habits
Celuy-là dont j'estois n'aguere. (I, 61-2)

But I am aware that I cannot
Attend to this sex when I am a woman,
And I am beginning to understand
That to love it one must not be it.
This is why I have decided
To readopt, with my clothes,
The sex to which I formerly belonged.

We notice that Monsieur's gender (and sex) depends here on his clothing. When he is dressed as a girl, he is a girl, and when he dresses once more as a boy, he becomes a boy again. To a large extent, his unstable gender identity may be attributed to his age. The sex of a prepubescent boy or girl was at this time thought to be indeterminate and, by this token, the adoption of different clothing might indeed be used as the ultimate indicator of sex. Cross-casting among prepubescent boys, particularly in a genre in which the emphasis is on real-life sexual identity, is thus very different from the cross-casting of adult men. On the one hand, it offers more scope for playing with issues of sex and gender, while on the other, as the above verses demonstrate, it is still coupled with the need to reassert the dancer's position within the standard heterosexual paradigm. Monsieur's experience of cross-dressing, we are told, inhibited his potential to practice heterosexual love and, for that reason, he will revert to masculine attire. When we consider that Philippe d'Orléans was homosexual in real life, an additional level of ambiguity and irony emerges from these verses, and their normative conclusion is a reminder of the same societal expectations that required him to marry.[17] Although it can be, cross-dressing is not usually about homosexuality (a common misconception), but it is interesting to note that it can be used to comment on various types of supposedly deviant behavior, including early signs of same-sex desire.

Five years later, Philippe d'Orléans took the ambiguously gendered role of Talestris, Queen of the Amazons, in the *Ballet de Psyché* (1656). His verses address him in the feminine form and insist upon the similarities between the performer and his adopted role, using "comme" (*like*) three times in four lines. In a celebration of the Amazon's combination of feminine beauty and manly courage, for example, Benserade writes "Comme vne veritable & parfaite Amazône / Vous auez la beauté tout ensemble & le Coeur" (I, 315) (*like a true and perfect Amazon, you combine beauty and courage*). Whereas the young Louis had to be distanced from the coquette's flirtatiousness and his kingly qualities reasserted in the *Ballet des Fêtes de Bacchus*, Monsieur is determinedly likened to the Amazon whose characteristics he is purported to share. The level of double-entendre is introduced when Benserade describes Monsieur's hatred of husbands: whereas Amazons wished to be free from patriarchal authority, Monsieur's aversion to husbands stems from his supposed love of women. Where the Amazons fight with their real arrows, Monsieur's metaphorical arrow comes from cupid. Once again, his verses offer a combination of gender ambiguity followed by a reassertion of normality.

The Marquis de Genlis

Whereas Benserade was expected to flatter Louis XIV and, to a lesser extent, his younger brother (especially when they were cross-cast), he was clearly accorded a surprising degree of liberty when it came to the court dancers who did not belong to the royal family. One of the most striking examples (and certainly the most recurrent) concerns the Marquis de Genlis, who performed regularly in court ballets under Louis XIV and who played an Amazon alongside Monsieur's portrayal of Talestris in the *Ballet de Psyché*. Genlis had been left severely scarred by smallpox and, far from politely ignoring this fact, Benserade alludes to his unsightliness at almost every opportunity. If Genlis's physical appearance was not a joke at court beforehand, it rapidly became one. The verses for Genlis's performance as an Amazon are no exception:

> Amazône discrete & sage,
> Sans que vostre pudeur en soit blessée en rien,
> I'oserois assurer & ie gagerois bien
> Que vous auez le corps plus beau que le visage. (I, 315)

> *Discreet and wise Amazon,*
> *Without offending your sense of modesty at all,*
> *I would dare to affirm, and I would confidently wager,*
> *That your body is more beautiful than your face.*

The discrepancy between Genlis and his role lies not in this instance with his sex, but with his pockmarked face that diverges from the image of the beautiful Amazon woman. In the case of a male dancer, such a lack of good looks is treated with humor. For a female dancer, such a commentary would be unthinkable, not only because it would have been considered un-*galant* to speak of a woman in such terms, but also because it served the male agenda to uphold the image of a woman as a beautiful object. Because he is ugly, Genlis cannot be a woman (not even an Amazon woman), however he may dress. Monsieur, on the other hand, could be an acceptable Amazon because he was thought to be attractive.

In view of the repeated references to the Marquis de Genlis's unattractiveness, the decision to cast him in the role of a "Belle Inconnue" (*unknown female beauty*) in the first entry of the *Ballet de la Galanterie du Temps* (1656) can only be understood as an ironic joke, highlighting the disparity between his adopted role and his real status as neither attractive, unknown, nor female.[18] In this instance, it is clear that the convention of cross-casting is being employed as a persuasive comic device. In a similar way, the Comte du Plessis had become the target of the court's humor when he played a Nereid in the *Ballet de la Nuit* (1653). Greeted as a "Beauté de figure estrange" (*strange-looking beauty*),

Plessis's appearance, according the Benserade, led the spectator (and here the spectator is clearly male) to conclude,

> Si toute vostre troupe a la mesme beauté,
> Il n'est point dans la Mer de Triton qui ne fasse
> De bon coeur voeu de chasteté. (I, 103)

> *If all your troupe has the same beauty*
> *There is not a Triton in the sea who would not*
> *Willingly take a vow of chastity.*

Once again, it is not so much owing to the count's conflicting gender signals that the spectators would gladly become celibate (although this could potentially have provided ample material for similar jokes), but rather owing to his physical unattractiveness. The message is that it is not worth pursuing a woman who is without beauty.

Pursuing the Feminine Ideal

However paradoxical it may seem, the imperative that women be beautiful is discernible in many of the verses for cross-cast roles. The verses for the Marquis de Monglas, playing a "Bourgeoise" in the *Ballet de la Nuit*, for example, draw attention to the lack of correspondence between the performer and his role:

> Vous meriteriez quelques voeux,
> Et seriez d'assez bon vsage,
> Si vous auiez le blanc dessus vostre visage
> Que vous auez dans les cheueux:
> Oüy, je vous le diray, deussay-ie émouuoir noise;
> Vous estes vn braue Seigneur,
> Vn fort bon Gentilhomme & d'esprit & d'honneur,
> Mais vne fort laide Bourgeoise. (I, 113)

> *You would deserve some greeting*
> *And you would be quite well bred*
> *If you had the same white color on your face*
> *That you have in your hair:*
> *Yes, I will tell you, even if I provoke an argument:*
> *You are a fine lord,*
> *A truly good gentleman of spirit and honor,*
> *But a really ugly bourgeois woman.*

Monglas fails to make a pleasing *bourgeoise* not because he is of a different class or even because he is of a different biological sex, but because the qualities he displays do not coincide with the notion of the young, beautiful woman.[19] His signs of ageing (notably his white hair) are perfectly acceptable for a *gentilhomme*, but they are incongruent with his female courtly counterpart and even, it seems, with a bourgeois woman. The suggestion is that gender imperatives are to be firmly enforced, more than even those of social status.

In many cross-cast entries, the requirement that women be beautiful lies at one remove from the text of the verses. In others, the imperative is more explicit. In the *Ballet d'Alcidiane* (1658), Monsieur Hesselin played the wife of a courtier preparing a grotesque dance. His verses are lighthearted and heavily ironic, but they are also deeply revealing:

> Comme il est dangereux de s'attacher aux hommes,
> Ie me tiens à mon Sexe, & ie m'en trouue bien.
> Il faut de la beauté comme de la ieunesse,
> Les Femmes ne sont rien sans ce tresor exquis;
> Aussi ces deux talens m'accompagnent sans cesse,
> S'ils ne sont naturels, au moins ils sont acquis. (I, 395–96)

> *Since it is dangerous to become attached to men,*
> *I remain steadfast to my own sex and find that it suits me well.*
> *It is necessary to have beauty and youth,*
> *Women are nothing without this exquisite treasure.*
> *Now these two qualities are my constant companions,*
> *If they are not natural, at least they have been acquired.*

The verses are, of course, humorous, and their emphasis is undoubtedly on the irony of Hesselin's casting and on his temporary espousal of the female sex. At the same time, they spell out in no uncertain terms what is expected of real women ("Il faut de la beauté comme de la ieunesse") and how women who do not display those attributes will be overlooked ("Les Femmes ne sont rien sans ce tresor exquis"). For all their playfulness, Benserade's verses are insidious in their insistence on youthful, feminine beauty.

The close association between beauty and youth is asserted in a number of cross-cast roles. In the mascarade ballet, the *Ballet des Plaisirs troublés* (1657), Monsieur d'Heureux played a coquette (a role that we saw was deemed inappropriate for Louis XIV) and his verses are enlightening:

> Afin de paroistre coquette,
> Les rides sur le front, et les cheveux tout gris,
> Je radoucis mes yeux et fais mille souris;

Mais si quelque galant à me parler s'arreste,
Tout aussitost je m'apperçoy
(S'il me dit des douceurs) que ce n'est pas pour moy. (Fournel, II, 460)

In order to appear attractive,
With wrinkles on my forehead and my hair all gray,
I soften my eyes and smile a thousand times;
But if some suitor stops to talk to me,
I notice immediately
(If he says sweet nothings to me) that it is not for me.

Once again, Benserade focuses not on d'Heureux's biological sex as an obstacle to his being a convincing coquette but on his wrinkled brow and gray hair. The suggestion is that, at a distance, he could pass as a coquette if he softens his eyes and smiles, but, on closer inspection, it is his signs of ageing that will give him away (rather than his evident masculinity). In the performance, of course, there was no question of d'Heureux making a convincing coquette at any distance, and therein lies much of the humor of his appearance. But it is significant that what is gently mocked is not the fact of his cross-casting so much as the more specific fact of his looking beyond his physical prime. The primary complicity here is not between female spectator and male performer but between all men present who have a collective interest in upholding the imperative of youthful beauty for women.

In this context, the Duc de Damville's personification of Beauty in the *Ballet de Psyché* (which featured a number of female dancers) becomes less surprising. Benserade justifies Damville's impersonation in his first stanza in terms of the notion of a lover coming to assume the form of his loved one. But the words of the second stanza are, if indirectly, even more revealing in this regard:

C'est moy qui suis le but de chaque Demoiselle,
C'est de moy seulement qu'elles font vn grand cas;
Telle m'a sans le croire, & telle
Pense m'auoir qui ne m'a pas. (I, 304)

I am the goal of every young lady,
They make much of me only.
Some have me without believing it, while others
Think they have me when they do not.

The first line is something of a self-fulfilling prophesy: if women are repeatedly told that they must be beautiful (or repeatedly praised for being beautiful, which is almost the same thing), even in entries performed by cross-cast men, they will come to believe it for themselves. In a sense, it is wholly appropriate that the role of Beauty be impersonated by a male performer, for it is members of the male sex who demand that their female counterparts be beautiful. This is true even if one might also argue that the women inevitably became complicit in the men's demand.

The verses for various cross-cast roles teach us that, in addition to being young and attractive, the ideal woman was also expected to be chaste. In the *Ballet de la Nuit*, for example, the mildly risqué reference to the cross-cast shepherdesses' unchaste appearance offers an implicit lesson to the female spectator:

> Ces Bergeres n'ont pas la mine fort modeste,
> Et ie m'imagine à leur geste
> Qu'elles auront gardé leurs brebis auec eux,
> Et n'auront point gardé le reste. (I, 106)

> *These shepherdesses do not have a very modest appearance*
> *And I imagine from their behavior*
> *That they have kept their flocks*
> *Without keeping the rest.*

Such a comment would have been unthinkable had the shepherdesses been performed by female dancers, a fact that draws our attention to the enduring disparity between sexual standards for men and women. Where flattering allusions to male sexual prowess were of course welcomed, vulgar references to the loss of female virginity were not. Here it is particularly ironic that the fact that these roles were played by men should provide Benserade with the opportunity to comment more freely on what was, and was not, considered acceptable female behavior.

The fact that members of the male sex should desire a virginal (and of course female) lover is made explicit in the verses for the young Messieurs de la Chesnaye and de Joyeux enacting nymphs from *L'Astrée* in the *Ballet des Plaisirs*. Their verses read as follows:

> Nous n'aymons point du tout les hommes,
> Et le souhait que nous formons
> Est que celles que nous aymons
> Soient chastes comme nous le sommes. (I, 254)

> *We do not like men at all*
> *And the wish that we are developing*

Is that those whom we love
Should be as chaste as we are.

Benserade eliminates any homoerotic potential associated with their cross-casting by immediately establishing the boys as (future) heterosexual men. He then uses their genuine sexual innocence (associated with their youth) as a means to comment on the desirability for men of a chaste female lover. Thus in four short lines, homoeroticism is shunned, the heterosexual paradigm is reestablished and upheld, and the women present are reminded that they should remain chaste for the enjoyment of their future male lovers.

We have seen that cross-casting operates very differently in French court ballet from both spoken professional drama and school drama (see chapters I and II). The constant play in Benserade's ballet verses on dramatic illusion and courtly reality, and the ultimate inclination toward the latter, establishes a theatrical environment in which almost every example of cross-casting is self-conscious (i.e., a device). The ballet audience is actively encouraged to reflect upon the relationship between a dancer and his role, and to notice both correlations and discrepancies between the two. In the case of cross-casting, certain discrepancies are flagrant, although a correspondence may be argued in the case of an attractive and youthful young man, notably Philippe d'Orléans. In the special case of Louis XIV, both discrepancies, and especially correlations, are manipulated in order to enforce his official image as glorious king. The way these discrepancies are commented on in the accompanying verses for Louis's courtiers is sometimes surprising. Although the verses often include lighthearted, teasing references to the fact that the performer is cross-cast, their emphasis is not on the fact of cross-casting per se, but rather on the performer's inability to impersonate convincingly owing to his unattractiveness or to his signs of ageing. The overwhelming message is that sought-after women are young and beautiful. While on one level this is a means of flattering the ladies of the court, it is also, on another, a means of imposing upon them a man-made feminine ideal. In Benserade's verses, any unwanted homoerotic associations of cross-casting are cleverly eschewed, but they are replaced, more insidiously, by repeated affirmations of the standard patriarchal model. The cross-cast men's deviance from the model of feminine beauty is gently mocked, but they are permitted to deviate precisely because they are not real

women. It is clear, however, that real women are expected to conform to that model. In this sense, the female spectator is the target
of a commentary on the feminine ideal. In the next chapter, we
examine the extent to which this ideal was pursued when real
women appeared on the ballet stage.

CHAPTER IV

FEMALE ROLES IN COURT BALLET II: WOMEN PLAYING WOMEN

I n chapter III it was seen that the appearance of cross-cast men in female roles in no way banished the notion of the feminine ideal from court ballet under Louis XIV. Quite the contrary, the discrepancies between a male dancer and his female role were often highlighted as a means of commenting precisely on that ideal. The model of the perfect woman is established in the verses for cross-cast men as someone who is beautiful, youthful, and chaste—but ultimately also seducible. In the present chapter, I examine the verses written to accompany female roles that were performed by women. I discuss whether or not the appearance of female dancers altered the nature of the feminine ideal (as described in chapter III), and their impact on the discussion in the ballet *livrets* of male-female relations, particularly regarding the role of women.

Female Dancers

In the previous chapter, I examine the widespread phenomenon of men dancing female roles. This was a convention inherited by Louis XIV from his father's generation, but one that was rapidly called into question by the increasingly frequent appearances of female dancers. While a number of the early ballets from the 1650s (especially the more lighthearted mascarade ballets) continued to feature all-male casts, female courtiers, and occasionally female professionals, were also beginning to appear. In *Les Noces de Pélée et de Thétis* (1654), for example, female courtiers danced in the opening and closing entries of the ballet; in the *Ballet de Psyché* (1656), they were a more pervasive presence appearing in five entries, and, in 1658, the professional dancer Mlle Verpré (to whom we shall return below) appeared in the final entry of the *Ballet d'Alcidiane*—she was the first adult professional female dancer ever to perform in a court ballet.[1] Throughout the late 1650s and the 1660s, alongside the occasional all-male ballet, female dancers appeared with increasing frequency. They did not, however, take over *every* female role, and male dancers continued to appear cross-cast until the genre's disappearance after 1669. The fact that cross-casting persisted long after the arrival of women on the ballet stage is important for a number of reasons: first and most interestingly, it reminds us that Benserade's ballets continued to feature some female roles that were not considered appropriate for portrayal by women. These included, for example, the "Quatre femmes sauvages" (*four wild women*) in the *Ballet des Muses* (1666) and the "vieille" (*old woman*) in the *Ballet de Flore* (1669).[2] Secondly, it suggests that men were still more willing and more able to perform than their female counterparts (be it for personal, physical, or political reasons)— a fact that accounts for the cross-cast portrayal of a number of female roles that do not seem to run counter to the feminine ideal. Whatever the reasons, the result was that the majority of court ballets between the mid 1650s and the late 1660s included both cross-cast female roles *and* straight-cast female roles, in varying proportion. The curious coexistence of two different casting conventions (one of which was being used predominantly as a device) is, of course, consistent with the principle of diversity associated with the *ballet de cour* genre (see chapter III).

The fact that certain unfeminine roles appear to have been considered inappropriate for portrayal by female dancers indicates that the relationship between role and performer was worked out differently for women and for men. In chapter III, we saw that, with the exception of the royal family, it was acceptable for male dancers to perform a variety of masculine roles, including those that would have been considered socially unacceptable for them in real life. Such impropriety is treated in Benserade's verses with humor and irony. In the case of female dancers, however, it appears that a much closer correspondence between the qualities the women were supposed to possess and those of the characters they were performing was expected. In both cases, the person of the performer takes precedence over his/her role, but the implication is that the feminine ideal must be upheld at every possible opportunity, whereas men are accorded more freedom to impersonate. Benserade's repeated references to it suggest a deeper level of anxiety with regard to the feminine ideal that is perhaps not as ubiquitous as the author and the men at court would like. The fact that the female dancers, unlike their male counterparts, *never* performed cross-cast suggests that their image might have been contaminated by such a performance, and that their femininity was not as stable as might have been wished.[3] Alongside its conventional compliments aimed at flattering the women of the court, this discrepancy also reveals a strong urge to control female behavior in order precisely that it might conform as closely as possible to the desires of the heterosexual male courtiers. The arrival of female dancers on the ballet stage tended, at least to begin with, to enforce, rather than to challenge, women's position as beautiful objects. In addition to their verses, their physical presence on stage further emphasized the weight given to the women's physical qualities and established them as legitimate objects of the gaze for all men present (coperformers and audience members alike).

The Feminine Ideal

The female dancers who performed in court ballets were expected to correspond to the feminine ideal described above, and many of them, or so their verses tell us, did exactly that. One such was Mlle de Neuillan who played one of the three Graces in the *Ballet de Psyché* and of whom Benserade wrote,

> Cette belle a de la fraischeur,
> De l'embonpoint, de la blancheur,
> Sa modestie est sans seconde,
> Et son Amant sans doute aura
> La meilleure grace du monde
> Alors qu'il la possedera.[4] (I, 304)

> *This beauty is youthful,*
> *Plump, with pale skin*
> *Her modesty is second to none*
> *And doubtless her lover will*
> *Be delighted indeed*
> *When he possesses her.*

Neuillan is complimented on her beauty, her youth, her shapely figure, and the paleness of her skin. She is also praised for her exemplary virginity, and especially on the sexual pleasures that she will soon be able to offer her husband (this is an allusion to her forthcoming marriage to the Marquis de Froulay). According to her verses, she is the epitome of the feminine ideal.

Although perhaps nowhere written as succinctly as for Mlle de Neuillan, many verses compliment female dancers on the feminine qualities that they were expected to possess, of which beauty is by far the most important. The best kind of beauty is that which is superlative, a quality with which, paradoxically, many of the female courtiers seem to be endowed. The Duchesse de Mercœur's face, we read, is second to none: "Ce visage en beauté surpasse tous les autres" (I, 295) (*This face surpasses all others in beauty*). Mlle Mancini's verses also salute her superlative qualities: "Croyez qu'en agrément nulle ne vous seconde, / Que vous estes parfaite, & de corps, & d'esprit" (I, 296) (*Please believe that no-one is more charming than you, that you are perfect both in body and in mind*). Sometimes Benserade's verses comment specifically on the physical attributes of the women. The verses for Mlle de Gourdon, for example, allude to a number of different aspects of her beauty but focus above all on her shapely legs: "vous auez la jambe admirablement belle" (I, 305) (*you have wonderfully beautiful legs*). Owing to the long skirts of her costume, Mlle de Gourdon's legs were not intended to be on view during a court ballet, and it seems likely that, as he often did, Benserade was drawing on his in-depth knowledge of life at court and on the reputation of individual dancers, and then applying it to his ballet verses. In the case of Mlle de la Porte, Benserade comments on the more visible parts of her body, selecting her eyes, mouth, hair, arms, and breast for particular praise and extended commentary over four stanzas. This attention to her physical attributes, combined with her physical presence dancing onstage, is clearly an invitation to the male spectator (and male coperformer) to gaze admiringly and desiringly upon her. This idea is spelled out in the fourth stanza in which Benserade, employing the first person pronoun "nous," identifies with the gazing, desiring men of the audience and expresses their desire for the dancer:

Et dont les bras blancs, gros, & ronds,
Et la gorge à nous mettre en cendre,
Sont veus de l'oeil dont les Larrons
Regardent ce qu'ils n'osent prendre. (I, 306)

Whose plump, round, white arms,
And whose breast, capable of burning us to a cinder,
Are seen by the thieving eye that
Looks at what it would not dare to take.

The desiring men are cautious about approaching Mlle de la Porte because they are touched by her vulnerability and her virginity.

However, it is clear that this hesitancy will not last long, and her verses conclude with the anticipation of a liaison of some kind: "Que c'est vn poste auantageux / Que d'estre dans vos bonnes graces!" (I, 306) (*What a wonderful position it is to be in your good graces!*). The women whose verses tell us that they conformed to the feminine ideal did so at a number of levels. First, at the general level of gender identity, they behaved appropriately for women. At the more local level of the French court, they behaved as women who were expected to find (or to have found) a marriage partner within that court. Those who appeared alongside the dancing Louis XIV fulfilled an additional function: that of helping establish the king's own sexual identity. We saw in chapter III that Louis's future exploits, both heroic and amorous, were alluded to in some of his early cross-cast roles. In his role as Apollo in the first entry of *Les Noces de Pélée et de Thétis* (1654), the onstage presence of nine female courtiers playing the nine Muses undoubtedly enhanced in a very tangible way Louis's image as future lover of women. His verses establish first his unparalleled qualities as a glorious monarch: "Ie cours sans cesse apres la gloire / Et ne cours point apres Daphné" (I, 181) (*I continually run after glory, But I do not run after Daphne*), but by the third and final stanza Louis admits,

Toutefois il le faut, c'est vne Loy commune,
Qui veut que tost ou tard je coure apres quelqu'vne,
Et tout Dieu que je suis je m'y voy condamné. (I, 182)

However, I will have to, as it is a universal law
Which means that sooner or later I will run after some woman,
And even though I am a god, I am condemned to this fate.

The onstage combination of a future king who is also susceptible to love and a group of attractive young women is, in terms of courtly convention, gratifying for both parties: the women are alluring enough to attract the attention of the king, while the king exudes enough monarchical, but above all sexual magnetism to be surrounded by nine beautiful women. The emphasis in the women's verses is, as we would expect, precisely on their beauty, while those for Mlle de Gourdon specifically invite Apollo (i.e., Louis) to decide which of the women is the most attractive: "La difference entre nous, / Qu'Apollon la détermine" (I, 187) (*Let Apollo decide what difference there is between us*). The fifteen-year-old Louis-Apollo is already established as the ultimate arbiter in matters of female beauty.

A less sexual and more stately image of Louis XIV was put forward by his appearance in the hybrid opera-ballet, *Hercule amoureux* (1662),[5] in which he was supposed to have appeared alongside Marie-Thérèse of Austria, whom he had married in 1660. In the event, Marie-Thérèse was pregnant and did not play the role that had been written for her, but her incarnation of the House of Austria alongside his incarnation of the House of France would have been less of an allegory than a factual commentary on a politically expedient alliance between two countries that had until recently been at war. In an entertainment that was officially—albeit belatedly—celebrating the royal wedding, it was clearly not appropriate to be praising the young king for his seductive powers. Although a passing reference to the power of love (as well as marriage) is made, the verses for Louis and Marie-Thérèse (their verses, symbolically and unusually, are combined) are not concerned with the customary agenda of seduction. Rather they reflect the more official nature of the entertainment by focusing on the king's official image as a glorious monarch who has recently made a glorious alliance.

Long after the formal entertainments commemorating the royal wedding were over, Benserade would again apply the seductive esthetic to the king. When Louis XIV appeared as a shepherd alongside Mlle de la Vallière (who was playing a shepherdess) in the first entry of the *Ballet des Arts* (1663), his verses emphasize the fact that he is a conscientious shepherd whose love of pleasure will always take second place to his heroism. In La Vallière's verses, however, in addition to being hailed as the most beautiful of the shepherdesses—"il n'est point de Bergere plus belle" (II, 607) (*there is no shepherdess more beautiful*), we find some surprisingly indiscreet allusions to her extramarital relationship with Louis XIV (to whom she bore four children):

Elle a dans ses beaux yeux vne douce langueur,
Et bien qu'en apparence aucun n'en soit la cause,
Pour peu qu'il fût permis de foüiller dans son coeur,
On ne laisseroit pas d'y trouuer quelque chose.
. . .
Et je ne pense pas que dans tout le village,
Il se rencontre vn coeur mieux placé que le sien. (II, 607–608)

In her beautiful eyes she has a sweet languor,
And although it seems that no-one is the cause,

If we were only allowed to search her heart
We would undoubtedly find something.
...
And I do not think that in the whole village
There is anyone whose heart is better placed than hers.

Once again, the compliments are to the mutual benefit of both parties. Louis XIV may simultaneously uphold his official image as heroic king, while enjoying the reflected glory of being involved with the most beautiful shepherdess in whom he inspires a sweet languor that is perceptible to his courtiers. La Vallière may rejoice in her beauty and in the fact that she has won the heart and body of the aforementioned heroic king. A thin veneer of moral virtue is preserved while the more truthful reality is alluded to in the familiar terms of courtly seduction.

Later in the same ballet, Benserade makes further references to the king's relationship with La Vallière when she reappears as an Amazon:

Ie voy luire dans vos beaux yeux
Vn certain air imperieux,
Fatal au repos des plus Braues,
Et ne conte pas moins qu'Alexandre & Cesar,
En me figurant des Esclaues
A la suite de vostre Char. (II, 624)

I can see, gleaming in your beautiful eyes,
A certain imperious manner,
Fatal to the repose of the bravest of men
And who include no lesser figures than Alexander and Caesar
When they show me who the slaves are
Following your chariot.

Again, Benserade takes the opportunity to flatter La Vallière's good looks and her justifiably imperious air at the same time that he hails Louis XIV as a great hero, likening him to Alexander and Caesar, so that the culture of complicity within this courtly genre is upheld even with regard to the not-so-private life of the king. In addition, we note in this entry a new method of treating the figure of the Amazon woman. In chapter III, we noted the sexual ambiguity of the Amazon and the fact that the Amazons in the *Ballet de Psyché* were performed by male dancers. Their sexual identity was not, however, presented as being unequivocally masculine; rather, it comprised a fitting blend of masculine and feminine traits in so far as the male dancers (at least Philippe d'Orléans) displayed some recognizably feminine qualities.

Here, on the other hand, the amazons are fully feminized. Although their verses include several references to their warring tendencies, these are closely linked with the language of love and should be understood as being more allegorical (referring to life at court) than literal (referring to the pursuits of the amazon women). The familiar rhyme of "armes" with "charmes," for example (II, 623) is a particularly apt way to describe the portrayal of warrior women by courtly ones, and the emphasis in their verses is quite clearly on the "doux regards" of these "ieunes Beautez" (II, 623) and not on the warring tendencies of their adopted roles.

The language of love is of course very tightly bound up with the notion of female beauty. This is perhaps best exemplified in the *Ballet des Amours déguisés* (1664) in which a group of *amours* (loves or cupids) appears in a series of different disguises. It is important to note that only the second level of disguise is upheld in the ballet costumes (that is to say that the dancers appear, for example, not as cupids disguised as blacksmiths, but simply as the blacksmiths), although references are made in Benserade's text to the supposed cupid beneath the costume. In the case of the Marquis de Rassan playing one of the cupids disguised as a sea god in the eleventh entry, for example, Benserade suggests that his unwitting embodiment of love stems from his superlative abilities as a dancer (and not, we note, from his physical attractiveness): "Icy malaisément l'Amour se peut cacher, / Le moindre de ses pas en donne connoissance" (II, 680) (*Cupid can hide himself here only with great difficulty, For the least of his steps makes his presence known*). But Benserade's commentary on cupid's inability to disguise himself is far more frequently and more forcefully made with regard to the female dancers.

The suggestion that to disguise love/cupid as an attractive woman is a profoundly inadequate disguise is made in the fourth entry from the first set of relevant verses, those for the Comtesse de Soissons, about whom Benserade comments, "l'Amour n'est pas si bien caché / Qu'il ne soit facile à cognestre" (II, 663) (*Cupid is not so well hidden that he isn't easy to recognize*). Similarly, in the next set of verses, written for Mlle de Nemours, Benserade observes that love, though disguised as a charming and youthful princess, is fully recognizable. The intriguing paradox, whereby the charms of a beautiful mortal woman are a more eloquent expression of love than his usual portrayal as a divine male youth, is spelled out in the verses for the Duchesse de Crequy in the same entry:

Pour estre encor plus beau vous pristes l'apparence
D'vne Femme la Gloire, & l'Honneur de la France,

Les delices des yeux, mais vne Femme enfin,
Ne valoit-il pas mieux sans faire tant le fin
D'vn air plus ingenu conduire cette affaire
En jeune Adolescent vostre forme ordinaire?
Vous ne cachiez pas tant vostre Diuinité,
Et vray-semblablement Rome en eut moins douté. (II, 664)

In order to be even more handsome you took the form
Of a woman, the glory and honor of France,
A delight to the eyes, but a woman after all.
Would it not have been better, without being so clever,
To have done this deed in a more natural way
In your customary form as a male youth?
You did not disguise your divinity so well
And it is likely that Rome would have been less suspicious.

The repetition of "femme" (and its echo in the word "enfin") stresses the dancer's biological sex and cleverly implies an equation between love and women. This direct correspondence is articulated in the verses for Mlle de Sévigné (daughter of the celebrated letter writer), who appeared in the eleventh entry:

Vous trauestir ainsi c'est bien estre ingenu
Amour, c'est comme si pour n'estre pas connu,
Auec vne innocence extresme
Vous vous déguisiez en vous-mesme,
Elle a vos traits, vos feux, & vostre air engageant. (II, 682)

To disguise yourself in this way is to be very ingenuous,
Oh Love, it is as if, in order not to be recognized,
With extreme naivety
You were disguised as yourself.
She has your features, your fire, and your engaging manner.

To disguise cupid as Mlle de Sévigné is, Benserade writes, to effect no disguise at all, for she *is* love, and vice versa. While in chapter III we saw that cross-cast female characters allowed for the discussion of women's roles at court, it can be seen here that the appearance of women in female parts allowed this discussion to be developed further as their roles were compellingly illustrated when, literally, performed on stage. In case there were still any doubt regarding the role of the ideal woman, Mlle de Sévigné is presented not simply as an object of beauty, but also, quite specifically, as an object of love (or even sex).

The presence of women onstage inevitably invited comparisons between them, a trend that was of course encouraged by Benserade's repeated references to individual women being the *most* beautiful. This in turn heightened a latent spirit of competition among the women, a spirit that Benserade came to articulate in their verses. In the first ballet entry of the *Ballet de la Naissance de Vénus* (1665), Vénus (played by the first wife of Philippe d'Orléans, Henriette d'Angleterre, known as Madame) is surrounded by her twelve Nereids, all played by female courtiers. Madame's verses celebrate her superlative beauty and, alluding to an unspoken competitiveness among women to be the most beautiful, confirm that it is she who enjoys supremacy in this domain. As he compares Madame to her beautiful, female companions, Benserade writes that "Ces Beautez à qui rien que leur beauté ne plaist / Luy cedent neantmoins"(II, 696) (*These beauties who are pleased only by their own beauty, still yield to her*). The suggestion is that beauty is the only possible means of pleasing not just the women but, more importantly, their male suitors as well. More revealing still are the terms in which Benserade formulates the question of beauty. On the subject of Madame's primacy, he writes,

> Mais par qui luy seroit cet honneur disputé
> Lors qu'il est question du prix de la Beauté,
> Et que le Iuge est vn Homme? (II, 696)
>
> *But who would dispute with her this honor*
> *When it is a question of a beauty contest*
> *And when the judge is a man?*

Not only does the poet write of the women's appearance on stage in terms of a beauty contest for which there is a prize, he also states quite unambiguously that the judge of this contest is a man ("un homme" here refers both to a human being and also specifically to a human of the male sex). There can be no doubt that the assembly of women appears onstage to delight the eye of the male courtiers and to stir their fantasy. If the first prize in the contest has already been awarded to Madame as Venus, the twelve Nereids still have an incentive to battle it out for the second and the third prizes.

Their verses, unusually, begin in the form of a dialogue and are headed "Conversation des nereides" (II, 697) (*Conversation of the Nereids*). The dialogue structure is introduced by Mlle d'Elbeuf and proceeds in the form of mutual compliments exchanged between the first three ladies who comment on each other's qualities. While the direct competitive nature of this exchange is subsumed by its outward form (the compliments), comparisons between the ladies are inevitably invited. Whenever a woman comments on the beauty of another woman, she cannot but invoke her own physical appearance by implicit comparison, whether intentionally or not. The dialogic structure begins to break down with the fifth set of verses as the links between them become more tenuous. In his search for suitable material for the verses of these twelve women, it seems that Benserade came to write about more than just their physical appearance. Many of their verses draw on the details of the real lives of the dancers, including those for the Comtesse de Vivonne that refer to the fact that her husband is away fighting Turkish pirates in the Mediterranean. The question of marital relations is examined in the verses for the Marquise de Vibraye that politely express her contentment with her husband and present a model of the perfect male spouse:

> Et de tant de Maris qui regnent aujourd'huy,
> Ie tien que le mieux fait, & le plus raisonnable
> Ne laisse pas toûjours d'estre vn peu redeuable
> A sa chaste Moitié qui ne pense qu'à luy. (II, 700–01)

> *And among all the husbands who reign today,*
> *I hold that the most handsome and the most reasonable*
> *Is still a little indebted*
> *To his chaste other half who thinks only of him.*

We notice that the perfect husband is required only to be *a little* indebted toward his wife, whereas she is expected to be *wholly* virtuous and think only of him. The suggestion that the postnuptial relationship should be reciprocal in some way is welcome, but the gender imbalance remains flagrant.

The embryonic female dialogue of the *Ballet de la Naissance de Vénus* was followed in the *Ballet des Muses* by a more sustained dialogue between the nine Muses and their rivals, the nine Pierides. In place of a dialogue of mutual compliments, theirs is a dispute between the two groups regarding who among them displays the finer qualities, including the proverbial question of whether blonds or brunettes are more attractive (see I, 798). In the *livret*, this entry is headed "Contestation des Pierides et des Mvses" (II, 792) (contest between the Pierides and the Muses). In mythological terms, the Pierides were indeed the rivals of the Muses whom they wanted to outshine and whom they challenged to a singing contest (that they lost). The finer details of his classical sources are often overlooked or changed by Benserade, who here focuses the contest not on singing (we remember that female courtiers did not sing in courtly entertainments) but on various other qualities. In his alternating verses for Pierides and Muses, we notice that Benserade focuses far less on the question of beauty than he had ever done before. Much of their debate is centered on the question of who will decide between them, mortals or gods. In the midst of this somewhat uninspired debate, Mlle d'Arquien's verses suggest that beauty might not be a woman's sole priority and moreover that it might not even be her first priority:

> Mais je tien qu'estre Muse aussi n'empesche pas
> Qu'on n'ait lieu de pretendre aux plus charmans apas,
> Ce seroit grand pitié que pour estre vn peu Belle
> On dût aprehender d'estre spirituelle,
> Qu'il falut renoncer à ces diuins thresors,
> Et que l'Esprit donnast l'exclusion au Corps. (II, 793–94)

> *But I maintain that to be a Muse does not prevent one*
> *From wanting to aspire to more charming attributes.*
> *It would be a real pity if, being attractive,*
> *One should shy away from being clever,*
> *If one had to renounce these divine treasures*
> *And if the mind and body were mutually exclusive.*

No verses for cross-cast female roles include any serious indication that a woman might wish to pursue her own intellectual development. For Benserade to write about such things, it took the arrival of *real* women whose repeated appearances onstage forced him to explore new ways of writing about the female condition. It is no coincidence that this surprisingly empathetic set of verses should feature in the most extensive set of verses for female dancers that Benserade had yet been required to write. I am not suggesting that having to write for real women turned Benserade into some kind of protofeminist. However, it does seem to be the case that his search for new material led the poet, on occasion, to think more sympathetically about what it was to be a woman and to understand for instance that the ladies of the court might wish to be educated as well as beautiful. We shall return below to the question of female emancipation from the tyranny of love and beauty in our discussion of Benserade's final two ballets, the *Ballet de Flore* (1669) and the belated *Ballet du Triomphe de l'Amour* (1681).

While Benserade's verses for the courtly women dancers tend to invite the men present to gaze upon them, they also contain multiple references to the female gaze. Where the male gaze is desiring and predatory (and very real), the female gaze is more a topos of courtly gallantry. A reference to a woman's gaze is a reference to her beauty and to her power to attract; but this suggestion of power is deceptive as it in fact signals her compliance with the man's desire, indicating that she is ready to be seduced by him. Benserade's references to the failure of a courtly woman to return the male gaze (which indicates her refusal to be seduced by him) are couched in teasing, gallant tones that nonetheless reveal a modest degree of lighthearted frustration with her behavior in response to the male spectators. This frustration is most apparent in the verses for Mlle de Sévigné's appearance as Omphale in the *Ballet de la Naissance de Vénus* (1665):

Elle verroit mourir le plus fidelle Amant
Faute de l'assister d'vn regard seulement,
Injuste procedé, sotte façon de faire,
Que la Pucelle tient de Madame sa Mere. (II, 727)

She would see the most faithful lover die
Because she has not deigned to look upon him once,
Unjust behavior, foolish conduct
That the virgin has inherited from Madame her mother.

Here the future Madame de Grignan is openly, if teasingly, reprimanded for her behavior that is seen to be deviant in its refusal to follow the requisite pattern of male-female relationships. Similarly, the refusal of her mother, Madame de Sévigné, to respond to the overtures of her admirers is described as being "au détriment du Genre humain" (II, 727) (*to the detriment of the human race*). As always, the flattery in Benserade's ballet verses is double-edged: where references to beauty are usually coupled with an expectation of seducibility, here the allusions to the charms of Mlle and Mme de Sévigné are coupled with a gentle reproach for their failure to be seduced.

Mlle Verpré

So far our discussion has been limited to the onstage appearance of female courtiers for the simple reason that only courtiers were given verses. We therefore strongly lack any material for the discussion of professional women dancers. Before embarking on an examination of Benserade's final two ballets, however, I would like to consider the case of one exceptional professional female dancer, Mlle Verpré. It was noted above that Mlle Verpré's appearance in the final entry of the *Ballet d'Alcidiane* (1658) constituted the first appearance by a professional (adult) woman dancer in French court ballet. More than that, it also represented an important challenge to traditional boundaries of both rank and gender. First, Mlle Verpré was the only female dancer to perform in the *Ballet d'Alcidiane* in which the small number of other female roles were performed cross-cast. Furthermore, her role was an important one, that of the Moorish princess who is the key character of the final entry. The *livret* suggests that Mlle Verpré first danced a solo chaconne and was then joined by a group of male dancers, including Louis XIV, who represented her suite of Moorish followers. Because she was a professional dancer, no verses are provided for Mlle Verpré to guide our interpretation, but it is clear that her inclusion as the sole female dancer of the ballet, and her appearance alongside no less a figure than the king, is remarkable. The *Ballet de la Raillerie* (1659), interestingly, included male and female courtiers and male and female professionals in its female roles, and Mlle Verpré appeared in the final entry again in close proximity to the dancing king. As in the *Ballet d'Alcidiane*, hers is an important solo role, prominently characterized as Spanish (the *livret* tells us that she performed with castanets and was accompanied by eight guitars), and she is once again the only female dancer of the entry.

Following on from her evident success in the earlier ballets, Mlle Verpré appeared again alongside Louis XIV in the opening entry of the *Ballet de l'Impatience* (1661). Louis XIV played "un grand amoureux" whose suite included a group of eleven men (both courtiers and professionals), as well as Mlle Verpré. Her appearance as the only female dancer together with a group of men is noteworthy of its own accord. But her appearance in what is evidently a male role is doubly remarkable. No female courtier *ever* performed cross-cast in these ballets, and Mlle Verpré is the only professional female to do so. There is nothing in the *livret* to suggest that her biological sex was even an issue in this entry: her name features unobtrusively at the bottom of the list of dancers, next to the names of the two other professionals appearing in the entry. It seems, therefore, that Mlle Verpré was required to perform as though she were a *male* dancer, and that she would have performed the same steps as her male codancers. Unfortunately, we do not know what costume she wore and can only speculate to what extent her legs were in view. It is likely that her costume closely resembled that of the men, perhaps with a skirt made out of the same material and with the same design as the men's breeches. This is the only instance of female-to-male cross-casting in a dancing role in ballet under Louis XIV. It is perhaps also the only example of a cross-cast role in ballet that the spectator is expected to treat as a pure convention (that is, to accept that it is a masculine role, despite knowing that it is played by a woman).

Mlle Verpré appeared again in the third entry of Part III of the same ballet, playing the solitary lady opposite eight knights who impatiently vie for her attentions. The only amateur dancer in this entry is the king, while the only female dancer is Mlle Verpré. Louis XIV is set apart by virtue of his real identity and is accorded an extensive set of verses emphasizing his heroic grandeur, while Mlle Verpré is set apart by virtue of her biological sex and by the gender of her role. It is ironic that her role should be that of a courtly lady and one to whom a group of men are making romantic overtures; the scene's solid grounding in courtly affairs is felt even when played out by a group of professionals (and the king). In the seventh entry of the *Ballet des Saisons* (1661), Mlle Verpré danced a solo sarabande. She is accorded no gender-specific role, and her purpose was undoubtedly to demonstrate her exceptional skills as a dancer—skills that must surely account for the exceptional status she held within these ballets. Similarly, in the sixteenth entry of *Hercule Amoureux* (1662), Mlle Verpré performed the solo role of the dawn. This part served a particularly important function, for it heralded the spectacular and allegorical arrival of Louis XIV in his celebrated role as the sun that constituted the official climax of the ballet. Finally, Mlle Verpré played the wife of the governor of Egypt in the *Ballet des Amours déguisés* (1664). As indicated above, this ballet included a large number of courtly women who performed the more glamorous and ladylike female roles. All the female roles of this Egyptian entry were played by men apart from that of Mlle Verpré. Once again we see that her position is exceptional. Throughout her career as a dancer in French court ballet, we see that Mlle Verpré played roles that encompassed a whole spectrum of gender markers including masculine, feminine, and neuter. She also transcended some of ballet's gender conventions and devices, taking on a role that might otherwise have been cross-cast and another that was, but whose cross-casting was apparently to be overlooked. Mlle Verpré's position as a professional dancer turns out in some ways to be more liberating than if she had been a courtier. On the one hand she was absolved from the pressures of conforming to courtly expectations of women owing to her inferior social status, while on the other, she still had the opportunity to dance with the king.

The Ballet de Flore

The *Ballet de Flore* (1669) marks a turning point both in Benserade's career as a creator of ballets and in the wider history of French *ballet de cour*. In the inside cover of the *livret*, before the ballet itself begins, we find the following Rondeau written by Benserade and addressed "Avx Dames":

> Ie suis trop las de joüer ce rolet,
> Depuis long-temps je trauaille au Ballet,
> L'Office n'est enuié de personne,
> Et ce n'est pas office de couronne
> Quelque talent que pour couronne il ait:
> Ie ne suis plus si gay, ny si folet,
> Vn noir chagrin me saisit au colet,
> Et je n'ay plus que la volonté bonne,
> Ie suis trop las.
> De vous promettre à chacune vn couplet,
> C'en est beaucoup pour vn homme replet,
> Ie ne le puis (Troupe aymable & mignonne)
> A tout le sexe en gros je m'abandonne,
> Mais en détail; ma foy, vostre valet,
> Ie suis trop las. (II, 830)

> *I am too tired of playing this role.*
> *I have been working on ballets for a long time:*
> *It is a task envied by no-one*
> *And is not an office of the crown,*
> *Whatever ways in which it may serve the crown.*
> *I am no longer so cheerful or so wild,*
> *A dark sorrow has seized me by the throat*
> *And all I am left with is my good intentions.*
> *I am too tired.*
> *To promise each of you a couplet*
> *Is a lot for a man who is sated:*
> *I cannot (oh delightful and sweet troupe).*
> *I give myself in general to the whole sex,*
> *But in particular to none; in truth, I am your servant;*
> *I am too tired.*

Benserade uses the tradition of addressing verses to the female spectator to discuss the more recent phenomenon of female courtiers appearing onstage and the requirement that he write verses for them. He specifically states that it is the duty of composing verses for *female* performers that he no longer feels able to discharge. While it is in keeping with the gallantry of the age that Benserade should excuse himself before the ladies of the court, the ageing poet is also suggesting that he is too old, too tired, and too entrenched in his habitual methods of composition to adapt to the fresh demands made by the presence of female courtly dancers on stage and to the gradual and inevitable evolution of their verses. Even before it has begun, the *Ballet de Flore* is thus set up as his farewell to the women of the court and to the genre in general.

An interesting counterpart to his supposed difficulty in writing for the courtly women is found in Benserade's verses for Louis XIV. In the verses for the king playing the sun in the first entry, Benserade expresses the conviction that his art is no longer up to the task of praising such an admirable king:[6]

L'Art ne peut plus traiter ce sujet comme il faut,
Et vous estes monté si haut
Que l'Eloge, & l'Encens ne vous sçauroient plus joindre. (II, 833)

Art can no longer address the subject appropriately,
And you have climbed so high
That praise and incense can no longer reach you.

In a similar way, Benserade frames the verses for the ladies in the second entry with explanatory stanzas. Before their individual verses, we read,

I'en ay bien de la honte, il est vray, mais helas,
Ie vous l'ay déja dit, Belles, je suis trop las
Pour vous faire vne digne offrande,
Et vous rendre séparément
Ce qu'il est juste qu'on vous rende,
Receuez donc mes voeux confusément. (II, 835)

I am very ashamed, it is true, but alas,
I have already told you, oh beauties, I am too tired
To make a suitable offering to you
And to give to each of you separately
What it is right that you should be given—
So receive my salutations together.

And at the end:

> D'vn Eloge plus long taschez de vous passer,
> Est-ce à moy de vous encenser?
> Il me faudroit écrire vos loüanges
> D'vn stile de sucre & de miel,
> Et me fondre en douceurs étranges,
> Vous estes toutes de vrais Anges,
> Les Graces mesmes dans le Ciel
> Ne font rien de meilleure grace,
> Mais que voulez-vous que j'y fasse? (II, 836)

> *Try to make do without a longer tribute.*
> *Is it up to me to praise you?*
> *I would have to write your praises*
> *In a sugary, honeyed style*
> *And to plunge myself into unfamiliar pleasantries.*
> *You are all true angels:*
> *The Graces themselves in the sky*
> *Do nothing with better grace—*
> *But what do you want me to do?*

Whereas Louis XIV's exploits are perceived to be so great that the art of poetry is rendered inadequate to the task of praising him, it is the poet himself who is seen to fall short of the task of praising the ladies. He claims that he no longer has the energy to write appropriate verses for the female courtly dancers, that he is incapable of writing in the sweet, honeyed style that is required of him.[7]

Benserade pursues the idea of his own inadequacy in his verses for the nymphs of the third entry that open with his complaint that they are an embarrassment to him and an unsuitable subject for him to write about:

> Quoy pour m'embarasser encore sept Déesses,
> Ou Nymphes plaines d'apas?
> Que de brillantes richesses
> Qui ne me conuiennent pas! (II, 837)

> *To discomfit me we have seven more goddesses—*
> *Or delightful nymphs?*
> *All these brilliant riches*
> *Do not suit me at all!*

In the next two stanzas he explains why this is such a difficult task for him:

Vous loüer dignement est vne tasche honneste
Qui demande vn grand labeur,
Pour l'auoir bien dans la teste
Il faut l'auoir dans le coeur.

Il faut estre vn Amant qui soûpire, qui brûle,
Et le suis-je à vostre endroit?
Trouuez-vous pas ridicule
La loüange de sens froid? (II, 837)

To praise you appropriately is a worthy task
That requires a lot of work.
In order to have it in one's head
One must have it in one's heart.

One must be a lover who sighs, who burns—
And am I such a one before you?
Do you not find
Such unfeeling praises ridiculous?

Benserade himself is no longer inclined to love and for this reason, he claims, he can no longer write in an appropriately gallant style on behalf of the lovesick male suitor. His words have interesting implications regarding the question of empathy in poetic writing and remind us of the requirement that verses for courtly female dancers should flatter their good looks and uphold the role of the appreciative male admirer gazing upon a beautiful woman. Having made his excuses, Benserade does provide a short stanza for each of the seven ladies dancing in this entry in which his traditional compliments are couched in rather diffident terms (we note, for example, his frequent use of the future and past conditional tenses that lend an air of reluctance to his writing). He concludes the verses with another stanza dealing with the problem of praising such women:

Vos Eloges me sont des écüeils ou j'auoüe
Que je craindrois d'échoüer,
Il faut aimer ce qu'on loüe
Afin de le bien loüer. (II, 838)

Your praises are stumbling blocks that I admit
I am afraid to trip over.

One must love what one praises
In order to praise well.

While Benserade is at pains to stress the problem of praising a king who is beyond praise and the (different) problem of praising the beauty and love-inspiring demeanor of courtly ladies, his verses for the male dancers in the ballet (whether in male or female roles) apparently pose him no difficulty. It is the specific presence of *women* in the *ballet de cour* that contributed to Benserade's wish to retire. Just as it was an exacting task to praise a supposedly superlative dancing king, so it was too much of a challenge to praise the supposedly superlative dancing courtly ladies.

What is striking about the *Ballet de Flore* is the absence of female dancers after the Third Entry combined with Benserade's categorical expression of his reluctance to write for them and his subsequent retirement from ballet. The decline of the *ballet de cour* was brought about by a number of factors. The fact that Louis XIV gave up dancing in ballets at much the same time that Benserade gave up writing them is no coincidence. By this time, the king needed to focus more on his foreign policy and was, at over thirty years of age, now beyond his physical prime. Since the foundation of the Académie Royale de Danse in 1661, ballet had become increasingly professionalized, with the result that the ballet steps were simply more difficult, and therefore less accessible to the courtly amateurs.[8]

The Ballet du Triomphe de l'Amour

One final ballet should be considered here: the *Ballet du Triomphe de l'Amour* (1681), performed to celebrate the marriage of the Dauphin to Marie-Anne-Christine de Bavière. For this special event, Benserade was brought out of retirement to write the verses for the courtly participants. The fact that the overall design of the ballet and the texts of the extensive singing parts were the work of Philippe Quinault (1635–88), Lully's principal librettist for his *tragédies-lyriques* at the Académie Royale de Musique, is highly significant, as is the incorporation of a substantial amount of vocal music. The *Ballet du Triomphe de l'Amour* is essentially a French opera, but one reminiscent of the now outmoded genre of the *ballet de cour* in its inclusion of royal and courtly participants in the ballet entries.

With regard to the question of female dancing roles, two aspects are noteworthy: firstly, female dancers are an important presence, appearing in eight ballet entries (compared with only two in the *Ballet de Flore*). Secondly, we note the lingering, but dwindling, presence of cross-casting in a single entry where male dancers played the parts of Orithya and four Athenian girls (for whom no verses are given). A large proportion of Benserade's verses for the female dancers is, as we would expect, dedicated to a commentary on the performers' beauty, and the new dauphine is encouraged in her commentary to produce the necessary male heir. Some verses, however, do stray from the conventional model of male-female relations and hint at a degree of female empowerment. A group of nereids opposite a group of sea-gods appear in the sixth entry in which we notice a shift in emphasis away from men gazing upon women in favor of the female participants gazing desiringly upon the attractive male. This is alluded to in two instances, the first of which is in the verses for the sea-gods:

Les froides Nymphes des eaux,
Trouvent ces Dieux marins beaux,
Ou pour mieux dire, estimables. (II, 906)

The cold water-nymphs
Find these sea-gods attractive
Or, to put it more accurately, admirable.

And then again in the verses for Mlle de Pienne we read the following:

Examinons bien la bande
De ces gens si dangereux,
Le seul que l'on apprehende
N'est pas peut-estre avec eux. (II, 908)

Let us look closely at this group
Of very dangerous people.
The only one whom we fear
Is perhaps not with them.

Here the suggestion is that, though gazing upon an attractive group of men is a hazardous exercise (just as gazing upon an attractive female was frequently presented as hazardous in earlier ballets), the real threat is posed by one of their number who is absent, presumably the Dauphin. What is interesting is the fact that the traditional operation of the male gaze is now seen to extend to its female counterpart: women are no longer uniquely the object of the desiring male gaze, they too may gaze with desire (and not just admiration) upon an attractive male.

The ninth entry was for Diana's nymphs, led by the Dauphine. The verses for her nymphs also challenge the conventions of traditional gallantry, warning the women present of the dangers of male suitors:

> Evitez bien ces gens qui font les doucereux;
> Beaux ou laids, tous sont dangereux,
> Et souvent on se perd quand on se les attire:
> Deffiez-vous également
> De tout ce qui s'apelle Amant,
> Soit le Berger, soit le Satyre. (II, 911)

> *Be careful to avoid these people who pretend to be so sweet,*
> *Handsome or ugly, they are all dangerous,*
> *And often we are lost when we attract them.*
> *Equally, beware*
> *Of anything claiming to be a lover,*
> *Be he a shepherd or a satyr.*

Whereas in earlier ballets men were warned of the alluring powers of women, here the procedure is reversed as women are advised to shun contact with amorous males, for this can lead to a loss of self-control, and therefore of power. It is remarkable that women are invited to take control of this aspect of their lives, rather than simply to prepare themselves for love by being beautiful. This ethic, given an importance hitherto unseen in the ballets of Louis XIV, is enforced by Diana's song, which begins with the following verse:

> Un Coeur maistre de luy-mesme
> Est toûjours heureux.
> C'est la liberté que j'ayme,
> Elle comble tous mes voeux,
> Vn Coeur maistre de luy-mesme
> Est toûjours heureux.
> Fuyons la contrainte extréme
> D'un esclavage amoureux.
> Vn Coeur maistre de luy-mesme
> Est toûjours heureux. (II, 877–78)

> *A heart that is its own master*
> *Is always happy.*
> *It is liberty that I love*
> *And that fulfils all my desires.*

A heart that is its own master
Is always happy.
Let us shun the extreme constraint
Of the slavery of love.
A heart that is its own master
Is always happy.

This call to independence and freedom is partly, of course, a means of characterizing Diana, but it also reflects a modest development in the prevailing attitude toward the extent to which women could take control of their lives (at least in ballet verses, if not in real life). If earlier ballets preached a message of imperative beauty to women, the message preached in the *Ballet du Triomphe de l'Amour* is, in part, one of the assumption of a certain degree of control by women over matters of the heart and, by implication, over their choice of marriage partner.

The question of a woman's experience of marriage features in the verses for the Duchesse de Mortemart in the fourteenth entry. These lines comment upon the particular difficulty of being the female partner:

Deux Espoux qui s'aiment fort
Sont separez dés l'abord;
Luy s'en va faisant sa plainte,
Elle beaucoup plus contrainte
Sous les loix d'un dur devoir,
Pour le suivre, & pour le voir
Dans l'ennuy qui la consomme
Auroit esté jusqu'à Rome. (II, 913)

Two spouses who love each other very much
Are separated from the outset.
He goes away with regret
While she, much more constrained
Under the laws of a harsh duty,
To follow him and to see him
In the chagrin that consumes her,
Would have gone as far as Rome.

Benserade is here taking his empathy with women onto a new level as he describes their constraints in marriage, its harsh obligations, and the misery married women may experience. While these surprisingly sensitive remarks are based on the assumption that the relationship between husband and wife is a loving and happy one, they nevertheless mark a significant step away from the traditional concept of women as beautiful objects and a movement toward a more in-depth engagement with some of the realities of their daily conjugal existence. These intermittent examples of apparent empathy, while remarkable and important, remain unusual, however, and it is significant that the *Ballet du Triomphe de l'Amour* should end with a reminder of the importance of youthful feminine beauty and with a corresponding call to love. While the texts of this ballet have displayed some evidence of a departure from the model according to which women are above all objects of male desire, it is nevertheless this status quo that is ultimately upheld, even in this late (final) example of the genre.

In the course of this examination we have noted a general trend toward the inclusion of ever more female dancers in French ballets, particularly female courtiers who featured in spectacular entries (often the first and last of the work), frequently as attractive female companions of the young dancing king. Although other qualities are mentioned, we have noted in their accompanying verses a compelling emphasis on physical beauty as the ultimate feminine quality imposed by men and to be sought by women. In this way, far from serving the feminine cause, the early appearances of female dancers in the *ballet de cour* tended to confirm their status as beautiful objects to delight the male.

The delicate division between male performer and female spectator (noted in chapter III) is disrupted by the appearance of female dancers, as men (whether as audience members or as coperformers) are invited to gaze admiringly upon their beauty and, finally, we assume, to seduce them. We have noted the breaking down of traditional barriers not only of gender but also of rank, as male and female dancers, as well as professionals and amateurs, shared the stage. One professional female dancer was singled out for particular distinction: Mlle Verpré, who several times danced with Louis XIV and whose participation on apparently equal terms with male dancers is remarkable — all the more so for the fact that it remained an exception. One can only regret that, owing to her status as a professional, no verses were written for Mlle Verpré who, it seems, performed the only female-to-male cross-cast role of French court ballet under Louis XIV.

The presence of female dancers on stage performing female roles did not exclude the continued appearance of male dancers in female roles, as men continued to take women's parts, not only the comic or grotesque roles, but also, occasionally, those of serious female characters. Impertinent comments in the ballet verses for female characters were reserved for those performed by male dancers only, and any possibility of identification with these dubious female roles on the part of female spectators was eschewed by the combination of the cross-casting and the very inclusion of such impudent observations. Similarly, when Louis XIV played female roles, any suggestion of homoeroticism was shunned by Benserade, thanks to the serious nature of his verses, and to an emphasis that was not on the sex or gender of his adopted roles but rather on their symbolic qualities and their specific relation to his qualities as king.

The inclusion of female courtly dancers and the phenomenon whereby they were required to attract the male onlooker by means of their beauty led to the fascinating development of ballet verses expressing overt competition between the ladies as they vied for male attention. This was seen in the extraordinary dialogues of the *Ballet de la Naissance de Vénus* and the *Ballet des Muses*. More advantageous developments too occurred as the importance of additional feminine qualities besides beauty came to be acknowledged more and more. The *Ballet de Flore*, in which French court ballet's principal poet, Benserade, articulated an inability to write suitable verses in praise of its female dancers, was representative of the decline of French court ballet, and the *Ballet du Triomphe de l'Amour* of its demise. In this concluding example of the genre, we noted the appearance of a large number of female dancers and the appearance of male dancers in female roles in only a single entry. Moreover, we observed a number of verses that challenged the traditional presentation of male-female relationships by, for example, describing the phenomenon of women gazing upon an attractive male, by encouraging women to take control over their amorous relationships, and by alluding to the difficulties of marriage and to the possibility of an equal partnership between man and woman. These seemingly radical remarks are of course few in comparison with the number of conventional comments offered, but are none the less significant for that. The status quo may be reasserted at the end of the ballet, but the fact that it has been brought into question at a number of points along the way means that it is now just a little more precarious.

CHAPTER V

CROSS-CASTING AND GENDER AMBIGUITY IN OPERA

One of the most striking aspects of the early French operatic tradition as established by Jean-Baptiste Lully in the 1670s and 1680s is its deliberate rejection of the figure of the castrato. In this chapter I shall explore the gender ambiguity exemplified by the castrato (who often performed cross-cast) and French responses to visiting castrati from Italy who performed in a number of court spectacles that took place between 1645 and 1662. I shall speculate why the French chose not to incorporate the castrato voice into their nascent genre, despite there being a small number of castrati at the Chapelle Royale at Versailles throughout the period in question. The peculiarly French phenomenon of the high tenor (known as the *haute contre*) will be explored, and then each of the small number of cross-cast roles included in Lully's operas will be examined in turn.

The Castrato

The castrato owes his existence largely to the Church of Rome (which, incidentally, threatened anyone found performing such an operation with excommunication).[1] In 1 *Corinthians* 14.34, Saint Paul writes that "women should remain silent in the churches." This decree was understood to apply to singing as well as to speaking, and women and girls were thus excluded from church and chapel choirs. The upper voices were, however, needed to achieve musical balance. Prepubescent boys were employed in this task with a certain degree of success, although their voices were sometimes thin and weak (as could be those of the male falsettists) and their career as treble singers was of an uncertain but limited duration. It seems, then, that the mutilation of the genitalia of young boys offered a solution to this problem, a solution that was somehow preferable to the participation of women and/or girls. As the tradition took hold, the castrato, whose voice was strong and compelling, had the additional advantage of being exceptionally well-trained as a singer. A good castrato thus offered a highly desirable combination of vocal brilliance and power, a wide vocal range, and exceptional breathing capacity. Additionally, the unearthly (i.e., unfamiliar and unusual) timbre of his voice brought to church music a "sense of asceticism and angelic asexuality."[2] The sexuality of the castrato is discussed in greater detail below, but the question of asceticism merits further comment here. As Roger Freitas has pointed out, the rise of the castrato coincided with a period of economic hardship in Italy and a resulting increase in the number of men who dedicated their lives to the church and thus to celibacy (a less expensive occupation than supporting a family).[3] At a time when asceticism was admired, the castration of a young boy destined for a career as a church chorister might have plausibly been understood as a noble—if rather extreme—form of piety.

While the majority of castrati remained in the service of the church throughout their working lives, a number of them took to the stage to perform opera—where their outstanding vocal training and exceptional voice quality were highly prized. The operatic roles assigned to castrati in Italian opera varied widely, depending on the availability of other singers, but also on location and time period. In seventeenth-century Venice (where the first public opera house, the Teatro San Cassiano, opened in 1637), for instance, castrati tended to play male characters, although, as Wendy Heller has observed, "most of the characters played by castrati were feminized either literally (by cross-dressing) or figuratively (by falling victim to love)."[4] The correspondence between falling in love and effeminacy recalls the Jesuits' fears for their students (see chapter II) and is important for our understanding of contemporary perceptions of the castrato, as will be seen below. The castrato's fascinating feminization should, however, be understood as part of a wider phenomenon of gender ambiguity prevalent in the operas of mid-seventeenth-century Venice, in which disguise plots abounded.[5] Whereas in seventeenth-century Venetian opera, the female roles were sung by women, in Rome and the majority of the papal States, women were not permitted to appear on stage.[6] In the absence of female singers, women's roles in Roman opera were always cross-cast and usually taken by castrati.

Toward the end of the seventeenth century and well into the eighteenth, the advanced technique of the castrato contributed to the developing vogue for elaborate coloratura singing in Italian opera. A series of highly trained, highly skilled castrati became renowned for their dazzling technique that they would display in virtuosic *da capo* arias, often written specially for the individual singer.[7] The founding of the Arcadian Academy in Rome in 1690 impelled, among other things, the reform of Italian opera by favoring the production of *opera seria*, based on historical and mythological plots. Toward the end of the seventeenth century and throughout the heyday of eighteenth-century serious Italian opera, it was customary for the male lead (*primo uomo*) to be sung by a castrato.[8] Thus it was not at all unusual to find a castrato playing the noble, heroic, and apparently masculine roles of Caesar, Alexander, or Achilles. The practice of casting castrati as male heroes raises some important issues regarding contemporary perceptions of gender and sexual difference as well as, more specifically, of the esthetics of Italian opera. In turn, France's remarkable rejection of the castrato suggests both that the French were less comfortable with the ambiguity he (literally) embodied and that they were less inclined to accept him as a viable operatic hero. Let us now examine more closely some of the sexual issues raised by this mutilated male.

The castrato is a paradoxical and perplexing figure who resists easy definition in terms of traditional sex and gender designations. Owing to his mutilation, the castrato is physically an incomplete man, a man with a distinct lack. He is the literal embodiment of the fulfillment of Freud's castration complex and thus liable to be a powerful source of castration anxiety in the adult male. Like a woman, the castrato lacked a properly functioning penis. His detractors were quick to identify this defect and to associate his uncomfortably graphic deficiency with all that is bad and, conversely, to link the possession of a fully functional penis with all that is good. In this way, anticastrato discourse graphically maintained the importance of a (phallic) male-dominated society in which the castrato represented a large step down the sliding scale away from sought-after masculinity and toward an unwelcome femininity. His association with femininity was further enforced by the fact that, in addition to his unnaturally high voice, the castrato tended to display a number of secondary female sexual characteristics, owing to an absence of androgen stimulation by the Leydig cells in the testes and the resultant condition known as primary hypogonadism. These traits included a tendency to put on weight around the hips, thighs, and breasts, and a lack of facial hair (as well as a tendency to grow disproportionately long limbs).[9] In his description of the physical attributes of the castrati he encountered during an extended stay in Italy in the mid–eighteenth century, the Frenchman Charles de Brosses revealingly commented on precisely this feminized physique, remarking that most castrati had "des hanches, une croupe, les bras, la gorge, le cou rond et potelé *comme des femmes*" (*the hips, the rump, the arms, the throat, and the round, plump breasts of women*).[10]

Disrupting as he does the traditional binary opposition of male and female, how might the castrato then be categorized? One way to accommodate the castrato is to try to make him fit the preexisting categories as de Brosses does when he refers to castrati as "demi-virs" (De Brosses, 36) (*half-men*). Another way is to create an additional category for him, rather like Freud's "third sex" or Marjorie Garber's "third term." If for Garber the transvestite is the third term, then

Figure 5.1   The Famous Castrato: II Farinelli, Recto. Ghezzi, Pier Leone (1674–1755). Pen and brown ink, over traces of black chalk, on paper. 12 x 8 1/8 inches (305 x 207 mm.). The Pierpont Morgan Library, New York, NY, U.S.A.

Source: Gift of Mr. Janos Scholz. 1985.87. The Pierpont Morgan Library/Art Resource, NY

perhaps the infinitely more perplexing castrato is the fourth? Such a solution to the problem of categorization is no invention of the modern era, however. As the author of the *Traité des Eunuques* reminds us, eunuchs had long been considered "une troisiéme sorte d'hommes," that is to say, a third sex, in addition to the male and female sexes.[11] In his autobiography, the castrato Filippo Balatri (c.1676–1756) struggles to define his own sex. He narrates how, when asked if he was male or female, he composed a short ditty that included the following lines:

> Resto imbrogliato allor per dar risposta.
> Se maschio, dico quasi una bugia,
> femmina men che men dirò ch'io sia,
> e dir che, son neutral, rossore costa.
>
> *I remain confused about how to reply.*
> *To say I am male is almost a lie,*
> *to say I am female is true even less,*
> *and to say I am neuter makes me blush.*[12]

Balatri clearly identifies himself as more male than female and is uncomfortable with the label "neuter." Perhaps de Brosses's half-man coinage was nearest the mark after all.

In addition to the binary opposition of male and female, the castrato disrupts the assumed correspondence between sex, gender, and vocal tessitura. Broadly speaking, a higher vocal tessitura is, of course, associated with women and a lower vocal tessitura is associated with men. With the castrato, a high tessitura corresponds in reality to a mutilated male, and, according to the fiction of the opera, to a man or woman, depending on his role. The disruption in traditional associations of tessitura brought about by the castrato (be he an alto or a soprano) is of course particularly noticeable in a theatrical genre in which such a strong emphasis is placed on voice quality. Interestingly, Dympna Callaghan reminds us of the impact of tessitura and vocal quality with regard to the spoken theatre of the English Renaissance, noting that "there are no recorded complaints about the *appearance* of male actresses . . . , only about their sound."[13] Unlike the boy actress, the castrato did not have to worry about his voice breaking, but he did have to contend with the apparent incongruity between his voice and his official masculine identity. One might argue that the castrato is vocally cross-cast when playing a male role (he performs as a man but sounds more like a woman) and more conventionally cross-cast when playing a female one (he sounds like a woman but his body is known to be that of a man, albeit a disfigured man). Ultimately, however, the inherent instability of the castrato's gender (and the ambiguity regarding his sex) means that he is different from any other cross-cast actor: he cannot play his biological opposite because he does not have one. At the same time, the pervasive presence of the castrato on the public stage in Italy during the seventeenth and eighteenth centuries raised some uncomfortable questions regarding sexual relations between men and women and, in particular, regarding female desire. The attraction that famous castrati singers held for their female audience is well documented. Despite his peculiar physical attributes, the castrato was clearly an object of erotic fascination for many female members of his audience. More than this, he was sometimes a serious object of female sexual desire. The extent to which a castrato could enjoy a "normal" sex life is a matter of some debate. Barbier writes that a castrato's penis was generally smaller than average but that

> La plupart des castrats pouvaient connaître une relation sexuelle à peu près normale, la castration ne leur empêchant ni l'érection ni l'émission de sperme et de liquide prostatique, sans spermatozoïds bien entendu. (*Histoire des castrats*, 21)
>
> *Most castrati could enjoy more or less normal sexual relations as their castration did not prevent them from achieving an erection or from discharging sperm and prostatic liquid (without spermatozoa, of course).*

He notes, however, that "la puissance et la régularité de cet acte sexuel devaient être passablement diminuées par rapport à celles des autres hommes" (Barbier, 21) (*the power and regularity of the sex act must have been somewhat below that of other men*). Thomas McGeary, on the other hand, writes that "it is, of course, physiologically impossible that the castrato—castrated well before puberty and, hence, with an infantile phallus—could engage in such heterosexual acts [i.e., vaginal sex],"[14] and Enid and Richard Peschel are of the same opinion. The Peschels also rightly point out that this mystery cannot be solved, as we do not know exactly of what the operation consisted ("Medicine and Music," 31, 32–33). Whatever the phallic potency of the castrato, the fact that he could be an object of female sexual desire (and, furthermore, that at least the famous castrati did have relations of some kind with some of their female admirers) remained a significant additional source of anxiety for the supporters of the dominant phallic ideology.

The undeniable fact that some women were, for whatever reason, attracted to these mutilated men raised the unwelcome possibility that female sexual desire could be satisfied without the aid of a penis (a possibility that, incidentally, is not even acknowledge by Peschel and Peschel in their articles). Not only did this mean that these castrated men might after all pose a genuine threat to the fully intact male by being able to satisfy a woman despite their lack, it offered the genuine prospect of nonreproductive sex. As Ancillon wrote in the *Traité des Eunuques* in 1707, castrati are "plus recherchez par les femmes débauchées, parce qu'ils leur donnent le plaisir du mariage sans qu'elles en courent les risques" (Ancillon, 159–60) (*more sought after by debauched women because they give them the pleasure of marriage without the risks*). The threat of unwanted pregnancy acted as a convenient check on the sexual mores of would-be respectable women, and the obviation of this impediment was as threatening to the male sex as it was liberating to the female one. Thus, the attraction of the castrato may have been precisely his *lack* of potency—a phenomenon that subverted the assumed power and dominance of normal male virility.

The castrato also raises some interesting questions with regard to sexual relations between men. Once again, it must be acknowledged that his possession of a deficient penis need not preclude his participation in sex acts, particularly as an object of sodomy. Freitas argues that, in the context of a vertical hierarchy of the sexes (with men at the top and women at the bottom), a feminine boy was widely considered to be superior to a woman (who was intrinsically contaminated and contaminating). Sexual relations with minors, however, were legally and morally problematic. One solution lay with the castrato who like the boy also offered a combination of feminine appeal and masculine superiority but who, as an adult, posed none of the legal or moral issues associated with pederasty (Freitas, 173–78). This is not to say, of course, that all Italian men during this period had as their sex object of choice a castrato. What is important is the fact that castrati were sometimes objects of desire for both men and women and that they could participate in a number of sex acts, their physical mutilation notwithstanding. Freitas hints at a possible conflation of musical and sexual services offered by castrati in Italy, citing as his prime example an apparent relationship between the castrato Atto Melani (to whom we shall return) and one of his patrons, the Duke of Mantua (Freitas, 150–51 and 183). It is perhaps no coincidence that evidence of Atto Melani's sexual relationships with men concern only his time in Italy, whereas he was forced to leave France by the

Duc Mazarin who was jealous of Melani's attachment to his wife (Hortense Mazarin, niece of the Cardinal) (Freitas, 154–55). I am not suggesting that sexual relations between men did not take place in seventeenth-century France, but it does seem that French and Italian attitudes toward sodomy differed at this time. In France, sodomy was commonly referred to as "le vice Italien" (*the Italian vice*), an association and attitude that must have influenced French responses to the sexually ambiguous Italian figure of the castrato.

In Italy, the castrato was a feature of an operatic tradition that demonstrated a strong esthetic bias in favor of the upper voices (soprano and, to a lesser extent, alto). Moreover, these higher voices were generally better endowed with the vocal agility required by contemporary composers. In Rome, as we saw, castrati were strongly identified with female roles, whereas in Venice or Naples they tended to sing male parts alongside female singers. Paradoxically, then, the all-male Roman opera retained some degree of correspondence between vocal tessitura and the fictional sex of the role, whereas other operatic centers in Italy, with their mixed casts of predominantly high voices, confused them. What all Italian operatic traditions of the time thus share in their different ways is a world in which the binary opposites of male/female sex, masculine/feminine clothing and high/low pitch are only partially operative. This sense of gender flexibility was further enforced (outside Rome) by the interchangeability of contemporary casting practices. Although the voice quality of a castrato differed from that of a female singer, the overlap in vocal range was sufficient for a woman to sing, when the need arose, a role originally written for a castrato. While Italian opera thrived in this environment of sexual indeterminacy, French opera, as will be seen, was to follow a more unambiguous path.

Italian casting practices also drew the audience's attention to the illusive and artificial nature of opera. Although written a century after our chosen time period, Goethe's responses to the theatre in Rome are enlightening and pertinent to our discussion. He commends the Roman tradition of cross-casting in spoken drama, commenting that its artificial nature enhanced and complemented the artifice inherent in theatrical production.[15] On the subject of the cross-cast castrato, Goethe's observations are even more intriguing. He writes that "the beautiful and beguiling voices of the *castrati*—who moreover seem more suitably dressed in women's clothes than in men's—reconcile one to whatever may appear inappropriate in that disguise" (Goethe, 48). Paradoxically, these lines suggest both that the castrato is a lesser source of anxiety for the audience when seen in women's clothing *and* that his seductively beautiful voice compensates for his disquieting appearance in female attire. While the peculiarity of the cross-cast actor for Goethe is more than compensated for by the heightened sense of artifice he brings with him, it is the cross-cast castrato's voice that amply compensates for his particular peculiarities. Goethe's comment regarding the suitability of female clothing for the castrated male might be understood in terms of his own castration complex. By assigning to the castrato a more feminine identity, Goethe distances himself from this too literal embodiment of the possibility of castration.

Before moving on to an examination of how he fared in France, it is worth remarking that, despite his evident operatic success, the castrato did not escape censure even in his mother country. Ellen Rosand notes that in Italy "the castrato was a favorite butt of sexual satire throughout the seventeenth century."[16] She mentions in particular the poem by Francesco Melosio, "Difesa di un musico castrato amante" and the "Lamento del castrato" by Fabrizio Fontana, while Peschel and Peschel draw our attention to two burlesque madrigals by the Italian musician Benedetto Marcello (1686–1739), author of *Il teatro alla moda* ("Medicine and Music," 32). For the Italian historian Lodovico Antonio Muratori (1672–1750) the castrato was a significant part of the pernicious effect of listening to opera. He rages against the effeminacy caused by ornamentation and by "the voices of the singers, who are all either naturally or artificially womanlike, and consequently inspire undue tenderness and languor in the souls of the audience."[17] It was precisely the ornamented and supposedly effeminizing style associated with Italian opera (and especially with castrati) that Lully (himself of Italian birth and training) sought to avoid when he carefully laid the foundations for French opera.[18]

The Castrato in France

The dominant attitude toward castrati in Louis XIV's France differed significantly from that which prevailed in musical circles in Italy (and indeed in England). We note that the French displayed an attitude toward castrati that was more hostile than anywhere else in Europe. Individual patrons, including Anne of Austria, occasionally took a castrato into their service and Louis XIV is reported to have loved the castrato Favalli (who arrived in 1674) "à cause de sa belle voix et du plaisir qu'il lui faisait en chantant" (*because of his beautiful voice and of the pleasure his singing brought him).*[19] For all their success in the private realm of the court during the Regency and the early part of Louis XIV's reign, however, castrati never became a feature of French opera. They did however make an important contribution to the music of the Chapel Royal and, to a lesser extent, to the Musique de la Chambre. Female voices were excluded from the music of the Chapel Royal for much the same reason that they were forbidden to sing in religious ceremonies in Italy. Similarly, castrati were brought in to reinforce the weaker voices of the male falsettists and the young boys. Maral notes that "selon le *Cérémonial historique* de l'abbé Chuperelle, c'est parce que le roi ne supportait plus les voix des pages de la Musique qu'il fit venir d'Italie 'sept ou huict jeunes Italiens qui eussent de très beaux hauts et bas dessus'" (*according to the Abbé Chuperelle's* Cérémonial historique, *it was because the king could no longer stand the voices of the pages from the* Musique *that he sent to Italy for "seven or eight young Italians who had very beautiful first and second soprano voices"*).[20] It seems, then, that Louis XIV was prepared to welcome castrati into his chapel in the interests of a music that he found esthetically pleasing. The importance of the castrati's contribution is attested to in the *Etat de la France* (1702), which includes, among the list of officers of the Chapel, "hauts et bas-dessus . . . 9, dont 6 Italiens (castrats)" (*nine first and second sopranos, including six Italians (castrati)*).[21] The fact that the castrati were designated "Italiens" reminds us of the lack of any homegrown French variety.[22] Despite their notoriety, it seems that for the imported castrati in the service of the king, "rien ne porte atteinte à leur reputation" and that "ils écoulent des jours tranquilles à la Cour de France" (Benoît, 187) (*nothing tarnished their reputation; they passed their days peacefully at the French Court*). Several of them lived together in a house built at Versailles around 1704, and there were still castrati living there as late as 1748.[23]

The person largely responsible for bringing Italian opera (and thus castrati) to the French court was the Italian-born Cardinal Mazarin. As early as 1642, Mazarin was encouraging his contacts in Italy to recruit singers and musicians for a trip to France as part of a wider program to consolidate his own power and influence. Among his various efforts, Mazarin oversaw, in 1647, eight performances of the Roman composer Luigi Rossi's opera, *Orfeo* (with a text by the Abbé Buti). In an attempt to woo the reluctant French audience, the work included a series of French ballet entries, but Italian casting practices were retained for the opera. The lead role of Orpheus was taken by the famous castrato Atto Melani (who had already enjoyed an extended visit to the French court in the winter of 1644–45), while Euridice was sung by the female soprano, Anna Francesca Costa.

Another castrato, the virtuoso Marc-Antonio Pasqualini, sang the role of Aristée (the son of Bacchus and Orfeo's rival), while yet another castrato, named Bentivoglio (or in the service of a gentleman of that name) played the part of an old nurse. While the spectacular stage machinery involved in the production was heralded as impressive, *Orfeo* was widely criticized by the public for the great expense it entailed. In the buildup to the civil war known as the Fronde, Mazarin was blamed for many things, including this excess, and he and his Italians (especially the castrati, who were an easy target) soon became an object of satire and ridicule.²⁴ The *Traité des Eunuques* cites an anonymous French ditty mocking the visiting Italian castrati who took part in *Orfeo*:

Je connois plus d'un Fanfaron
A crête & mine fiére,
Bien dignes de porter le Nom
De la Chaponardiére.
Crête aujourd'hui ne suffit pas
Et les plus simples Filles,
De la Crête font peu de cas
Sans autres Béatilles. (Ancillon, 2, verso)

I know more than one braggart
With a crest and a proud demeanor,
Worthy enough to be named
Mr. Capon.
These days a crest is not enough
And the most simple girls
Will not be impressed by a crest
Without the other parts.

After the turbulence of the Fronde (1648–52) and his triumphant return to Paris, Mazarin set about organizing more productions of Italian opera in France. Star singer Atto Melani returned to Paris in 1656 at Mazarin's invitation, where he delighted not only Anne of Austria but also her son, the young Louis XIV. Atto Melani's proximity to the king is nicely illustrated by their joint appearance in the Franco-Italian opera-ballet by Lully and Buti, *Amor malato* (or *L'amour malade*) in January 1657. While Atto Melani sang the title role, Louis XIV danced the role of *Le Divertissement*. A letter from Melani to his patron Mattias de' Medici reveals the pleasure he derived from this interaction:

> Qui si attende a fare il balletto di S.M., che vien rappresentato, la Dominica et il Mercoledi, e mai mi toccherà a vedere una festa con tanta commodità, poi che dal principio sino al fine, rappresentando Amore Infermo, me ne sto in letto, sopra del quale riposa anche S.M., che balla in maniera che rapisce I Cori d'ogn'uno.[25]
>
> *Here we attend to performing the ballet of His Majesty, which was presented on Sunday and Wednesday. Never again will I have the chance to see a festivity with such comfort, since from beginning to end, playing* Amore Infermo, *I remain in bed, on which also rests His Majesty, who dances in a manner that steals the hearts of everyone.*

Mazarin's most ambitious project, however, was *Ercole Amante*, a new commission from the famous Venetian composer, Pietro Francesco Cavalli (1602–76), in honor of the marriage of Louis XIV to Marie-Thérèse of Spain (which took place in June 1660). During the prolonged preparations for the performance of Cavalli's *Ercole Amante*, it was decided to produce Cavalli's earlier opera, *Serse* (originally performed in Venice in 1654). *Serse* was performed in November 1660 at the Louvre with the title role transposed down an octave from the alto to the baritone range.[26] Despite this apparent—and important—concession to French tastes, castrato singers featured widely in the opera in both male and female roles: Xerxès's brother, Arsamène, for instance, was sung by Atto Melani, while the Princess Amastris was played by Melani's brother, Don Filippo. The cross-cast princess is a particularly interesting site of gender play, for within the opera she also appears in male disguise.[27]

On the subject of castrati playing both male and female roles in opera, Atto Melani wrote in a revealing letter to his patron in 1660 of his unwillingness to play anything other than a lead *male* role in the forthcoming production of *Ercole Amante*: "Non rappresenterei in alcun modo, a meno fare una delle principali parti, fuori anche di donne" (*I would not perform under any circumstances unless it were one of the principal parts, excluding women's roles too*).[28] Clearly he considered a woman's role to be less prestigious than a man's, an attitude that of course reflects contemporary views of the relative merits of men and women. It also suggests a desire on Melani's part to assert his own masculinity: if the castrato was an uncomfortable reminder for the intact male of the precariousness of his masculinity, so was the performance of female roles an uncomfortable reminder for the castrato of the far greater precariousness of his.

In the event, Atto Melani was excluded from the long-awaited and much-anticipated production of *Ercole Amante*, which finally took place on February 7, 1662 at the newly constructed Salle des Machines in the Tuileries Palace. Owing to the two-year delay, many of the Italian singers had left the French court by this time, and it is likely that the cast was not as it was originally conceived. While several castrati appeared in the opera in both male and female roles, what is striking about this production is their appearance in only secondary roles.[29] Prunières suggests that the reassignment of the principal roles in this opera may have had an esthetic component in order to "éviter le ridicule de guerriers et de héros à voix feminine" (Prunières, *L'Opéra Italien*, 237) (*avoid the ridiculous phenomenon of warriors and heroes with feminine voices*). It would certainly seem that the French remained generally unconvinced by the figure of the castrato and still much preferred the French ballet entries. An epigram by Pierre Perrin comments precisely on how much more pleasing it was to see young girls (who performed in the Entrée des Etoiles) dancing than to witness the performances of the Italian castrati:

Vive l'entrée de petites filles du Ballet
Rien n'est si mignon, rien n'est si follet
Non pas ces grands concerts de ces vieilles Laures De Signores
Et ces *non sunt* qui chantent leur *libera*
Pour la mémoire de leurs *et cœtera*. (Prunières, *L'Opéra Italian*, 303)

Hurrah for the ballet entry performed by a group of little girls,
Nothing is so sweet, nothing is so fun
Not these great concerts given by these old Signores Lauras
And these non sunt *who sing their* libera
In memory of their et cœtera.

In the pages that follow I consider a number of French responses to the castrato (including additional remarks by Perrin) as part of an attempt to understand why he never came to be an established feature of public operatic entertainment in France.

French Responses to the Castrato

As we have seen, the castrato was not met with universal distaste in France. In addition to several prominent individuals at court who took a genuine liking to the visiting castrati, the small number of French people who took their defense tended to be those who had heard performances by castrati in a more favorable context, that is to say, performing Italian opera in Italy. As early as 1639, for example, one of Richelieu's musicians, Maugars, wrote of the castrati whom he had heard perform in Rome in the following terms:

> Il faut avouer avec vérité qu'ils sont incomparables et inimitables en cette musique scénique, non seulement pour le chant, mais encore pour l'expression des paroles, des postures et des gestes des personnages qu'ils représentent naturellement bien. Pour leur façon de chanter, elle est bien plus animée que la nôtre: ils ont certaines flexions de voix que nous n'avons pas.[30]
>
> *In truth it must be admitted that they are incomparable and inimitable in this music drama, not just in their singing, but also in their expression of the text, and in the postures and gestures of the characters that they are naturally good at representing. As regards their singing style, it is much more animated than ours: they have certain inflections of the voice that we do not.*

He finds their acting convincing, or rather, appropriate (we remember that verisimilitude was not necessarily of prime importance in Italian opera), but above all, it seems, he is impressed by the nascent genre of opera, "cette musique scénique," which was far more developed in Italy than in France at this time.

Perhaps the most prominent advocate of the benefits of the castrato among the French was the Abbé Raguenet who had also seen castrati perform in Rome and who published his *Parallèle des Italiens et des François, en ce qui regarde la musique et les operas* in 1702. Raguenet's treatise is but one small contribution to the wider ongoing debate concerning the relative merits of French and Italian music that raged throughout the reign of Louis XIV (and beyond), and it is in the context of this deeply entrenched Franco-Italian rivalry that French responses to the castrato and to Italian opera must be understood. Although Raguenet is largely pro-Italian, he is quick to extol the virtues of certain aspects of French opera, notably the successful use of the *basse-contre*, particularly in the roles of gods and kings.[31] Later in his treatise he reiterates the importance of the *basse-contre* in French opera, but this time he goes on to comment,

> Mais quels avantages n'ont-ils pas sur nous, pour les Opéra, par leurs *Castrati* qui sont sans nombre, & dont nous n'en avons pas un seul en France? Les voix de femme sont à la vérité aussi douces & aussi

agréables, chez nous, que celles de ces sortes d'hommes; mais il s'en faut bien qu'elles soient aussi fortes & aussi perçantes; il n'y a point de voix ny d'homme ny de femme au monde si flexibles que celles de ces *Castrati*; elles sont nettes, elles sont touchantes, elles pénétrent jusqu'à l'ame. (Raguenet, 76–77)

But what advantages do they not have over us with regard to opera, with their countless castrati, while we do not have a single one in France? Women's voices are truly as soft and agreeable in France as those of these men, but they are far from being as strong or as penetrating. There is no man's nor woman's voice in the world that is as flexible at that of the castrato; his voice is clear and affecting, and it pierces the soul.

Here, Raguenet comments on the total absence of castrati in France (by which he means in French opera)—something that he deems regrettable. He remarks that the voices of the women who perform opera in France are as soft and agreeable as those of the castrati, but that they are less powerful and less penetrating. Moreover, the Italian castrati display a vocal flexibility second to none. His remark that "il n'y a point de voix ny d'homme ny de femme au monde si flexibles" suggests both that the castrato is superior to all other singers, male and female, and, more subtly, that the castrato is himself neither a male nor a female singer, but a separate additional category.

Raguenet elaborates further on the particular qualities of the castrato's voice. It is, he says,

une de ces voix qui, d'un son le plus éclatant & en même tems le plus doux, perce la symphonie & s'éléve au dessus de tous les Instrumens avec un agrément qu'on ne sauroit décrire, il faut l'entendre. Ce sont des gosiers & des sons de voix de Rossignol; ce sont des haleines à faire perdre terre, & à vous ôter presque la respiration, des haleines infinies par le moyen desquelles ils exécutent des passages de je ne sai combien de mesures, ils font des échos de ces mêmes passages, ils soutiennent des tenuës d'une longueur prodigieuse, au bout desquelles, par un coup de gorge semblable à ceux des Rossignols, ils font encore des cadences de la même durée. (Raguenet, 78–79)

one of those voices that, with a more vibrant yet at the same time softer sound, comes through the orchestra and rises above all the instruments with a pleasantness that is impossible to describe: it must be heard.... They have the throat and sound of a nightingale; they have astonishing breath control that almost takes the listener's breath away. In endless single breaths they perform passages of countless bars, then they repeat the same passages; they produce passages of a prodigious length, at the end of which, by a trick of the throat similar to that of the nightingale, they sing more cadenzas of the same length.

He insists on the strength and penetrating nature of the castrato's voice as well as its beauty and is clearly impressed by the exceptional breath control displayed by these highly trained singers. It is significant that Raguenet feels the advantages of Italian opera over its French counterparts particularly keenly when it comes to the figure of the male lover. On this subject, he writes,

> Au reste, ces voix douces & rossignolantes sont enchantées dans la bouche des Acteurs qui font le personnage d'amant; rien n'est plus touchant que l'expression de leurs peines formée avec ces sons de voix si tendres & si passionnez; & les Italiens ont, en cela, un grand avantage sur les Amans de nos Théatres, dont la voix grosse & mâle est constamment bien moins propre aux douceurs qu'ils disent à leurs Maîtresses. D'ailleurs comme ces voix sont aussi fortes qu'elles sont douces, on entend tres-distinctement tout ce qui se chante aux Théatres Italiens, au lieu qu'on en perd la moitié à ceux des François . . . Ce sont ordinairement de petites filles sans poumons, sans force, & sans haleine, qui chantent, en France, les Dessus; au lieu que cette même partie est toûjours chantée, en Italie, par des hommes forts dont la voix ferme & résonnante se fait entendre avec netteté dans les lieux les plus vastes, sans qu'on en perde une syllabe à quelqu'endroit qu'on soit placé. (Raguenet, 79–82)

For the rest, these sweet, nightingale-like voices are enchanting in the mouths of actors who perform the role of the male lover. Nothing is more moving than the expression of their plight with the tender and passionate sounds of these voices. The Italians have, in this respect, a great advantage over the lovers of our own theatres, whose big, male voices are always considerably less suitable for the sweet nothings they say to their mistresses. Furthermore, as these voices are as powerful as they are soft, everything that is sung in the Italian theatre is heard very clearly, whereas in French theatres half of it is lost. . . . Normally it is the little girls with no lung power, no strength, and no breath control who, in France, sing the soprano line, whereas in Italy it is always sung by strong men whose firm, resonant voices are heard clearly in the largest of spaces, without one syllable being lost, wherever one is seated.

This passage is particularly interesting as it highlights many of the paradoxes associated with the figure of the castrato. Raguenet states that the castrato's voice is better suited to the expression of a man's painful, tender, and passionate love than the "voix grosse & *mâle*" (my emphasis) found in French opera. His use of the word *"mâle"* is especially intriguing. We remember that in discussions of Jesuit school drama, expressions of erotic love were perceived to be dangerously feminizing (see chapter II). Raguenet's position is not as far removed from that of the Jesuits as it might appear, for he too perceives a correspondence between a certain femininity and men in love. The principal difference between Raguenet and the Jesuits is that, where the Jesuits disapprove of the performance of male love, Raguenet finds it wholly acceptable and pleasing when it is sung by a castrato. Just like the castrato, a man who is in love is an imperfect man. The "petites filles" of whom Raguenet writes (he must mean young women rather than young girls) may possess voices of an appropriate tessitura for the discussion of love, but they are lacking in force, musical training, and, like the men, good diction. The castrato, then, combines the essential qualities of non-maleness (being in love) with power, resonance, and clarity.

For Raguenet, the ambiguous gender of the castrato (a source of anxiety for many spectators) was a theatrical advantage as it enabled him to play female roles with just as much success as male ones:

D'ailleurs les Italiens ont encore un grand avantage sur nous par le moyen de leurs *Castrati*, en ce qu'ils en font le personnage qu'ils veulent, une femme aussi-bien qu'un homme, selon qu'ils en ont besoin; car ces *Castrati* sont tellement accoûtumez à faire des rôles de femme, que les meilleures Actrices du monde ne les font point mieux qu'eux; ils ont la voix aussi douce qu'elles, & l'ont avec cela beaucoup plus forte; ils sont plus grands que le commun des femmes, & ont par là plus de majesté qu'elles; ils sont mêmes ordinairement plus beaux en femme, que les femmes mêmes. FERINI, par exemple, qui, en 1698 faisoit, à Rome, le personnage de *Sibaris* à l'Opéra de *Thémistocle*, est plus grand & plus beau que ne le sont communément les femmes, il a je ne sai quoi de noble & de modeste dans la physionomie; habillé en Princesse Persanne, comme il étoit, avec le Turban & l'Aigrette, il avoit un air de Reine & d'Impératrice; & l'on n'a peut-être jamais vû une plus belle femme au monde qu'il le paroissoit sous cet habit. (Raguenet, 98–101)

Moreover, the Italians have an additional advantage over us in the figure of the castrato, as he can play the character that he wants, a female role as well as a male one, according to what is required. These castrati are so used to playing female roles that the best actresses in the world do not perform them better; the castrati have voices as soft as theirs but they are much stronger; they are taller than most women and thereby have more majesty; they are usually even more beautiful dressed as women than women themselves. Ferrini, for example, who in 1698 played the character of Sibaris in the opera, Thémistocle, in Rome, is taller and more handsome than the majority of women. He has something noble and modest in his countenance; dressed as a Persian princess, as he was, with a turban and a feather crest, he had the air of a queen or an empress. A more beautiful woman has perhaps never been seen in the world than he appeared dressed in this clothing.

His arguments are again paradoxical: the castrato is so well trained that he impersonates a woman better than any woman can. The fact that he is taller than the average woman bestows upon him a greater majesty that only enhances his beauty. Not only can the castrato impersonate a woman better than the real thing, but, when cross-dressed, he is even more beautiful than she! To support this assertion, he cites the example of the famous castrato, Ferrini, whose successful portrayal of a Persian princess clearly made quite an impression on Raguenet. There are several ways in which one might interpret Raguenet's account here. In response to his remarks suggesting that castrati make more convincing and more beautiful women than women themselves, one might well accuse him of misogyny. Equally, one might link him with Goethe and understand his assertions to mean that the artifice of art in this context should be prized above any (necessarily futile) attempts at verisimilitude. Or one might understand him to be unwittingly expressing a repressed homosexual desire or homoerotic fantasy. What is clear is that he joined the hundreds of spectators of Italian opera who, for whatever reasons (and these varied), *were* able to enjoy the performances of castrati.

It was undoubtedly more difficult to convince the French in France of the merits of Italian opera. Most of the small number of French who took some pleasure in hearing visiting castrati sing did so reluctantly or with surprise. Mme de Longueville's response on hearing a visiting castrato perform, as given by Tallemant des Réaux, is both revealing and representative: she is reported to have exclaimed "Mon Dieu, que cet *incommodé* chante bien!" (*My God, how well this ungainly man sings!*).[32] The fact that the castrati were exceptionally well-trained singers is not in dispute—a good number of skeptics were forced to admit that they possessed good singing voices. The stumbling block remained their peculiar physique and manner, something that was clearly much more of an issue on stage than in the chapel (where they were heard but not usually seen). Many French people were simply not convinced at all. Pierre Perrin famously described them as "l'hor-reur des Dames et la risée des hommes" (*the horror of women and the laughing stock of men).*[33] Again, Perrin's objection is not to their voices, but to their mutilation and gender ambiguity—a fact that is emphasized by his separation of men's and women's responses. His objections are surely sexual in nature: the women are physically repulsed by the castrati, while the (intact) men who consider the castrati from a position of phallic superiority, find them ridiculous. Such a response is particularly important in the case of a castrato playing a male hero: if the men present in the audience are expected to identify with that hero, then to have him played by a mutilated and sexually ambiguous man is almost tantamount to an attack on their own sexual capacities. Ridicule and the sense of superiority that accompanies it is a useful strategy for managing such a threat.

Regarding the women of France, we know of at least one who *was* susceptible to the mysterious allure of the castrato. As Charles d'Ancillon explains in the dedicatory epistle of his *Traité des Eunuques,*

Il y avoit autrefois ici plusieurs Eunuques Italiens, Musiciens, qui y faisoient grosse figure. Ils se flattérent de faire de grandes & d'illustres Conquêtes, mais ils se trompérent; nos Dames ne se laissérent point éblouïr, & ne se payérent point de la bagatelle. . . . Cependant il y en a eu une qui s'est laissé charmer, & qui a prêté l'oreille aux propositions de mariage qui lui ont été faites par un de ces Eunuques. Une Personne que je considére beaucoup, m'ayant prié de lui dire mon avis, & de le lui donner raisonné par écrit, en forme de consultation, pour détourner cette jeune fille sa parente du dessein qu'elle avoit d'entrer dans un tel engagement. (Ancillon, 2, verso and 3, recto)

In the past there were several Italian eunuchs here, musicians who were much celebrated. They flattered themselves that they could make great and illustrious conquests, but they were misguided: our women were not dazzled by them and did not get caught up in these trifles. . . . However, there was one who allowed herself to be charmed, and who listened to the proposals of marriage made to her by one of these eunuchs. A person whom I hold high in esteem asked me to give [her] my opinion and to provide a written account of it, in the form of a consultation, in order to dissuade this young girl, her relation, from entering into such a contract.

The purpose of his book, then, was to set forth as many arguments as he could think of against marrying a castrato and to anticipate any counterarguments that might be made in response.

One of the arguments that Ancillon does not use in this context is nonetheless one of the principal and most insidious objections to the castrato: his inextricable association with Italian opera. The long history of the Franco-Italian rivalry in terms of music and culture during this period is well-known and is founded on political as well as on patriotic and esthetic grounds. For the French, the castrato was a microcosm of Italian opera: he represented all that the French objected to in Italian opera, notably its implausibility, and its emphasis on dazzling virtuosity and its heavy ornamentation. To condone the castrato was to condone Italian opera and vice versa. Rather than adopt and adapt the flourishing Italian tradition, Lully (and it is Lully—himself of Italian extraction—who may be said to have established the foundations of the French operatic tradition) chose instead to create a specifically French style of opera. A large part of what made it French was that it was not Italian. Part of what made it not Italian was its lack of castrati.[34] Thus, French opera was consciously established in contradistinction to the Italian variety.

Cross-Casting in Early French Opera

The Académie Royale de Musique (informally known as the Opéra) was founded on the understanding that both men and women of all social classes could sing in the opera without any questions being raised regarding the morality and suitability of their actions. Ménestrier reminds us of this, citing the *Lettres patentes* of June 28, 1669:

[A l'opéra] les Gentilshommes chantent publiquement en Musique sans déroger, il [Louis XIV] voulut que tous Gentilshommes & Damoiselles pussent chanter ausdites pieces & representations de cette Academie Royale, sans que pour ce ils fussent censez deroger au titre de Noblesse, ny à leurs Privileges, Charges, droits, immunitez.[35]

[At the opera] gentlemen sing in public without abasing themselves. Louis XIV wanted all gentlemen and all ladies to be able to sing in the aforementioned plays and performances of the Académie Royale without losing their nobility or their privileges, charges, rights, or immunities.

From its inception, the Académie Royale de Musique was to include male and female singers (but no mention is made of the inclusion or exclusion of castrati).

The closest the French operatic tradition comes to gender ambiguity is perhaps in its frequent use of the *haute contre*, a light tenor with a high range, close to that of the female contralto but with a very different vocal quality. The *haute contre* is a naturally high tenor who might occasionally use his falsetto range (rather than a full falsettist, like the English alto). The popularity of the *haute contre* is demonstrated by the fact that Lully assigned the principal male role in eight of his fourteen operas to this voice part.[36] In addition, as will be seen below, the majority of Lully's cross-cast roles were given to the *haute contre*. James Anthony has suggested that the French custom of having an *haute contre* play a nurse or a confidante "challenged verisimilitude as much as did the use of the castrato in Italy."[37] While it is clear that having an *haute contre* singing a female role would have created a certain amount of gender ambiguity, I cannot agree with his claim that the cross-cast *haute contre* was anything like as challenging a figure as the castrato. The cross-cast nurse was a time-honored tradition that was often employed to serve the drama by emphasizing certain characteristics of that person, whereas the castrato, as we have seen, was potentially highly destabilizing in any role, male or female. While it is true that the range of the *haute contre* might sound unnaturally high (especially to modern ears), there was never any doubt in the minds of Lully's audience regarding the singer's biological sex.

For the purposes of this investigation, I shall be looking exclusively at Lully's operas, which were all written between 1673 and 1687.[38] As was the case in spoken theatre of the period (see chapter I), instances of cross-casting in Lully's operas are decidedly rare and all the more interesting for that. After the unsuccessful attempts of Perrin and Cambert to establish a French national opera in 1669, the royal patent was passed exclusively to Lully in 1672, whereupon he rapidly began to establish his strict monopoly over all musical productions performed in French. His place in operatic history was thus secure (albeit at the expense of that of other would-be opera composers of the 1670s and 80s). With his librettist of choice, Philippe Quinault (1635–88), who wrote the libretti for all but two of his operas, Lully set about creating a French style of opera, known as *tragédie en musique* or *tragédie-lyrique*. Lully's operas were performed before both a private audience at court and the public in Paris. Unfortunately we have no cast lists for the public performances given before 1699 and so the following analyses are based on the performers named in the court *livrets* subsequently collected and published by Carl Schmidt.[39]

In an analysis of Lully's singing roles, a distinction should be made between solo parts and parts written for the chorus. Anthony notes that the French operatic chorus from Lully to Rameau was commonly divided into a *grand* and a *petit chœur*. The favored texture for the *petit chœur* was the trio, with two sopranos and one *haute contre*. The *grand chœur* included sopranos (mainly women but occasionally, it seems, some male sopranos, falsettists, and boy pages) and the three male voices of the *haute contre*, the tenor, and the bass (Anthony, 118). In direct contrast with the marked Italian preference for the soprano and contralto voices, what we notice in the French system is the distinct dominance of male voices and a marked lack of interest in the female contralto range.

Given the musical requirements of the ensemble vocal roles, too much emphasis should not be placed on the fairly frequent instances of cross-casting in the opera chorus. In the interests of maintaining a certain vocal balance, it is not unusual to find male and female performers singing together the roles of a single-sex group. This is the case, for example, in a 1677 *livret* for Lully-Quinault's *Thésée* (1675), in which we learn that one female singer sang alongside three men and two boy pages as the "six hommes déguisés en prêtresses" (Schmidt, 81) (*six men disguised as priestesses*). Similarly, on at least one occasion, the "dix femmes phyrgiennes" (*ten Phrygian women*) in Lully-Quinault's *Atys* (1676) were sung by five men and five women (Schmidt, 128). Perhaps the most important thing we learn from the cast lists of Lully's *tragédies en musique* is the fact that casting was flexible and, as we have already observed, very much dependent on who was available to perform at any given time. The casting of the ensemble vocal roles, in particular, varied from one performance to another, as the contents of Schmidt's *Catalogue raisonné* amply demonstrate.

The decision to have a cross-cast solo role, however, is clearly a significant choice, made for dramatic as well as for musical reasons. In Lully's operas, the cross-cast solo vocal roles are all male-to-female, a fact that supports both the notion that cross-casting was somehow inappropriate for women performers and the related idea that women were disinclined to perform certain unfeminine roles. It was also perhaps owing to the fact that there were a good deal more professional male singers available than female ones. Our cross-cast roles fall into three unequal categories: human beings, mythological beings, and allegories.

Lully and Quinault's first cross-cast role, and their only cross-cast human figure is the nurse in their first opera, *Cadmus et Hermione* (1673), a role that was sung by an *haute contre*. We remember that in the Italian *commedia* tradition and in Venetian opera it was customary for the comic older women to be played by men, and that this tradition was, to a very small extent, adopted by both Corneille and Molière (see chapter I). It is likely that Lully's nurse also descended from this tradition.[40] The fact that she is anonymous and referred to only as "La nourrice d'Hermione" (*Hermione's nurse*) reminds us that she is a comic type and that she is there primarily to serve a function rather than to advance the action or to offer any deep psychological insight. Her purpose is largely to provide a degree of comic relief in contrast with the more serious subject of the rest of the opera. The comic interplay between the cowardly servant, Arbas, and the cross-cast old nurse relies mainly on the inappropriate nature of the nurse's desire for him. She is old and ugly, while he is young and, presumably, more attractive, despite his cowardliness. Moreover, he is attracted to the youthful and beautiful Charite. This situation is strongly reminiscent, among others, of that of the old hags in Aristophanes's *Ecclesiazusae* (see Introduction). Having the unattractive and inappropriately libidinous old nurse played by a male singer, far from being out of place, cleverly and convincingly highlights what is most interesting and enjoyable about her character. The nurse is not, of course, one of the central characters of the opera. Buford Norman comments that "the nurse presents little interest beyond that of the standard aging woman in love, rejected by Arbas and ridiculed by her rival Charite."[41] And this is certainly true at the level of plot. But she is in her own modest way well-crafted as well as well-cast. In 2.3.283–288 for instance, she makes a wonderful response as Arbas runs away from her:

Il me quitte, l'ingrat, il me fuit, l'infidèle!
Ne crains pas que je te rappelle;
Va, cours, je te laisse partir;
Va, je n'ai plus pour toi qu'une haine mortelle:
Puisses-tu rencontrer la mort la plus cruelle,
Puisse le Dragon t'engloutir.[42] (I, 28)

He is abandoning me, he is fleeing from me, the ungrateful,
*   unfaithful one!*
Do not think that I shall call you back;
Go, run away, I shall let you go;
Go, I only feel for you a deadly hatred.
May you meet the most cruel death
May the dragon gobble you up.

As Norman observes, this is a delightful parody of the tragic French style, concluding with a comic change in tone in the last line (*Touched by the Graces*, 90).

By definition, mythological beings are otherworldly, and cross-casting is one of the best ways in which their otherworldliness can be conveyed on stage. Given that we are dealing with male-to-female cross-casting, it is perhaps not surprising that all of the cross-cast mythological beings of Lully's operas are somehow unfeminine (i.e., grotesque) in nature. This is the case, for example, of the Furies who are, in these operas too fierce, too demonic, and too closely associated with the darkness of the underworld to be considered anything other than unladylike. In *Alceste* (1674), the part of the fury, Alecton, is written for an *haute contre*. There is nothing in the music or the text to suggest that Alecton is in any way a comic character; rather, she is menacing and violent as she urges her underworld companions to attack the approaching interloper, Alcide. In Jean-Claude Malgoire's recording of *Alceste*, Alecton is sung by the high tenor, Douglas Nasrawi.[43] Malgoire renders this scene comic by means of the comical offstage barking sounds of Cerberus and the exaggerated vocal gestures of Alecton. It seems unlikely that Lully intended the scene to be performed that way, but the recording is convincing enough, and the fact that Lully did include some short comic episodes in his early operas gives a degree of credence to a comic reading of certain scenes.

In Lully-Quinault's *Isis* (1677), the fury Erinnys was also written for an *haute contre*. Erinnys, who is Io's chief torturer, plays a significantly more important part in the action of *Isis* than Alecton does in *Alceste*. For this reason, perhaps, she is even more clearly characterized. When Junon summons Erinnys from hell she addresses her as "barbare Erinnis" (I, 267; 3.7.699) and commands her:

Epouvante tout l'Univers
Par les tourments de ma rivale.
Viens la punir au gré de mon courroux.
Redouble ta rage infernale,
Et fais, s'il se peut, qu'elle égale
La fureur de mon cœur jaloux. (I, 268; 702–707)

Horrify the whole universe
With the torments of my rival.
Come and punish her according to my anger.
Intensify your infernal rage,
And, if it is possible, let it equal
The fury of my jealous heart.

Erynnis is as vindictive as her mistress could wish and appears to take a certain sadistic pleasure in Io's suffering. She sings, for example, in 4.2.725–726: "Soupire, gémis, pleure, crie, / Je me fais de ta peine un spectacle charmant" (I, 269) (*Sigh, groan, cry, shout, / Your pain is for me a charming spectacle*). Lully's other cross-cast furies appear in *Proserpine* (1680) in which they play a small role in Act V. The three Furies sing, "renversons toute la Nature" (II, 50; 925) (*let us overturn the whole of Nature*), and their cross-casting acts precisely as an illustration of this reversal of nature as well as of the otherworldliness of the underworld. These furies were sung by the three male voices of *haute contre*, tenor, and bass. The same three male voices were used for the Gorgons in *Persée* (1682). These are relatively substantial cross-cast roles, for the Gorgons dominate Act III of the opera. The role of the Gorgon leader, Méduse (or Medusa) is of particular importance. Act III opens in the Gorgons' lair as Medusa laments, at some considerable length, the loss of her beauty. She begins with the words "j'ai perdu la beauté qui me rendit si vaine" (II, 83; 3.1.441) (*I have lost the beauty that made me so vain*). Given the close association we have observed between beauty and womanhood, it is not surprising that these words were given to a male singer. Moreover, these are not typically feminine roles (Medusa is angry and irritable), and the fact that they are cross-cast can only serve to enforce this lack of femininity as the Gorgons rejoice in the pleasure they take at being frightening and destructive. We notice that Medusa, the principal Gorgon, is sung not by an *haute contre* but by a tenor, the voice "traditionally used for old or ridiculous female characters."[44] In Christophe Rousset's recording of *Persée*, the original pitches are maintained as Medusa is sung by the tenor, Laurent Slaars, Euryale by the *haute contre*, Cyril Auvity, and Sténone by the bass, Bruno Rostand.[45] Here, Medusa's cross-casting comes into particular relief when she is in dialogue with Mercure in 3.2. Mercure's music is cautiously soothing and calm, whereas Medusa's is enervated and frenzied. Moreover, Mercure sings at a higher pitch than she does, thereby enforcing the contrast between the two characters and between their respective moral outlooks.

Benoît Bolduc has noted that Medusa and her sisters continued to be played by men until 1746 when a woman began to play the role of the Medusa (Bolduc, par. 5.3). He also draws our attention to the 2001 Toronto production of *Persée* by the Opéra Atelier, in which "the rusty machine of the *merveilleux* was cranked up again, newly oiled by this era's poetics of camp" (Bolduc, par. 6.1). In other words, Medusa was performed as a drag queen. It is not especially difficult to imagine how she and her sisters might be camped up. Medusa's preoccupation with her physical appearance (specifically with the loss of her good looks), combined with her cattiness (and that of her sisters) has the potential to make a very entertaining drag queen. Judging by the reviews of this production, however, this transformation was not entirely successful. Jon Kaplan wrote "I'd like more from baritone Michael Chioldi's Medusa, too, either more comedy or more fearsomeness."[46] This comment would suggest that Chioldi's understanding of the role was that it was unclear or imbalanced: it is nigh impossible to be both fearsome and comic, so a choice between the two is necessary. Kamal Al-Solaylee simply felt that high camp was not the best way of resurrecting French baroque opera, and in particular noted that "a scantily clad drag-queen Medusa playing to the rafters" prevented the audience from becoming more emotionally involved with the production.[47] His comments are not so far removed from those of Jon Kaplan. It would seem that for many the decision to play Medusa as a drag queen was an obstacle to her fearsomeness that in turn limited audience involvement with her character and held back the development of the plot. For Bolduc, on the other hand, she "succeeded in restoring the luster and the profound shock and appeal of this character for an audience largely not invested in the rules of seventeenth-century poetics" (Bolduc, par. 6.3).

Lully's remaining cross-cast figure from mythology is the Déesse de la terre (*goddess of the earth*) who appears in 5.6 of *Phaëton* (1683) crying to Jupiter for help. Her music is written in the *haute contre* range and in Minkowski's recording of the opera, this role is sung by a suitably agitated tenor, Jean-Paul Fouchécourt.[48] The final cross-cast role that I would like to examine briefly is the allegorical figure of La Haine (*hatred*) who appears in III, 4 of *Armide* (1686). Unlike the majority of the cross-cast roles in Lully's operas, the music for La Haine is written for a low-pitched male voice, the baritone. In Philippe Herreweghe's recording, La Haine is sung by a bass-baritone, John Hancock, whose low pitch nicely evokes the "fond des Enfers" (*depths of hell*) of which s/he sings.[49] Rather like the scene between Medusa and Mercury in *Persée*, La Haine's interactions are all about contrasts. The deep, solemn music of La Haine's solos contrast with the more upbeat (and potentially mildly comical) music for the chorus of her companions as they gleefully anticipate their destruction of love. The contrast is even more striking as La Haine confronts the eponymous heroine Armide, at which point the music becomes particularly dark and menacing. Clearly the impact of this scene, and especially the characterization of La Haine, would have been far less striking had the role been played by a female soprano.

We have seen that French baroque opera was established in opposition to the Italian musical tradition. Italian opera rejoiced in the striking voice and gender ambiguity (and therefore flexibility) of the castrato and demonstrated a marked preference for the upper voices, particularly that of the soprano, both male and female. French opera, on the other hand, rejected the ambiguity and flexibility of the castrato and exhibited its own preference for men's voices, notably that of the naturally high tenor, known as the *haute contre*. While cross-casting was rife in Italian opera, the French taste for verisimilitude, combined with the fact that, throughout French operatic history, women had always been permitted to sing on stage, meant that very few roles were cross-cast. Each of Lully's cross-cast solo roles displays an absence of feminine traits or displays traits that are positively unfeminine according to the standards of the day. The fact that the majority of Lully's cross-cast roles were written for the *haute contre* (and not for lower pitched men's voices) moderates the impact of any improbability associated with their cross-casting and shifts the emphasis onto the positive impact of this choice. Thus we see that cross-casting was used in a modest but constructive way in order to enhance characterization and render the drama as a whole more convincing. There is no small amount of irony in the fact that something as seemingly far-fetched as cross-casting might render a drama *more* compelling. This is nonetheless the case in French baroque opera, where a fine balance was sought between the magic of otherworldly figures and their fantastic stage machinery on the one hand, and, on the other, traces of *vraisemblance*, inherited from classical tragedy.

CONCLUSION

In the course of this study we have examined a sample of different cross-cast roles, including spoken parts played by schoolboys, schoolgirls, and adult men, as well as dancing and singing parts in court ballet and opera. In addition, we have observed the rise of the professional actress and of the female ballet dancer, and reviewed French attitudes toward the most complex figure ever to have been associated with cross-casting: the castrato. It has been seen that no single evaluation of the phenomenon of cross-casting can be applied in all these instances, for the impact of the cross-cast actor is heavily dependent on performance context and theatrical genre, as well as on the response of each individual audience member. The phenomenon of cross-casting has been shown to be inextricably bound up with questions of theatricality and gender with which it finds itself in a reciprocal relationship: our reading of cross-casting is informed by our understanding of contemporary views regarding theatricality and gender, and vice versa. In a society in which women were widely understood in terms of what they were not (men), the conflation of woman and child (and, inversely, of child and woman) that we have witnessed at various points in this investigation is, when judged by its own standards, perfectly explicable. From this point of view, women, children, and castrati may all be considered as incomplete men. In their different ways, they each embody a threat to masculinity at the same time that they are potential objects of male desire. Similarly, in a society in which sex and gender were not always assumed to be as stable as people might have liked, cross-dressing was widely frowned upon and cross-casting was only tolerated under certain circumstances and in certain contexts.

Cross-casting is an inherently theatrical phenomenon and therefore an artificial one. It can be used variously for comic effect, to undermine or even to enforce traditional understandings of sex and gender roles, to convey a sense of otherworldliness, or simply out of practical necessity. Our examination of cross-casting during the early reign of Louis XIV has revealed a discernible, though uneven, movement toward the establishment of clear distinctions between male and female, man and woman, as well as masculine and feminine. At the same time, the practice of cross-casting continued to challenge those very distinctions. Seventeenth-century French theatre audiences knew that men and women were biologically different, and what they saw on stage encouraged them to speculate about the true causes and effects of those differences. Similarly, they knew that what they saw on stage was inherently false, an illusion, but understood that the theatre could nonetheless teach them something true about themselves and their own lives. The cross-cast figure, like every human being, is thus intrinsically paradoxical.

Cross-casting is of course a relatively rare phenomenon in present-day, mainstream European theatre. Public opinion regarding the presence of female actors on the public stage (and the acting profession in general) has evolved to the extent that it is now fully expected that women should play female roles and men male roles. Cross-casting thus no longer exists as a convention, although it may still be employed as a device. The notable exception to this trend lies with the genre of pantomime, which customarily features two central cross-cast figures: the pantomime dame and the breeches role of the principal boy. That the tradition of cross-casting should endure in a comic, lighthearted theatrical genre (and not in its more serious counterparts) is significant. In the early twenty-first century, a male actor may dress as woman (the pantomime dame) if s/he is made to be grotesque through the exaggeration of feminine signifiers (the forced falsetto voice, extravagant false breasts and makeup, a dress, and high heels), combined with clear and reassuring evidence of the male identity of the performer beneath the costume (visible facial and body hair, the constant adjustment of ill-fitting stockings and underwear, stocky legs, and an ungainly walk). Like Molière's cross-cast female characters, the modern pantomime dame is at no point intended to *pass* as a woman; nor is she supposed to be sexually attractive to the audience (apart from anything else, her age precludes this). Her grotesque and comical appearance is principally a source of laughter—a laughter that, in this instance, neutralizes any potential for transgression contained within the figure of the theatrical cross-dresser.

The cross-cast principal boy though is a more problematical figure whose transgressive potential must once again be offset by laughter and by the frivolous (and therefore nonthreatening) nature of the pantomime genre. The erotic potential of the female actress dressed in masculine attire (famously exploited in the plays of Restoration

England) is undoubtedly still operative today, although her impact must be strongly diminished owing to the comparative visibility and accessibility of the female body in modern western society. Where the pantomime dame is grotesque and highly comical, the principal boy is a more serious role, capable of provoking an erotic response among audience members. In both instances, the actors' cross-casting may be understood to contribute to the characterization of their roles: the pantomime dame is a postmenopausal, unfeminine figure, while the principal boy is youthful and ripe for sexual experience. This continued association of late boyhood with young womanhood subtly points to the continuation of a double standard regarding male and female sexuality according to which adult men should be sexually experienced, while desirable women are to remain chaste. At the same time, the suggestion that a man who has not yet reached full sexual maturity is still female implicitly perpetuates the notion that men are more complete versions of women. As Thomas Laqueur has argued at some length, the one-sex model, according to which women were thought to be inferior men (or inverts) and which dominated European sexual discourse until the end of the eighteenth century, is still not wholly eclipsed and now sits uncomfortably in the shadow of the modern two-sex model (*Making Sex*, passim).

In addition to the self-conscious and deliberate attempts of modern theatre to experiment with all manner of theatrical conventions and devices (including casting practices), the most important vestiges of cross-casting are to be found in projects to create "authentic" productions of early drama, such as all-male productions of Shakespeare. The New Globe Theatre in London, for example, has since its opening in 1997 been the site of a number of all-male Shakespeare productions, including Giles Block's *Antony and Cleopatra* in 1999. Audience responses to his use of cross-casting (an attempt to recreate the original convention) varied considerably. The reviewer for the *Daily Telegraph* (August 1999), echoing the English antitheatricalists of the Renaissance, perceived in this production a correspondence between cross-casting and effeminacy, complaining that Mark Rylance's appearance on stage as Cleopatra involved "a little too much drag comedy" and that the interaction between Antony and Cleopatra was "in danger of descending into a camp farce." The reviewer for the *Sunday Times* (August 8, 1999) however, noted that Rylance was "determined to avoid contemporary associations with drag" and that the cross-cast actors betrayed "not a whisper of camp."

Mark Rylance's performance as Olivia in Tim Carroll's 2002 production of *Twelfth Night*, on the other hand, met with almost universal acclaim (see figure C.1). Maddy Costa wrote in the *Guardian* on May 24, 2002,

> Mark Rylance's stammering, fluttery Olivia is exquisite: gliding across the stage, head in the clouds, she flinches at real, sullied life—uncle Toby drunk, Malvolio capering—and is left utterly breathless by her encounter with Viola/Cesario. Rylance's minute attention to detail renders Olivia's struggles to woo this mysterious boy, and her abashed amazement when Viola's identity is revealed, superbly comic and almost unbearably poignant.

Francine Brody, writing for the *Times Literary Supplement*, found his performance equally compelling:

> Mark Rylance's Olivia is quite simply wonderful. One never completely loses sight of the fact that he is not a woman but it is irrelevant. He brings new qualities to the role and does it so well that it is impossible to decide whether it is partly the masculine nuances or only that he is a magnificent actor. I have always been rather bored by Olivia, but here she is a wonderful mixture of strong and weak, noble and pathetic. She had us in fits of laughter and at the same time managed to gain our sympathy.

What is most interesting about this review is the fact that Rylance's performance here was convincing enough for Brody to accept his cross-casting as the convention that it originally was ("it is irrelevant"). That the issue of camp (so prominent in the reviews of *Antony and Cleopatra*) disappears from the reviews of this production is equally revealing, and it perhaps bears witness to the greater acceptability of cross-casting in comedy as opposed to tragedy. What we learn from Mark Rylance's cross-cast performances at the New Globe Theatre in London is that a highly skilled actor performing in a first-rate production *can* create an environment in which a modern device is experienced as (something approaching) a much older convention. We also learn that such an effect is never guaranteed.

As it did during the reign of Louis XIV, the practice of cross-casting continues to elicit divergent responses from theatre audiences and individual theatregoers. Seventeenth-century France grappled with the woman question at a very basic level, asking "what is a woman?" and "should women be permitted to perform in public?" and "should men be permitted to perform female roles?" We in the twenty-first

Figure C.1   **Mark Rylance playing Olivia in *Twelfth Night* (2002).**

Source: Shakespeare's Globe Theatre, photograph by John Tramper.

century believe that we know the answers to those fundamental questions, but still find ourselves perturbed and/or fascinated by behavior that is perceived as cross-gendered. While it is perfectly routine and acceptable to see a modern western woman wearing trousers (on or off the stage), for instance, the same cannot be said about men wearing dresses or skirts—even a Scotsman in a kilt still causes eyebrows to be raised. Our theatrical conventions have, of course, become more open to the participation of women, and modern theatre enjoys an experimental wing that permits almost anything in its performances. But mainstream audiences continue to be troubled by cross-casting, be it in the form of a modern device (e.g., in experimental theatre) or in the form of a convention revived from an earlier period of theatre history (e.g., an all-male production of Shakespeare). If it is ironic that an "authentic" production of Shakespeare should resemble in some ways modern experimental theatre, it is also a measure of how much and how little things have changed since Elizabeth I or Louis XIV. In the theatre in which everything is created and everything is at some level an illusion, new conventions may be established and new devices employed, but the distinction between the two will ultimately always remain somewhat hazy. It is the essence of theatre—this tension between reality and illusion, mediated by performance, and the discomfort it can still sometimes produce—that is so perfectly captured by the cross-cast actor.

Notes

Introduction: Cross-Dressing and Cross-Casting

1. Dorothy Keyser, "Cross-Sexual Casting in Baroque Opera: Musical and Theatrical Conventions," *Opera Quarterly* 5:4 (Winter 1987–88): 46–57 (46).
2. All quotations from *Ecclesiazusae* are taken from David Barrett's translation, Penguin Classics, London: Penguin, 1978.
3. Jeffrey Henderson, "Older Women in Attic Old Comedy," *Transactions of the American Philological Association* 117 (1987): 105–29 (118).
4. "The Myth of Shakespeare's Squeaking Boy Actor—Or Who Played Cleopatra?" *Shakespeare Bulletin* 19: 2 (Spring 2001), consulted online.
5. See their edited volume, *En travesti: Women, Gender Subversion, Opera*, New York: Columbia University Press, 1995, 3, 5.
6. See *Republic*, Books 3 and 10.
7. In the seventeenth century, the concept of homosexuality as such did not exist. A man might choose to participate in acts of sodomy, but he was not considered to be a homosexual. Same-sex relations between women were even less clearly understood or defined. See Joseph Harris, *Hidden Agendas: Cross-Dressing in 17th-Century France*, Biblio 17: 156, Tübingen: Gunter Narr, 2005, 27–28.
8. Judith Butler, *Gender Trouble: Feminism and the Subversion of Identity*, New York and London: Routledge, 1990, 137.
9. *Vested Interests: Cross-Dressing and Cultural Anxiety*, London: Penguin, 1993.
10. See her book *The First English Actresses: Women and Drama 1660–1700*, Cambridge: Cambridge University Press, 1992.
11. The related topic of disguise plots (i.e., cross-dressing as opposed to cross-casting) during much the same period is the subject of Georges Forestier's monumental tome *Esthétique de l'identité dans le théâtre français (1550–1680)*, Geneva: Droz, 1988. See also John D. Lyons, *A Theatre of Disguise: Studies in French Baroque Drama (1630–1660)*, Columbia, SC: French Literature Publications Company, 1978, and Joseph Harris, *Hidden Agendas*.

12. The first major study of cross-casting in Shakespeare was W. Robertson Davies's speculative and gloriously opinionated *Shakespeare's Boy Actors*, London: Dent, 1939. This was followed by, among others, Michael Shapiro's *Gender in Play on the Shakespearean Stage: Boy Heroines and Female Pages*, Ann Arbor: University of Michigan Press, 1994, Stephen Orgel's *Impersonations: The Performance of Gender in Shakespeare's England*, Cambridge: Cambridge University Press, 1996, and Dympna Callaghan's *Shakespeare Without Women: Representing Gender and Race on the Renaissance Stage*, London and New York: Routledge, 2000.

Chapter I   Unattractive Women: Cross-Casting in Comedy

1. For an excellent study of attitudes toward cross-casting in England, see Laura Levine, *Men in Women's Clothing: Anti-Theatricality and Effeminization, 1579–1642*, Cambridge: Cambridge University Press, 1994.
2. See Henry Phillips, *The Theatre and its Critics in Seventeenth-Century France*, Oxford: Oxford University Press, 1980, 174.
3. Tertullian, *De Spectaculis*, trans. Pierre de Labriolle, Paris: 1937, 26. Cited in Phillips, *The Theatre and its Critics*, 177.
4. Ph. Vincent, *Traité des théâtres*, La Rochelle, 1647, 8. Cited in Phillips, *The Theatre and its Critics*, 202.
5. For an equally excellent study of the impact of the professional actress in England, see Elizabeth Howe, *The First English Actresses: Women and Drama 1660–1700*, Cambridge: Cambridge University Press, 1992.
6. See Lynette R. Muir, "Women on the Medieval Stage: The Evidence from France," *Medieval English Theatre* 7:2 (1985): 107–19. Documents dealing with Passion plays produced in Mons in 1501 and in nearby Valenciennes in 1547 include a small number of roles for "junes filles" (*young girls*), but none for married women. Elsewhere in France, married women did perform, for instance in a 1509 production in Romans of the *Trois Doms*, which included eleven women in its cast, nine of whom were married. In this instance, only one female role was taken by a man: that of Proserpina. Similarly, women performed in a 1526 production of the *Trois Martyrs* in Valence. Muir also gives details of the one recorded example of a women playing Mary in a Passion play, of an actress of unknown age playing the eponymous saint in a production at Metz of *St. Catherine* in 1468, and a woman playing in the *Vie de Sainte Barbe* in Nancy in the early sixteenth century.
7. The rise of the Italian actress as a permanent fixture coincided almost exactly with the birth and development of the *commedia dell'arte* tradition in the sixteenth century, and her presence constituted an integral part of the originality of this particular brand of theatre. See Rosamond Gilder, *Enter the Actress: The First Women in the Theatre*, Boston: Houghton Mifflin, 1931; New York: Theatre Arts Books, 1960, 57.

8. See Gilder, *Enter the Actress*, 56. Unfortunately, Gilder provides no reference for this quotation.

9. I return to the effects of the papal ban on female performers in my discussion of castrati in chapter V.

10. Gustave Attinger, *L'esprit de la commedia dell'arte dans le théâtre français*, Paris: Librairie théâtrale/Neuchatel: A la Baconnière, 1950, 98.

11. Bernard Jolibert, *La commedia dell'arte et son influence en France du XVIᵉ au XVIIIe siècle*, Paris and Montreal: Harmattan, 1999, 39.

12. *La piazza universale di tutte le professioni del mondo*, Venice: Somasco, 1585. Cited in French in Attinger, *L'esprit de la commedia dell'arte*, 45.

13. *Le Théâtre de l'Hôtel de Bourgogne*, 2 vols., Paris: Nizet, 1968–70, I: 26. Deierkauf-Holsboer writes the "Hôtel de Bourbon," but she must mean the Hôtel de Bourgogne. The French parliament, however, disapproved of the performance, doubtless owing in part to the appearance of women on stage.

14. Isaac Du Ryer, *Le Temps perdu*, Paris: Du Bray, 1610, 65–66.

15. Léopold Lacour, *Les premières actrices françaises*, Paris: Librairie Française, 1921, 9.

16. See M. Barras, *The Stage Controversy in France from Corneille to Rousseau*, New York: Publications of the Institute of French Studies, 1933.

17. *Maximes et réflexions sur la comédie*, reproduced in Urbain and Levesque (eds.), *L'Eglise et le théâtre*, Paris: Grasset, 1930, 167–279 (267–68).

18. *Sentiments de l'Eglise et des saints Pères*, Paris, 1694. Cited in Phillips, *The Theatre and its Critics*, 187.

19. J. de Voisin, *La Défense du traitté de Monseigneur le prince de Conti*, Paris, 1671, Lettre I, 477. Cited in Phillips, *The Theatre and its Critics*, 188.

20. Jan Clarke, "Women Theatre Professionals in 17th-Century France" in *Women in European Theatre*, ed. Elizabeth Woodrough, London: Intellect, 1995: 23–31 (23). See Mme du Noyer, *Lettres historiques et galantes*, I: 15, in P. Mélèse, *Le Théâtre et le public à Paris sous Louis XIV (1659–1715)*, Paris: Droz, 1934; Geneva, 1976, 176.

21. See P. Mélèse, *Le Théâtre et le public*, 174.

22. See *Le Théatre François*, ed. Georges Monval, Lyon: Guignard, 1674; Paris: Bonnassies, 1875.

23. J. de Courbeville, *La Critique du Théâtre Anglois, comparé au Théâtre d'Athènes, de Rome et de France, et l'Opinion des auteurs tant profanes que sacrez, touchant les Spectacles*, Paris, 1715, v. See M. Barras, *The Stage Controversy in France*, 144.

24. It should be noted that the principal female roles in these plays were performed by actresses; probably by Mlle Le Noir and Mlle Villiers who were then the leading actresses of Mondory's troupe (soon to be called the Troupe du Marais).

25. Henry Lyonnet, *Les "Premières" de P. Corneille*, Paris: Delagrave, 1923, 28.

26. Such was Alizon's close association with playing grotesque, elderly women, he even lent his stage name to a number of contemporary plays, including Discret's *Alizon* (1637).

27. See Barbara C. Bowen, *Les Caractéristiques essentielles de la farce française et leur survivance dans les années 1550–1620*, Illinois Studies in Language and Literature 53, Urbana: University of Illinois Press, 1964, 14, 51 and 111.

28. See G. J. Mallinson, *The Comedies of Corneille: Experiments in the Comic*, Manchester: Manchester University Press, 1984, 1–7 (3).

29. Neither does he comment on the shift from cross-casting to straight casting, even when he refers to Corneille's own discussion of this very transition (77). Similarly, Théodore Litman cites Corneille's words and fails to comment on either the fact or the implications of the cross-casting mentioned. See Théodore A. Litman, *Les comédies de Corneille*, Paris: Nizet, 1981, 93.

30. Louis Rivaille, *Les débuts de P. Corneille*, Paris: Boivin, 1936, 194.

31. Unfortunately, we only have Chapelle's side of the correspondence in which he writes of "le déplaisir que vous donnent les partialités de vos trois grandes actrices pour la distribution de vos roles" (*the displeasure you felt at the preferences of your three great actresses with regard to the distribution of your roles*). Cited in G. Michaut, *La Jeunesse de Molière*, Paris: Hachette, 1922, 182.

32. "Discours à Cliton sur les Observations du Cid," in *La Querelle du Cid*, ed. Armand Gasté, Paris: Weller, 1898; Geneva: Slatkine, 1970, 241–82 (265).

33. In addition to stimulating the introduction of new types of female roles in comedy, actresses also encouraged the development of tragedy—the theatrical genre for which the century is probably best known today. Tragedy was for obvious reasons considered a more respectable genre than its comic counterpart and therefore a more appropriate genre for women to perform. While it is clear that early French actresses did perform in comedies and even in vulgar farces, their professional ambition appears to have centred around tragic drama, as they sought to gain their reputation from performing the female roles of playwrights such as Corneille and, later, Racine.

34. See Roger W. Herzel, *The Original Casting of Molière's Plays*, Ann Arbor, MI: UMI Research Press, 1981, 21.

35. Quoted in Claude and François Parfaict, *Histoire du Théâtre François depuis son origine jusqu'à présent*, 15 vols., Paris, 1745–49; New York: B. Franklin, 1968, XII: 474 and in Herzel, *The Original Casting*, 12.

36. See Herzel, *The Original Casting*, 67–68 for a discussion of the first production of *George Dandin*. He concludes, after some debate, that Mme de Sotenville was premiered by Béjart (and not, as others have suggested, by Hubert).

37. As Herzel reminds us, the 1685 cast lists were drawn up in the Autumn of 1684 and offer "the ideal casting for each play," showing us "the primary possessor of each role" (3). He describes the Repertory as "a prospectus for plays to be performed at the Court" (22). See also Henry Carrington Lancaster, *Actors' Roles at the Comédie Française*

According to the Repertoire des Comedies françoises qui se peuuent joüer en 1685, Baltimore: John Hopkins Press, 1953, xv.

38. See Lancaster, *Actors' Roles*, 35 and 45. In the 1685 Repertory, the cast lists are divided into "Damoiselles" and "Hommes." Interestingly, cross-cast characters appear under the heading that corresponds to the sex of the actor rather than to that of the role.

39. Richard Parish, "*Molière en travesti*: Transvestite Acting in Molière" in *Molière*, ed. Stephen Bamforth, Nottingham French Studies 33:1, Nottingham: University of Nottingham, 1994, 53–58 (56). In addition to the four parts we have identified, Parish suggests that Lucette in *Pourceaugnac* was also premiered by a man and that the eponymous countess in *La Comtesse d'Escarbagnas* "rapidly joined the transvestite camp" (55), although he gives no supporting evidence for this.

40. René Bray, *Molière, homme de théâtre*, Paris: Mercure de France, 1954, 81.

41. His article was originally given as a paper at a conference in Nottingham, U.K. in December 1993. It was then that the discussion points emerged.

42. This is one of many such lines that spell out Tartuffe's hypocrisy and that, one imagines, may have been added during revisions after *Le Tartuffe* was banned from public performance in 1664.

43. Stephen Dock, *Costume and Fashion in the Plays of Jean-Baptiste Poquelin Molière: A Seventeenth-Century Perspective*, Geneva: Slatkine, 1992, 148.

44. In his edition of the play, Parish notes that the 1938 production of *Le Tartuffe* at the Théâtre Pigalle included for "the first recorded time since the seventeenth century, a Madame Pernelle played by a man," *Le Tartuffe: Ou l'imposteur*, Bristol: Bristol Classical Press, 1994, xxiv.

45. Dock writes (correctly) in his discussion of *George Dandin* that the role of Mme de Sotenville was premiered by Béjart, but confuses the issue somewhat in his conclusion where he writes of Hubert playing the role. See Dock, 208, 343 and 344.

46. *George Dandin* has sometimes been interpreted as a serious play owing to its apparently bitter ending and the unhappiness of Dandin's marriage. This, however, is to overlook both the joyful ballet with which the play (or rather, *comédie-ballet*) originally ended and the spirit of Molière's œuvre. There is no doubt that the cross-cast Mme de Sotenville is a highly comical figure.

47. H. Gaston Hall, *Molière's Le Bougeois gentilhomme: Context and Stagecraft*, Durham Modern Languages Series FM5, Durham: University of Durham, 1990, 61.

48. Roland Bruyelle, *Les personnages de la comédie de Molière*, Paris: René Debresse, 1946, 118.

49. See Claude Abraham, *On the Structure of Molière's Comédies-Ballets*, Biblio 17:19, Paris: PFSCL, 1984, "From *Comédie-ballet* to Carnaval [*sic*]": 41–94.

50. *Molière: Le Bourgeois gentilhomme*, Critical Guides to French Texts 92, London: Grant and Cutler, 1992, 52.
51. Roger Herzel, "Problems in the Original Casting of *Les Femmes Savantes*," in *Actes de New Orleans*, ed. Francis L. Lawrence, Biblio 17:5, Paris, PFSCL, 1982: 215–31 (224–26).
52. *Lettres familières* (1661), 139, cited in Joseph Harris, *Hidden Agendas*, 89.
53. "Des Femmes," 52, in *Œuvres completes*, ed. Julien Benda, Pléiade, Paris: Gallimard, 1951, 123.
54. As Parish notes, "the distinction between Philaminte and the other (less dominant) 'femmes savantes' was well served by her travesty," 58n.
55. Bray also suggests that Bélise might have been played by a man, although there is no evidence to support this claim.
56. Dock comments on Pierre Brissard's 1682 engraving of *Les Femmes Savantes* in which Philaminte appears as an attractive young woman (Dock, 319–20). I wonder if this is not a depiction of Armande and Henriette, rather than of Philaminte and Bélise?
57. The play was so popular that the authors shared a staggering 5,651 *livres* in receipts for its first performance run, which is, according to Lough, "the record" for professional writers. See John Lough, *Seventeenth-Century French Drama: The Background*, Oxford: Clarendon Press, 1979, 47.
58. Gustave Reynier, *Thomas Corneille: Sa vie et son théâtre*, Paris: Hachette, 1892; Geneva, Slatkine, 1970, 380n.

Chapter II   Boys Will Be Girls: Cross-Casting in School Drama

1. This chapter was published in an earlier, shorter form as "Cross-Casting and Women's Roles in School Drama," *Seventeenth Century French Studies* 26 (2004): 195–208. It is reproduced here with permission.
2. Cited in *Le théâtre et l'opéra vus par les gazetiers Robinet et Laurent (1670–1678)*, ed. William Brooks, Biblio 17: 78, Paris: PFSCL, 1993, 87.
3. See William H. McCabe, *An Introduction to the Jesuit Theater*, St. Louis, Missouri: Institute of Jesuit Sources, 1983, 64, and Ernest Boysse, *Le théâtre des Jésuites*, Paris, 1880; Geneva: Slatkine, 1970, 31.
4. Cited in L.-V. Gofflot, *Le théâtre au collège du moyen âge à nos jours*, Paris: Champion, 1907, 96–97.
5. In the Latin original "nec persona ulla muliebris vel habitus introducatur." See *Ratio Studiorum: Plan raisonné et institution des études dans la Compagnie de Jésus*, ed. Adrien Demoustier, Dominique Julia et al., Paris: Belin, 1997.
6. *Responsa ad postulata congr. prov.* (Acta congr. Prov. 1599). Henri Fouqueray, *Histoire de la Compagnie de Jésus en France des origines à la suppression (1528–1762)*, 5 vols., Paris: Picard, 1910–25, II: 717.

7. All references to Jesuit repertoire, unless otherwise stated, are to productions at Louis-le-Grand/Collège de Clérmont.
8. *Opere edite e inedite in prosa ed in versi*, Venice, 1799–1801, XIX, 22 ff. Cited in McCabe, 191.
9. *Œuvres complètes*, ed. Georges Couton, 3 vols., Pléiade, Paris: Gallimard, 1980–87, III: 129.
10. Boysse provides a version of this scene in French, 171–76.
11. René Rapin, *Reflexions sur la poetique d'Aristote*, Paris: Muguet, 1674, 185.
12. Supporting this notion, Allardyce Nicoll has commented more recently that "the feminine in high tragedy . . . must either be made hard, approaching the masculine in quality, or else be relegated to a position of minor importance in the development of the plot." *An Introduction to Dramatic Theory*, London, 1923, 109. Cited in McCabe, 188. Interestingly, Nicoll nonetheless insists that a feminine element is important in tragic theatre and that "its absence mars the dramas of Marlowe" (108).
13. It is not, as Boysse rather patronizingly suggests "pour les mères, un plaisir suffisant, que de voir leurs fils dans des costumes d'empereurs ou de martyrs, gesticuler et déclamer agréablement sur le théâtre?" (*ample reward for the mothers to see their sons dressed as emperors and martyrs, performing and declaming well on stage?*). See Boysse, 89.
14. J. H. Phillips, "Le théâtre scolaire dans la querelle du théâtre au XVIIe siècle," *Revue d'histoire du théâtre* 35: 2 (1983): 190–221.
15. Ménestrier negotiates these difficulties with some deftness, writing:

> Si tout ce qui paroist sur les Theatres étoit de la nature de ces representations, il n'y auroit pas lieu de déclamer contre des actions où tout est grave & serieux, mais les mœurs ne sont pas toûjours aussi reglées, & souvent on a raison de deffendre le Théâtre, & les spectacles qu'on y represente, aux personnes qui font profession d'une vie un peu reguliere. J'écris pour ceux, qui bien loin d'en abuser s'en servent pour instruire la jeunesse & pour la former.
>
> *If everything that appeared in our theatres were like these performances, there would be no need to cry out against such activities in which everything is solemn and serious. But morals are not always regulated in this way and often there is good reason to prohibit people from entering the theatre and from attending its performances who choose to lead a somewhat steady life. I am writing for those who, far from abusing it, use the theatre to instruct the young and to help them in their growth.*

Des représentations en musique anciennes et modernes, Paris: Guignard, 1681, 4–5.
16. Voisin, *La Défense du traitté de Monseigneur le prince de Conti touchant la comédie et les spectacles*, 282. Cited in Phillips, *The Theatre and its Critics*, 205.

17. This is reproduced in Gofflot, 190–93n.
18. "Women on the Medieval Stage: The Evidence from France," *Medieval English Theatre* 7: 2 (1985): 107–19 (116–17).
19. Cited in Achille Taphanel, *Le Théâtre de Saint-Cyr (1689–1792) d'après des documents inédits*, Versailles: Cerf et fils; Paris: J. Baudry, 1876, 4.
20. This was the case for the boys at Jesuit schools too, although the question of the education of women was of course a good deal thornier than that of their male counterparts.
21. Fénelon, *Traité de l'éducation des filles*, Paris: Klincksieck, 1994, 81.
22. *Les Souvenirs de Madame de Caylus*, ed. Bernard Noël, Paris: Mercure de France, 1965, 95.
23. P. Manseau, *Mémoires*, cited in Anne Piéjus, *Le théâtre des demoiselles: Tragédie et musique à Saint-Cyr à la fin du grand siècle*, Paris: Société française de musicologie, 2000, 96–97.
24. Manseau, *Mémoires*, 111. Cited in Piéjus, 536.
25. F-V, ms. Rés. F.629, 92. Cited in Piéjus, 536.
26. F-Pn, ms.fr.23499, f.52. Cited in Piéjus, 536.
27. The girls in the audience dressed up in a more modest way, wearing special ribbons in their dormitory colors.
28. Interestingly, the 1689 privilege for the publication of *Esther* was made out not to Racine but to the Dames de Saint-Louis. The privilege for *Athalie*, on the other hand, was accorded to the author. See Jean Dubu, "Autour d'*Esther* et d'*Athalie*" in *La littérature et ses avatars*, ed. Yvonne Bellenger, Paris: Klincksieck, 1991: 241–48 (241).
29. P. Bardou, *Epitre sur la condamnation du théâtre*, reproduced in Urbain and Levesque (eds.), *L'Eglise et le théâtre*, Paris: Grasset, 1930: 279–84 (281).
30. *Œuvres*, III, 182. Cited in Jean Orcibal, *La Genèse d'Esther et d'Athalie*, Paris: Vrin, 1950, 45n.
31. *Correspondence de Quesnel*, ed. Le Roy, I: 129 and 123. Cited in Raymond Picard, *La Carrière de Jean Racine*, Paris: Gallimard, 1961, 423.
32. *Mémoires du Curé de Versailles, François Hébert, 1686–1704*, ed. G. Girard, Paris: Editions de France, 1927, 123. Cited in Picard, 425.
33. Mme de Maintenon's sexagenarian cousin, M. de Villette, apparently married one of the actresses who had performed in *Esther*—see Madame de Maintenon, *Comment la sagesse vient aux filles*, ed. Pierre-E. Leroy and Marcel Loyau, Paris: Bartillat, 1998, 24.
34. *Mémoires du Curé de Versailles*, 123. Cited in Picard, 425.
35. To Nicaise, ed. Le Roy, I: 123–24; see also his letter of July 1689 to P. du Breuil, I: 129. Cited in Orcibal, 45n. Also cited in Phillips, "Le théâtre scolaire," 210.
36. Mme de Maintenon, 423. Cited in Phillips, "Le théâtre scolaire," 207.
37. *Mémoires du Curé de Versailles*, 123. Cited in Phillips, "Le théâtre scolaire," 208.

38. *L'Instruction chrétienne*, 21. Cited in Phillips, *The Theatre and its Critics*, 113.
39. *Mémoires du Curé de Versailles*, 123. Cited in Picard, 424.
40. *Mémoires du Curé de Versailles*, 123. Cited in Phillips "Le théâtre scolaire," 208.
41. *Like Néron in Racine's* Britannicus (1669), they are moved by the sight of youthful innocence combined with feminine beauty.
42. *Mémoires et lettres de Madame de Maintenon*, ed. Voltaire, Maestricht: Dufour and Roux, 1778, VIII: 87.
43. The elimination of elaborate costumes is very important, but it is not strictly true to claim, as Jean Dubu has done, that without them "le problème du travesti ne se posait pas" (*the problem of transvestism was no longer an issue*) ("Autour d'*Esther* et d'*Athalie*," 245), for even in their school uniforms, the students playing male roles remained cross-cast, if not cross-dressed.
44. P. Manseau, *Mémoires*, 157. Cited in Piéjus, 551.
45. Manseau, *Mémoires*, 193 (March, 1692). Cited in Picard, 428.
46. Mme de Maintenon's private view of the male sex as expressed here is particularly striking when one considers that she was the morganatic wife of Louis XIV, the one man in the kingdom who was supposed, in theory, to be beyond the type of behavior she is alluding to.

Chapter III Female Roles in Court Ballet I: Men Playing Women

1. See "*Le Balet Comique*" by Balthazar de Beaujoyeulx, 1581: A Facsimile with an Introduction, ed. Margaret M. McGowan, Medieval and Renaissance texts and studies 6, New York: Center for Medieval and Early Renaissance Studies, 1982.
2. Mark Franko, *Dance as Text: Ideologies of the Baroque Body*, Cambridge: Cambridge University Press, 1993, 1.
3. *Des ballets anciens et modernes selon les règles du théâtre*, Paris: Guignard, 1682, 55.
4. For an investigation of French ballet before Louis XIV, see Margaret M. McGowan's *L'Art du Ballet de cour en France, 1581–1643*, Paris: CNRS, 1963.
5. See Marie-Françoise Christout, *Le Ballet de Cour de Louis XIV: 1643–1672*, Vie Musicale en France sous les Rois Bourbons 12, Paris: Picard, 1967, 17 and Charles I. Silin, *Benserade and his* Ballets de Cour, John Hopkins Studies in Romance Literatures and Languages, Extra volume XV, Baltimore, Maryland: John Hopkins Press, 1940, 203n.
6. Cross-cast singing roles in opera under Louis XIV are examined in chapter V.

7. Exceptionally, this same piece includes an instance of a male role being sung by a female singer: Mlle Bergerotti sang the part of the "gallant" in the closing entry. See *Les Contemporains de Molière*, ed. Victor Fournel, 3 vols., Paris: Firmin Didot Frères, 1863–75; repr. Geneva; Slatkine, 1967, II: 447.

8. "Herakles: The super-male and the feminine" in *Before Sexuality: The Construction of Erotic Experience in the Ancient Greek World*, ed. David M. Halperin, John J. Winkler, and Froma I. Zeitlin, Princeton: Princeton University Press, 1990, 21–52 (29).

9. Unless otherwise stated, all quotations of ballet verses are from Isaac Benserade, *Ballets pour Louis XIV*, ed. Marie-Claude Canova-Green, 2 vols., Toulouse: Société de Littératures Classiques, 1997. I retain the spelling given in this edition throughout.

10. I discuss this issue in some length in my article, "The Gendering of the Court Ballet Audience: Cross-Casting and the Emergence of the Female Ballet Dancer," *Seventeenth-Century French Studies* 24 (2002): 127–34.

11. See also my article "Conflicting Signals: Images of Louis XIV in Benserade's Ballets" in *Culture and Conflict in Seventeenth-Century France and Ireland*, ed. Sarah Alyn Stacey and Véronique Desnain, Dublin: Four Courts Press, 2004, 227–41.

12. She is reported to have said, "I know I have the body of a weak and feeble woman, but I have the heart and stomach of a king, and a king of England too."

13. See also my article "Conflicting Signals: Images of Louis XIV in Benserade's Ballets."

14. Much of this discussion of his appearance as a girl in the *Ballet des Fêtes de Bacchus* comes from my article "Cross-Casting in French Court Ballet: Monstrous Aberration or Theatrical Convention?" *Romance Studies* 21: 3 (November 2003): 157–68 (165–66). Reproduced here with permission.

15. Abbé de Choisy, *Mémoires pour servir à l'histoire de Louis XIV*, ed. G. Mongrédien, Paris: Mercure de France, 1966, 185.

16. From birth, both boys and girls wore dresses. Boys were normally "breeched" between the ages of five and seven, whereas Philippe d'Orléans continued wearing dresses until the age of twelve or thirteen.

17. For an interesting (though borderline homophobic) account of Monsieur's homosexuality, see Nancy Nichols Barker, *Brother to the Sun King: Philippe, Duke of Orléans*, Baltimore and London: John Hopkins University Press, 1989, 56–65.

18. Victor Fournel, II: 444.

19. See my article "Cross-Casting in French Court Ballet," 165.

Chapter IV Female Roles in
Court Ballet II: Women Playing Women

1. As Canova-Green has noted, the first appearance of a female professional in French court ballet was, strictly speaking, that of the child
   dancer, "La petite Molier," in the *Ballet des Fêtes de Bacchus* (1651) (see
   I: 67n). Rather confusingly, Canova-Green also states that the *Ballet de
   la Raillerie* (1659) was the first court ballet to include female professionals
   (see I: 26n). Undoubtedly, she means *adult* female professionals, but
   their appearance had, in any case, been preceded one year earlier by
   Mlle Verpré's performance in the *Ballet d'Alcidiane*.

2. We remember that the roles that professional actresses often refused
   to perform were those that were for old women—see chapter I.

3. The one exception appears to be Mlle Verpré's appearance in the
   king's suite in the *Ballet de l'Impatience* (1661), which I discuss below.

4. As in chapter III, unless otherwise stated, all quotations of ballet
   verses are from Isaac Benserade, *Ballets pour Louis XIV*, ed. Marie-Claude
   Canova-Green, 2 vols., Toulouse: Société de Littératures Classiques,
   1997. I retain the spelling given in this edition throughout.

5. *Hercule amoureux* (or *Ercole amante*) was an Italian opera with music by
   Cavalli, interspersed with French ballet entries—see also chapter V.

6. On the subject of praising the king, see also my article "The
   Problem of Praise and the First Prologue to *Le Malade imaginaire*" in
   Seventeenth-Century French Studies 23 (2001): 139–49.

7. Having stated that he will combine the ladies' praises, Benserade nevertheless goes on to write a stanza on each one of them, employing his
   customary references to their adopted roles as well as to their good
   looks, youth, and the powerful effect of the gaze.

8. Professional ballet featured in the new genre of French opera at the
   hands of Jean-Baptiste Lully, who took over the Académie Royale de
   Musique in 1672 (see chapter V).

Chapter V Cross-Casting and
Gender Ambiguity in Opera

1. Given the Catholic Church's inescapable—and uncomfortable—association with the castrato, it is perhaps fitting that long after the castrato
   had disappeared from the operatic stage he continued to perform in
   Italian churches. The last known castrato was Alessandro Moreschi
   (1858–1922) of the Sistine Chapel, whose voice features on the only
   known recordings of such a singer: in 1902 and 1904 Moreschi made
   recordings for the Gramophone and Typewriter Company.

2. Laurence Senelick, *The Changing Room: Sex, Drag and Theatre*, London:
   Routledge, 2000, 193–94.

3. See Roger Freitas, "*Un atto d'ingegno:* A Castrato in the Seventeenth Century," Unpublished Ph.D. dissertation, Yale University (1998), 18–21.

4. Wendy Heller, *Emblems of Eloquence: Opera and Women's Voices in Seventeenth-Century Venice*, Berkeley, Los Angeles, and London: University of California Press, 2003, 18.

5. In Pietro Ziani's *La Semiramide* (1670), for example, the principal male and female protagonists, Nino and Semiramide, are dressed in each other's clothing during the greater part of the opera. See Heller's chapter on "Semiramide and Musical Transvestism" in *Emblems of Eloquence*: 220–62 for an interesting analysis of the musical implications of this phenomenon.

6. Some popes had a more relaxed attitude toward the appearance of women on stage than others. See Patrick Barbier, *Histoire des castrats*, Paris: Bernard Grasset, 1989, 136–38.

7. These include Carlo Broschi (1705–82), known as Farinelli, who became famous again in the late–twentieth century thanks to Gérard Corbiau's excellent film, *Farinelli* (1994).

8. The second male role might also be taken by a castrato with tenors singing the parts of kings and old men. See John Rosselli's entry on "Castrato" in *The New Grove Dictionary of Opera*, ed. Stanley Sadie, 4 vols., London: Macmillan, 1992, 1: 766–68.

9. See Enid R. Peschel and Richard E. Peschel, "Medicine and Music: The Castrati in Opera," *Opera Quarterly* 4: 4 (Winter 1986/87): 21–38 (27), and, by the same authors, "Medical Insights into the Castrati in Opera," *American Scientist* (November–December 1987): 578–83.

10. Charles de Brosses, *Lettre d'Italie sur les spectacles et la musique*, Paris: La Flûte de Pan, 1980, 35, my emphasis. Later in his letter he describes a castrato whom he names "Porporino" (a student of the composer and singing teacher, Nicolas Porpora) as being "joli comme la plus jolie fille" (*as pretty as the prettiest girl*) (39)—words that are very similar to the Abbé Choisy's description of Phillipe d'Orléans (see chapter III).

11. Charles d'Ancillon, *Traité des Eunuques*, n.p.: 1707, 2.

12. Cited in Peschel and Peschel, "Medicine and Music," 34.

13. Dympna Callaghan, *Shakespeare Without Women: Representing Gender and Race on the Renaissance Stage*, London: Routledge, 2000, 71.

14. Thomas McGeary, " 'Warbling Eunuchs': Opera, Gender, and Sexuality on the London Stage, 1705–1742," *Restoration and 18th Century Theatre Research*, second series 7: 1 (Summer 1992): 1–22 (15).

15. Johann Wolfgang von Goethe, "Women's Parts Played by Men in the Roman Theater," trans. by Isa Ragusa, in *Crossing the Stage: Controversies on Cross-Dressing*, ed. Lesley Ferris, London: Routledge, 1993: 47–51 (49–50).

16. *Opera in Seventeenth-Century Venice: The Creation of a Genre*, Berkeley: University of California Press, 1991, 119n.

17. Lodovico Antonio Muratori, *On Perfect Italian Poetry* (1706); cited in Enrico Fubini, *Music and Culture in Eighteenth-Century Europe: A Source Book*, ed. Bonnie J. Blackburn, Chicago and London, 1994, 41.

18. Italian castrati were also a common object of satire in England. See Jill Campbell, " 'When Men Women turn': Gender reversals in Fielding's plays," in *Crossing the Stage: Controversies on Cross-Dressing*, ed. Lesley Ferris, London: Routledge, 1993: 58–79. As was the case with the cross-cast boys of Renaissance England (see chapter I), one of the principal preoccupations of English anticastrato discourse was the danger of effeminization. One of the most notorious detractors of Italian opera in Britain was John Dennis, author of an *Essay on the Opera's after the Italian Manner . . . with some Reflections on the Damage which they may bring to the Publick* (1706). Italian opera was thought to be effeminizing owing to its musical language, its association with luxury and decadence, and to its dependence on castrati. Moreover, it was foreign, and other, and thus "[struck] at the very heart of British Publick Spirit" (Thomas McGeary, 5).

19. J. Benjamin de Laborde, *Essai sur la musique ancienne et moderne*, Paris: 1780, 508. Cited in Barbier, 195.

20. Alexandre Maral, *La Chapelle Royale de Versailles sous Louis XIV: Cérémonial, liturgie et musique*, Sprimont: Mardaga, 2002, 76n.

21. Cited in Marcelle Benoît, *Versailles et les musiciens du Roi, 1661–1733*, Paris: Picard, 1971, 186.

22. An exception was a man named Blaise Berthod (or Bertaut) from Lyon, who was known as "Berthod le châtré." See Benoît, *Versailles et les musiciens du Roi*, 187.

23. See Rosselli, *Singers of Italian Opera*, Cambridge: Cambridge University Press, 1992, 47 and Benoît, 269–70, 324–29 and 348–50.

24. Freitas notes on the other hand that Atto Melani's singing had delighted Anne of Austria so much that she did not want him to leave after the performances of *Orfeo* were over and persuaded him to spend another two years in France. See Freitas, "*Un atto d'ingegno*," 63–64.

25. Letter of January 26, 1657. Cited in both Italian and English in Freitas, 221.

26. See Freitas, 227 and Lorenzo Bianconi, *Music in the Seventeenth Century*, trans. David Bryant, Cambridge: Cambridge University Press, 1987, 239.

27. Rosselli, *Singers of Italian Opera*, 36 (and, following him, Senelick) wrongly states that Don Filippo Melani played the part of a woman disguised as a man in Cavalli's *Ercole Amante* in 1660. Filippo Melani did play such a role in 1660, but it was in Cavalli's *Serse*.

28. Letter of March 1, 1660. Cited in Freitas, 225–26.

29. See Henry Prunières, *L'Opéra italien en France avant Lulli*, Paris: Champion, 1913, 278 and Norman Demuth, *French Opera: Its Development to the Revolution*, Sussex: Artemis, 1963, 86–87 for details of the cast.

30. Maugars, *Réponse faite à un curieux sur le sentiment de la musique d'Italie*, 1639; Paris: Claudin, 1865, 35. Cited in Barbier, 107. He was, incidentally, writing about two of the great castrati, Loreto Vittori and Marc-Antonio Pasqualini.

31. François Raguenet, *Parallèle des Italiens et des Français en ce qui regarde la musique et les operas*, Paris: Jean Moreau, 1702; Geneva: Minkoff, 1976, 13.

32. Tallemant des Réaux, *Historiettes*, 2 vols., Pléiade, Paris: Gallimard, 1960–61, II: 60.

33. Lettre à l'Archevesque de Turin. *Oeuvres de poésie*, 1661, 287. Cited in Prunières, *L'Opéra Italian*, 267.

34. Despite Lully's aversion to castrati and his deliberate decision to exclude them from his new form of French opera, the *tragédie en musique*, the resident castrati at Versailles were occasionally called upon to participate in the choruses of musical productions *at court*. According to Sawkins, the castrato Antonio Bagniera (born in Switzerland, and castrated in France, much to the horror of Louis XIV) performed in the chorus for the court performance(s) of Lully's *Alceste* in 1677. There is no reason to think that any castrati ever performed at the Paris Opéra, however, where the *dessus* parts were usually taken by women (and occasionally by boys or falsettists). Although the participation of castrati at court did not translate to the town productions of Lully's (and subsequent) operas, Lionel Sawkins observes an interesting phenomenon whereby "the presence of the falsetti and castrati in the choruses of opera performances at court resulted in fewer female sopranos being employed than at the Paris Opéra." See Sawkins, "For and Against the Order of Nature: Who Sang the Soprano?" *Early Music* 15: 3 (August 1987): 315–24.

35. Claude-François Ménestrier, *Des représentations en musique anciennes et modernes*, Paris: Guignard, 1681, 236.

36. These were *Atys*, *Psyché* (Cupid), *Bellérophon*, *Persée*, *Phaëton*, *Amadis*, *Armide* (Renaud), and *Acis et Galatée*.

37. James R. Anthony, *French Baroque Music, from Beaujoyeulx to Rameau*, revised and expanded edition, Oregon: Amadeus Press, 1997, 105–06.

38. Lully's *tragédie en musique* is well-known for having displayed a strong emphasis on dance, a tradition inherited from the *ballet de cour* and from the *comédie-ballet* (two genres for which Lully had previously composed music). Since I have already written at length about cross-cast dancing roles in the *ballet de cour* in chapters III and IV, here I shall focus uniquely on the small number of cross-cast singing roles in Lully's operas.

39. Carl B. Schmidt, *The livrets of Jean-Baptiste Lully's* tragédies-lyriques: *A catalogue raisonné*, New York: Performers' Editions, 1995.
40. Quinault and Lully were criticized for their inclusion of comic elements in their early *tragédies en musique*, and it was largely in response to those criticisms that they came to eliminate all such episodes from their later works.
41. Buford Norman, *Touched by the Graces: The Libretti of Philippe Quinault in the Context of French Classicism*, Birmingham, Alabama: Summa, 2001, 89.
42. All references to the *livrets* of Lully-Quinualt's *tragédies en musique* are to Philippe Quinault, *Livrets d'opéra*, ed. Buford Norman, 2 vols., Toulouse: Littératures Classiques, 1999.
43. Lully-Quinault, *Alceste*, La Grande Ecurie et la Chambre du Roy et l'Ensemble Vocal Sagittarius, dir. Jean-Claude Malgoire (Montaigne/ Auvidis, 1992/1994, 3CD).
44. Benoît Bolduc, "From Marvel to Camp: Medusa for the Twenty-First Century," *Journal of Seventeenth-Century Music* 10: 1 (2005): par. 5.3; http://www.sscm-jscm.org/jscm/v10/no1/bolduc.html.
45. Lully-Quinault, *Persée*, Maîtrise du Centre de Musique Baroque de Versailles, les Chantres de la Chapelle et Les Talens Lyriques, dir. Christophe Rousset (Astrée, 2001, 3CD).
46. *Now* 20: 9 (November 2–8, 2000).
47. *Eye Weekly* (November 2, 2000).
48. Lully-Quinault, *Phaéton*, Ensemble vocal Sagittarius et Les Musiciens du Louvre, dir. Marc Minkowski (Erato, 1994, 2CD).
49. Schmidt, 414 and Lully-Quinault, *Armide*, Chœur et Orchestre du Collegium Vocale et de la Chapelle Royale, dir. Philippe Herrewegghe (Harmonia Mundi, 1993, 2CD).

BIBLIOGRAPHY

Early Sources (Pre-1800)

Ancillon, Charles d'. *Traité des Eunuques*. n.p., 1707.

Aristophanes. *Ecclesiazusae*. Translated as *The Assemblywomen* by David Barrett. Penguin Classics. London: Penguin, 1978.

Aristophanes. *Plutus*. Translated as *Wealth* by Alan H. Sommerstein. Penguin Classics. London: Penguin, 1978.

Bardou, P. *Epistre sur la condamnation du théâtre, A Monsieur Racine*. Paris and Poitier, 1694. Rpt. in *L'Eglise et le théatre*, ed. Ch. Urbain and E. Levesque. Paris: Grasset, 1930: 279–84.

Beaujoyeulx, Balthazar de. *Le Balet Comique*, ed. Margaret M. McGowan. Medieval and Renaissance texts and studies 6. New York: Center for Medieval and Early Renaissance Studies, 1982.

Benserade, Isaac. *Ballets pour Louis XIV*, ed. Marie-Claude Canova-Green, 2 vols. Toulouse: Société de Littératures Classiques, 1997.

Bossuet, Jacques-Bénigne. *Maximes et réflexions sur la comédie*. Paris: 1694. Rpt. in *L'Eglise et le théatre*, ed. Ch. Urbain and E. Levesque. Paris: Grasset, 1930: 167–276.

Boyer, Claude. *Jephté*. Paris: Coignard, 1692.

Brosses, Charles de. *Lettre d'Italie sur les spectacles et la musique*. Paris: La Flûte de Pan, 1980.

Caffaro, Père. *Lettre d'un théologien illustre* (1694). Rpt. in *L'Eglise et le théatre*, ed. Ch. Urbain and E. Levesque. Paris: Grasset, 1930: 67–119.

Caylus, Madame de. *Les Souvenirs de Madame de Caylus*, ed. Bernard Noël. Paris: Mercure de France, 1965.

Chappuzeau, Samuel. *Le Théatre François*, ed. Georges Monval. Lyon: Guignard, 1674; Paris: Bonnassies, 1875.

Choisy, Abbé de. *Mémoires pour servir à l'histoire de Louis XIV*, ed. G. Mongrédien. Paris: Mercure de France, 1966.

Corneille, Pierre. *Œuvres completes*, ed. Georges Couton. 3 vols. Pléiade, Paris: Gallimard, 1980–87.

Corneille, Thomas. *Le Festin de Pierre, Thomas Corneille*, ed. Alain Niderst. Paris: Champion, 2000.

De Visé, Donneau and Thomas Corneille. *La Devineresse*, ed. P. J. Yarrow. Textes Littéraires, 4. Exeter: University of Exeter Press, 1971.

Discret, L. C. *Alizon*. Paris: Guignard, 1637.

Du Ryer, Isaac. *Le Temps perdu*. Paris: Du Bray, 1610.

Fénelon, François de Salignac de la Mothe. *Traité de l'éducation des filles*. Paris: Klincksieck, 1994.

Fournel, Victor (ed.). *Les Contemporains de Molière, recueil de comédies rares ou peu connues, jouées de 1650 à 1680, avec l'histoire de chaque théâtre*. 3 vols. Paris: Firmin Didot, 1863–75; Geneva: Slatkine, 1967.

Gasté, Armand (ed.) *La Querelle du Cid*. Paris: Weller, 1898; Geneva: Slatkine, 1970.

Goethe, Johann Wolfgang von. "Women's Parts Played by Men in the Roman Theater." Trans. Isa Ragusa, in *Crossing the Stage: Controversies on Cross-Dressing*, ed. Lesley Ferris. London: Routledge, 1993: 47–57.

La Bruyère. *Œuvres completes*, ed. Julien Benda. Pléiade, Paris: Gallimard, 1951.

Lauze, F. De. *Apologie de la danse by F. De Lauze 1623: A Treatise of Instruction in Dancing and Deportment Given in the Original French*, ed. Joan Wildeblood. London: Frederick Muller, 1952.

Loret. *La Muze historique, ou Receuil des lettres en vers à son Altesse Mademoiselle de Longueville*, ed. J. Ravenel and E. D. V. de la Pelouze. 4 vols. Paris: P. Jannet, 1857–78.

Maintenon, Madame de. *Mémoires et lettres de Madame de Maintenon*, ed. Voltaire. Maestricht: Dufour and Roux, 1778.

———. *Comment la sagesse vient aux filles*, ed. Pierre-E. Leroy and Marcel Loyau. Paris: Bartillat, 1998.

Ménestrier, Claude-François. *Des représentations en musique anciennes et modernes*. Paris: Guignard, 1681; Geneva: Minkoff, 1972.

———. *Des ballets anciens et modernes selon les règles du théâtre*. Paris: Guignard, 1682; Geneva: Minkoff, 1972.

Molière. *Œuvres complètes*, ed. Georges Couton. 2 vols. Pléiade, Paris: Gallimard, 1971.

———. *Le Tartuffe, ou l'imposteur*, ed. Richard Parish. Bristol: Bristol Classical Press, 1994.

Parfaict, Claude and François. *Histoire du Théâtre François depuis son origine jusqu'à present*. 15 vols. Paris, 1745–49; New York: B. Franklin, 1968.

Prynne, William. *Histrio-Mastix: The Player's Scourge or Actor's Tragedy*. New York: Garland Publishing, 1974.

Pure, Michel abbé de. *Idée des spectacles anciens et nouveaux*. Paris: Brunet, 1668.

Quinault, Philippe. *Livrets d'opéra*, ed. Buford Norman. 2 vols. Toulouse: Littératures Classiques, 1999.

Racine, Jean. *Œuvres complètes I: Théâtre-poésie*, ed. Georges Forestier. Pléiade, Paris: Gallimard, 1999.

Raguenet, François. *Parallèle des Italiens et des Français en ce qui regarde la musique et les operas*. Paris: Jean Moreau, 1702; Geneva: Minkoff, 1976.

Rapin, René. *Reflexions sur la poetique d'Aristote et sur les ouvrages des poetes anciens et modernes.* Paris: Muguet, 1674.

Ratio Studiorum: Plan raisonné et institution des études dans la Compagnie de Jésus, ed. Adrien Demoustier, Dominique Julia et al. Paris: Belin, 1997.

Scudéry, Georges de. *La Comédie des comédiens,* ed. J. Crow. Exeter: University of Exeter Press, 1975.

Sévigné, Mme de. *Correspondence,* ed. Roger Duchêne. 3 vols. Pléiade, Paris: Gallimard, 1972–78.

Tallemant des Réaux. *Historiettes,* ed. Antoine Adam. 2 vols. Pléiade, Paris: Gallimard, 1960–61.

Modern Sources

Abraham, Claude. *On the Structure of Molière's Comédies-Ballets.* Biblio 17: 19. Paris: PFSCL, 1984.

Alm, Irene. "Winged Feet and Mute Eloquence: Dance in Seventeenth-Century Venetian Opera." *Cambridge Opera Journal* 15: 3 (November 2003): 216–80.

Anthony, James R. *French Baroque Music, from Beaujoyeulx to Rameau.* Revised and expanded edition. Portland, Oregon: Amadeus Press, 1997.

Apostolidès, Jean-Marie. *Le roi-machine: Spectacle et politique au temps de Louis XIV.* Paris: Minuit, 1981.

Astier, Régine. "Louis XIV, 'Premier Danseur,' " in *Sun King: The Ascendancy of French Culture during the Reign of Louis XIV,* ed. David Lee Rubin. Washington: Folger Shakespeare Library; London & Toronto: Associated University Presses, 1992: 73–102.

Attinger, Gustave. *L'esprit de la commedia dell'arte dans le théâtre français.* Paris: Librairie théâtrale/Neuchatel: A la Baconnière, 1950.

Barbier, Patrick. *Histoire des castrats.* Paris: Bernard Grasset, 1989.

Barish, Jonas. *The Antitheatrical Prejudice.* Berkeley: University of California Press, 1981.

Barker, Nancy Nichols. *Brother to the Sun King: Philippe, Duke of Orléans.* Baltimore and London: John Hopkins University Press, 1989.

Barras, M. *The Stage Controversy in France from Corneille to Rousseau.* New York: Publications of the Institute of French Studies, 1933.

Beaussant, Philippe. *Lully, ou le Musicien du Soleil.* Paris: Gallimard, 1992.

———. *Louis XIV: Artiste.* Paris: Payot, 1999.

Benoît, Marcelle. *Versailles et les musiciens du Roi, 1661–1733.* Paris: Picard, 1971.

Bianconi, Lorenzo. *Music in the Seventeenth Century.* Trans. David Bryant. Cambridge: Cambridge University Press, 1987.

Blackmer, Corinne E., and Patricia Juliana Smith (eds.). *En Travesti: Women, Gender Subversion, Opera.* New York: Columbia University Press, 1995.

Bolduc, Benoît. "From Marvel to Camp: Medusa for the Twenty-First Century." *Journal of Seventeenth-Century Music* 10: 1 (2005), http://www.sscm-jscm.org/jscm/

Bowen, Barbara C. *Les Caractéristiques essentielles de la farce française et leur survivance dans les années 1550–1620*. Illinois Studies in Language and Literature, 53. Urbana: University of Illinois Press, 1964.

Boysse, Ernest. *Le théâtre des Jésuites*. Paris: Vaton, 1880; Geneva: Slatkine, 1970.

Bray, René. *Molière, homme de théâtre*. Paris: Mercure de France, 1954.

Brooks, William (ed.). *Le théâtre et l'opéra vus par les gazetiers Robinet et Laurent (1670–1678)*. Biblio 17: 78, Paris: PFSCL, 1993.

Bruyelle, Roland. *Les personnages de la comédie de Molière*. Paris: René Debresse, 1946.

Bruzzi, Stella. *Undressing Cinema: Clothing and Identity in the Movies*. London and New York: Routledge, 1997.

Butler, Judith. *Gender Trouble: Feminism and the Subversion of Identity*. London and New York: Routledge, 1990.

Callaghan, Dympna. *Shakespeare Without Women: Representing Gender and Race on the Renaissance Stage*. London and New York: Routledge, 2000.

Campbell, Jill. " 'When Men Women turn': Gender reversals in Fielding's plays," in *Crossing the Stage: Controversies on Cross-Dressing*, ed. Lesley Ferris. London: Routledge, 1993: 58–79.

Canova-Green, Marie-Claude. "La parole écrite et chantée dans le ballet de cour," in *La Rochefoucauld, Mithridate, Frères et sœurs, Les Muses sœurs*, ed. Claire Carlin. Biblio 17: 111. Tübingen: Gunter Narr, 1998: 319–27.

— — —. "Ballet et comédie-ballet sous Louis XIV ou l'illusion de la fête." *Papers on French Seventeenth-Century Literature* 17: 32 (1990): 253–62.

Cervantes, Xavier. " 'Tuneful Monsters': Les Castrats et le Public Lyrique Londonien au début du XVIIIe Siècle." *Bulletin de la Société d'Etudes Anglo-Américaines des XVIIe et XVIIIe Siècles* 39 (1994): 227–54.

Christout, Marie-Françoise. *Le Ballet de cour de Louis XIV, 1643–1672*. La Vie Musicale en France sous les Rois Bourbons, 12. Paris: Picard, 1967.

Clarke, Jan. "Women Theatre Professionals in 17th-Century France," in *Women in European Theatre*, ed. Elizabeth Woodrough. London: Intellect, 1995: 23–31.

— — —. "Female Cross-Dressing on the Paris Stage, 1673–1715." *Forum for Modern Language Studies* 35: 3 (1999): 238–50.

Cohen, Sarah R. "Masquerade as Mode in the French Fashion Print," in *The Clothes That Wear Us: Essays on Dressing and Transgressing in Eighteenth-Century Culture*, ed. Jessica Munns and Penny Richards. Newark: University of Delaware Press and London: Associated University Presses, 1999: 174–207.

— — —. *Art, Dance, and the Body in French Culture of the Ancien Régime*. Cambridge: Cambridge University Press, 2000.

Davies, W. Robertson. *Shakespeare's Boy Actors*. London: Dent, 1939.

Deierkauf-Holsboer, S. Wilma. *Le Théâtre du Marais*. 2 vols. Paris: Nizet, 1954–58.

— — —. *Le Théâtre de l'Hôtel de Bourgogne*. 2 vols. Paris: Nizet, 1968–70.

Delcourt, Marie. *Hermaphrodite: Mythes et rites de la Bisexualité dans l'Antiquité classique*. Paris: Presses Universitaires de France, 1958.

Demoris, René. "Le corps royal et l'imaginaire au XVII⁰ siècle: *Le Portrait du Roy* par Félibien." *Revue des sciences humaines* 172 (1978): 9–30.

Demuth, Norman. *French Opera: Its Development to the Revolution.* Sussex: Artemis, 1963.

Doane, Mary Ann. "Film and the Masquerade: Theorizing the Female Spectator," in *The Sexual Subject: A "Screen" Reader in Sexuality.* London and New York: Routledge, 1992: 227–43.

Dock, Stephen Varick. *Costume and Fashion in the plays of Jean-Baptiste Poquelin Molière: A Seventeenth-Century Perspective.* Geneva: Slatkine, 1992.

Dolan, Jill. *The Feminist Spectator as Critic.* Ann Arbor: University of Michigan, 1991.

Dubu, Jean. "Autour d'*Esther* et d'*Athalie*," in *La littérature et ses avatars*, ed. Yvonne Bellenger. Paris: Klincksieck, 1991: 241–48.

Duhamal, Jean-Marie. "La grande vogue des castrats." *L'Histoire* 93 (October 1986): 28–36.

Dusinberre, Juliet. "Squeaking Cleopatras: Gender and Performance in *Antony and Cleopatra*," in *Shakespeare, Theory, and Performance*, ed. James C. Bulman. London and New York: Routledge, 1996: 46–67.

Ferrier-Caverivière, Nicole. *L'image de Louis XIV dans la littérature française de 1660 à 1715.* Paris: Presses Universitaires de France, 1981.

Ferris, Lesley (ed.) *Crossing the Stage: Controversies on Cross-Dressing.* London and New York: Routledge, 1993.

Forestier, Georges. *Esthétique de l'identité dans le théâtre français (1550–1680).* Geneva: Droz, 1988.

Fouqueray, Henri. *Histoire de la Compagnie de Jésus en France des origines à la suppression (1528–1762).* 5 vols. Paris: Picard, 1910–25.

Franko, Mark. *Dance as Text: Ideologies of the Baroque Body.* Cambridge: Cambridge University Press, 1993.

— — —. "The King Cross-Dressed: Power and Force in Royal Ballets," in *From the Royal to the Republican Body: Incorporating the Political in Seventeenth- and Eighteenth-Century France*, ed. Sara E. Melzer and Kathryn Norberg. Berkeley, Los Angeles and London: University of California Press, 1998: 64–84.

Freitas, Roger. "*Un atto d'ingegno*: A Castrato in the Seventeenth Century." Unpublished Ph.D. dissertation. Yale University (May 1998).

Frontisi-Ducroux, Françoise and François Lissarrague. "From Ambiguity to Ambivalence: A Dionysiac Excursion through the 'Anakreontic' Vases," in *Before Sexuality: The Construction of Erotic Experience in the Ancient Greek World*, ed. David M. Halperin, John J. Winkler, and Froma I. Zeitlin. Princeton: Princeton University Press, 1990: 211–56.

Fubini, Enrico. *Music and Culture in Eighteenth-Century Europe: A Source Book.* Trans. Bonnie J. Blackburn. Chicago and London: Chicago University Press, 1994.

Garber, Marjorie. *Vested Interests: Cross-Dressing and Cultural Anxiety.* London: Penguin, 1993.

Garlick, Fiona. "Dances to Evoke the King: The Majestic Genre Chez Louis XIV." *Dance Research* 15: 2 (Winter 1997): 10–34.

Gaumy, Christian. "Le chant des castrats." *Opéra international*, 76 (December 1984): 26–29 and 77 (January 1985): 24–27.

Gilder, Rosamond. *Enter the Actress: The First Women in the Theatre*. New York: Theatre Arts Books, 1960.

Gofflot, L.-V. *Le théâtre au collège du Moyen Age à nos jours*. Paris: Champion, 1907.

Greenberg, Mitchell. *Subjectivity and Subjugation in Seventeenth-Century Drama and Prose: The Family Romance of French Classicism*. Cambridge: Cambridge University Press, 1992.

Hall, H. Gaston. *Molière's* Le Bourgeois gentilhomme: *Context and Stagecraft*. Durham Modern Languages Series, FM5. Durham: University of Durham, 1990.

Halperin, David M., John J. Winkler, and Froma I. Zeitlin (eds.). *Before Sexuality: The Construction of Erotic Experience in the Ancient Greek World*. Princeton: Princeton University Press, 1990.

Harris, Joseph. *Hidden Agendas: Cross-Dressing in 17th-Century France*. Biblio 17: 156. Tübingen: Gunter Narr, 2005.

Heller, Wendy. *Emblems of Eloquence: Opera and Women's Voices in Seventeenth-Century Venice*. Berkeley: University of California Press, 2003.

Henderson, Jeffrey. "Older Women in Attic Old Comedy." *Transactions of the American Philological Association* 117 (1987): 105–29.

Heriot, Angus. *The Castrati in Opera*. New York: Da Capo, 1975.

Herzel, Roger W, " 'Much Depends on Acting': The Original Cast of Le Misanthrope." *Publications of the Modern Language Association of America* 95: 3 (May 1980): 348–66.

———. *The Original Casting of Molière's Plays*. Ann Arbor, MI: UMI Research Press, 1981.

———. "Problems in the Original Casting of Les Femmes Savantes," in *Actes de New Orleans*, ed. Francis L. Lawrence. Biblio 17: 5. Paris: PFSCL, 1982: 215–31.

Hilgar, Marie-France. "Théâtralité du travestissement au XVIIe siècle." *XVIIe Siècle* 33: 1 (1981): 53–62.

Hogwood, Christopher. *Handel*. London: Thames and Hudson, 1984.

Hourcade, Philippe. "Louis XIV travesti." *Cahiers de Littérature du XVIIe siècle* 6 (1984): 257–71.

Howard, Jean E. "Cross-Dressing, the Theater, and Gender Struggle in Early Modern England," in *Crossing the Stage: Controversies on Cross-Dressing*. London: Routledge, 1993: 20–46. Originally published in *Shakespeare Quarterly* 39: 4 (1988): 418–40.

Howe, Elizabeth. *The First English Actresses: Women and Drama, 1660–1700*. Cambridge: Cambridge University Press, 1992.

———. "*A State of Undress*. The first English actresses on stage: 1600–1700," in *Women in European Theatre*, ed. Elizabeth Woodrough. London: Intellect, 1995: 15–21.

Isherwood, Robert M. *Music in the Service of the King: France in the Seventeenth Century*. Ithaca and London: Cornell University Press, 1973.

Jardine, Lisa. "Boy Actors, Female Roles, and Elizabethan Eroticism," in *Staging the Renaissance: Reinterpretations of Elizabethan and Jacobean Drama*, ed. by David Scott Kastan and Peter Stallybrass. New York and London: Routledge, 1991: 57–67.

Jolibert, Bernard. *La commedia dell'arte et son influence en France du XVIᵉ au XVIIIᵉ siècle*. Paris and Montreal: Harmattan, 1999.

Kahn, Madeleine. *Narrative Transvestism: Rhetoric and Gender in the Eighteenth-Century English Novel*. Ithaca and London: Cornell University Press, 1991.

Kantorowicz, Ernst H. *The King's Two Bodies: A Study in Mediaeval Political Theology*. Princeton: Princeton University Press, 1995.

Keyser, Dorothy. "Cross-Sexual Casting in Baroque Opera: Musical and Theatrical Conventions." *Opera Quarterly* 5: 4 (Winter 1987/88): 46–57.

Kowaleski-Wallace, Beth. "Shunning the Bearded Kiss: Castrati and the Definition of Female Sexuality." *Prose Studies* 15: 2 (August 1992): 153–70.

Lacour, Léopold. *Les premières actrices françaises*. Paris: Librairie Française, 1921.

La Gorce, Jérôme de. *L'Opéra à Paris au temps de Louis XIV: Histoire d'un théâtre*. Paris: Editions Desjonquères, 1992.

———. *Féeries d'opéra: Décors, machines et costumes en France, 1645–1765*. Paris: Editions du Patrimoine, 1997.

Lancaster, Henry Carrington (ed.). *Actors' Roles at the Comédie Française According to the Repertoire des Comedies françoises qui se peuuent joüer en 1685*. John Hopkins Studies in Romance Literatures and Languages, 47. Baltimore: John Hopkins Press, 1953.

Laqueur, Thomas. *Making Sex: Body and Gender from the Greeks to Freud*. Cambridge, MA: Harvard University Press, 1990.

Levine, Laura. *Men in Women's Clothing: Anti-Theatricality and Effeminization, 1576–1642*. Cambridge Studies in Renaissance Literature and Culture, 5. Cambridge: Cambridge University Press, 1994.

Litman, Théodore A. *Les comédies de Corneille*. Paris: Boivin, 1936.

Loraux, Nicole. "Herakles: The Super-Male and the Feminine," in *Before Sexuality: The Construction of Erotic Experience in the Ancient Greek World*, ed. David M. Halperin, John J. Winkler, and Froma I. Zeitlin. Princeton: Princeton University Press, 1990: 21–52.

———. *The Experiences of Tiresias*. Princeton: Princeton University Press, 1995.

Lough, John. *Seventeenth-Century French Drama: The Background*. Oxford: Clarendon Press, 1979.

Lowe, Robert W. *Marc-Antoine Charpentier et l'opéra de collège*. Paris: Maisonneuve and Larose, 1966.

Lyonnet, Henry. *Les "Premières" de P. Corneille*. Paris: Delagrave, 1923.

Lyons, John D. *A Theatre of Disguise: Studies in French Baroque Drama (1630–1660)*. Columbia, SC: French Literature Publications Company, 1978.

McCabe, William H. *An Introduction to the Jesuit Theater*, ed. Louis J. Oldani. St. Louis: Institute of Jesuit Sources, 1983.

186 ❦ *Bibliography*

McGeary, Thomas. " 'Warbling Eunuchs': Opera, Gender, and Sexuality on the London Stage, 1705–1742." *Restoration and 18th Century Theatre Research*, 2nd series, 7: 1 (Summer 1992): 1–22.

McGowan, Margaret M. *L'art du Ballet de cour en France, 1581–1643*. Paris: Centre National de la Recherche Scientifique, 1963.

Mallinson, G. J. *The Comedies of Corneille: Experiments in the Comic*. Manchester: Manchester University Press, 1984.

Maral, Alexandre. *La Chapelle Royale de Versailles sous Louis XIV: Cérémonial, liturgie et musique*. Sprimont: Mardaga, 2002.

Marin, Louis. *Le portrait du roi*. Paris: Minuit, 1981.

Mélèse, Pierre. *Le Théâtre et le public à Paris sous Louis XIV, 1659–1715*. Paris: Droz, 1934; Geneva, 1976.

Michaut, G. *La Jeunesse de Molière*. Paris: Hachette, 1922.

Muir, Lynette R. "Women on the Medieval Stage: The Evidence from France." *Medieval English Theatre* 7: 2 (1985): 107–19.

Munns, Jessica and Penny Richards (eds.). *The Clothes that Wear Us: Essays on Dressing and Transgressing in Eighteenth-Century Culture*. Newark: University of Delaware Press and London: Associated University Presses, 1999.

Néraudau, Jean-Pierre. *L'Olympe du Roi-soleil: Mythologie et idéologie royale au Grand Siècle*. Paris: Les Belles Lettres, 1986.

Newman, Joyce. *Jean-Baptiste de Lully and his Tragédies Lyriques*. Michigan: UMI Research Press, 1979.

Norman, Buford. *Touched by the Graces: The Libretti of Philippe Quinault in the Context of French Classicism*. Birmingham, Alabama: Summa Publications, 2001.

Orcibal, Jean. *La Genèse d' Esther et d' Athalie*. Paris: Vrin, 1950.

Orgel, Stephen. "Gendering the Crown," in *Subject and Object in Renaissance Culture*, ed. Margreta de Grazia, Maureen Quilligan, and Peter Stallybrass. Cambridge Studies in Renaissance Literature and Culture 8. Cambridge: Cambridge University Press, 1996: 133–65.

———. *Impersonations: The Performance of Gender in Shakespeare's England*. Cambridge: Cambridge University Press, 1996.

Parish, Richard. "*Molière en travesti*: Transvestite Acting in Molière," in *Molière*, ed. Stephen Bamforth. Nottingham French Studies 33: 1. Nottingham: University of Nottingham, 1994: 53–58.

Peschel, Enid R., and Richard E. Peschel. "Medicine and Music: The Castrati in Opera." *Opera Quarterly* 4: 4 (Winter 1986/87): 21–38.

———. "Medical Insights into the Castrati in Opera." *American Scientist* (November–December 1987): 578–83.

Phillips, Henry. *The Theatre and its Critics in Seventeenth-Century France*. Oxford: Oxford University Press, 1980.

———. "Le théâtre scolaire dans la querelle du théâtre au XVIIe siècle." *Revue d'histoire du théâtre* 35: 2 (1983): 190–221.

Picard, Raymond. *La carrière de Jean Racine*. Paris: Gallimard, 1961.

Piéjus, Anne. *Le théâtre des demoiselles: Tragédie et musique à Saint-Cyr à la fin du grand siècle*. Paris: Société française de musicologie, 2000.

Prest, Julia. "Dancing King: Louis XIV's Roles in Molière's *Comédies-ballets*, from Court to Town." *The Seventeenth Century* 16: 2 (2001): 283–98.

———. "The Problem of Praise and the First Prologue to *Le Malade imaginaire*." *Seventeenth Century French Studies* 23 (2001): 139–49.

———. "The Gendering of the Court Ballet Audience: Cross-Casting and the Emergence of the Female Ballet Dancer." *Seventeenth Century French Studies* 24 (2002): 127–34.

———. "Cross-Casting in French Court Ballet: Monstrous Aberration or Theatrical Convention?" *Romance Studies* (November 2003): 157–68.

———. "Conflicting Signals: Images of Louis XIV in Benserade's Ballets," in *Culture and Conflict in 17th-Century France and Ireland*, ed. Sarah Alyn Stacey and Véronique Desnain. Dublin: Four Courts Press, 2004: 227–41.

———. "Cross-Casting and Women's Roles in School Drama." *Seventeenth Century French Studies* 26 (2004): 195–208.

Prunières, Henry. *L'Opéra italien en France avant Lulli*. Paris: Champion, 1913.

———. *Le ballet de cour en France avant Benserade et Lulli*. Paris: Laurens, 1914.

Reynier, Gustave. *Thomas Corneille: Sa vie et son théâtre*. Paris: Hachette, 1892; Geneva: Slatkine, 1970.

Rivaille, Louis. *Les débuts de P. Corneille*. Paris: Boivin, 1936.

Rosand, Ellen. *Opera in Seventeenth-Century Venice: The Creation of a Genre*. Berkeley: University of California Press, 1991.

Rosenberg, Marvin. "The Myth of Shakespeare's Squeaking Boy Actor—Or Who Played Cleopatra?" *Shakespeare Bulletin* 19: 2 (Spring 2001), consulted online.

Rosselli, John. *Singers of Italian Opera: The History of a Profession*. Cambridge: Cambridge University Press, 1992.

———. "The Castrati as a Professional Group and a Social Phenomenon, 1550–1850." *Acta musicologica* 60 (1988): 143–79.

———. "Castrato." in *The New Grove Dictionary of Opera*, ed. Stanley Sadie. 4 vols. London: Macmillan, 1992. I: 766–68.

Rubin, David Lee (ed.). *Sun King: The Ascendancy of French Culture during the Reign of Louis XIV*. Washington: Folger Shakespeare Library; London and Toronto: Associated University Presses, 1992.

Sawkins, Lionel. "For and Against the Order of Nature: Who Sang the Soprano?" *Early Music* 15: 3 (August 1987): 315–24.

Schmidt, Carl B. *The livrets of Jean-Baptiste Lully's tragédies-lyriques: A catalogue raisonné*. New York: Performers' Editions, 1995.

Schwartz, I. A. *The commedia dell'arte and its Influence on French Comedy in the Seventeenth Century*. Paris: H. Samuel, 1933.

Senelick, Laurence. *The Changing Room: Sex, Drag and Theatre*. London and New York: Routledge, 2000.

Sergent, Bernard. *L'homosexualité dans la mythologie grecque*. Paris: Payot, 1984.

Shapiro, Michael. *Gender in Play on the Shakespearean Stage: Boy Heroines and Female Pages*. Ann Arbor: University of Michigan Press, 1994.

Silin, Charles I. *Benserade and his Ballets de Cour*. John Hopkins Studies in Romance Literatures and Languages. Extra volume XV. Baltimore, Maryland: John Hopkins Press, 1940.

Snyders, Georges. *La pédagogie en France aux XVIIe et XVIIIe siècles*. Paris: Presses Universitaires de France, 1965.

Stallybrass, Peter. "Worn Worlds: Clothes and Identity on the Renaissance Stage," in *Subject and Object in Renaissance Culture*, ed. Margreta de Grazia, Maureen Quilligan, and Peter Stallybrass. Cambridge Studies in Renaissance Literature and Culture 8. Cambridge: Cambridge University Press, 1996: 289–320.

Taphanel, Achille. *Le Théâtre de Saint-Cyr (1689–1792) d'après des documents inédits*. Versailles: Cerf et fils; Paris: J. Baudry, 1876.

Tastu, Amable. "Esther à Saint-Cyr." *Revue de Paris* 53 (1833): 84–96.

Tessier, André. "Les répétitions du *Triomphe de l'Amour* à Saint-Germain-en-Laye." *La Revue musicale* 6: 4 (1925): 123–31.

Twycross, Meg. "Transvestism in the Mystery Plays." *Medieval English Theatre* 5: 2 (1983): 123–80.

Verhoeff, Han. *Les comédies de Corneille: Une psycholecture*. Paris: Klincksieck, 1979.

Whitton, David. *Molière: Le Bourgeois gentilhomme*. Critical Guides to French Texts, 92. London: Grant and Cutler, 1992.

Williams, Clifford John. *Theatres and Audiences: A background to dramatic texts*. London: Longman, 1970.

Wood, Caroline. *Music and Drama in the tragédie en musique, 1673–1715: Jean-Baptiste Lully and his Successors*. New York and London: Garland, 1996.

——— and Graham Sadler. *French Baroque Opera: A Reader*. Aldershot: Ashgate, 2000.

Woodrough, Elizabeth (ed.). *Women in European Theatre*. London: Intellect, 1995.

Woshinsky, Barbara. "La musique parlante: La fonction du chœur dans l'*Esther* de Racine." *Littératures classiques* 21 (1994): 149–61.

Discography

Lully-Quinault. *Alceste*. La Grande Ecurie et la Chambre du Roy et l'Ensemble Vocal Sagittarius. Dir. Jean-Claude Malgoire (Montaigne/Auvidis, 1992/1994, 3CD).

———. *Armide*. Chœur et Orchestre du Collegium Vocale et de la Chapelle Royale. Dir. Philippe Herrewegghe (Harmonia Mundi, 1993, 2CD).

———. *Persée*. Maîtrise du Centre de Musique Baroque de Versailles "les Chantres de la Chapelle" et Les Talens Lyriques. Dir. Christophe Rousset (Astrée, 2001, 3CD).

———. *Phaéton*. Ensemble vocal Sagittarius et Les Musiciens du Louvre. Dir. Marc Minkowski (Erato, 1994, 2CD).

Filmography

Farinelli. Gérard Corbiau (1994).

Monty Python's Life of Brian. Terry Jones (1979).

Le Roi danse. Gérard Corbiau (2000).

Saint-Cyr. Patricia Mazuy (2000).

INDEX